THE WISDOM OF GEORGE SANTAYANA

The
Wisdom
of
George
Santayana

[ATOMS OF THOUGHT]

selected and edited by IRA D. CARDIFF

PHILOSOPHICAL LIBRARY

NEW YORK

To Douglas, Edward and Robert

Author's Preface

THIS COLLECTION of passages marked in my books by the keen and judicial eye of Dr. Cardiff was planned and well advanced before I had heard of it; and even now, when it goes to the press, I have seen only a few pages of his selections, which suffice to assure me that he would not peel off the baroque facade of my philosophy without also displaying in patches the prehistoric blocks of the substructure.

The merits of a baroque philosophy are clearly distinguished by Spinoza, himself an austere writer. "If the mind in its fictions," he says, "recognized them for fictions, it would regard this power of invention as a virtue, not as a vice; particularly if this faculty flowed from the very nature of the mind, that is to say, if it was free."[1]

Now all images of sense, all instincts and passions are original fictions of the animal psyche, formed according to the structure and condition of its organs; and it is the free exercise of these organs and active powers that clothes the world with the images and values which we find in it. It was therefore by a notable exhibition of vital liberty and power that the baroque architects, when once the material stability of their buildings was assured according to well-tried practice and experiment (which alone touch material reality) were pleased to vivify their prescribed pavilions with a wealth of twisted columns, scrolls, shells, grotesque masks, heraldic monsters, river-gods, garlanded urns, acrobatic statues and broken pediments rising boldly into empty air. Though materially useless and frankly theatrical, these accretions were usually suggested by something festive and liberal proper to the occasion: just as the images and sentiments hatched in

---

[1] Ethics, Part II, Prop. XVII, Schollum (abridged).

a living brain, ethereal as they are, normally have a clear relevance to the physical surroundings and human impulses that provoke them.

So, too, a philosophy that has touched bottom and has once stripped itself naked, by either a thorough scepticism or a fearless self-scrutiny, when it again gathers its forces together to face the world, will not stint the imagination. Regenerate judgment can never be so crude as to mistake appearance for reality or the human moral world for the universe. Our language is poetic, figurative, symbolic essentially; why should we not allow it to become poetic artistically? Words and thoughts can never be the very object that has aroused them and to which they impulsively address fancy names and rhetorical epithets. These names and epithets must always vary: why should they not be trained to cling more closely to their object and at the same time to express more fully and justly the human emotions that it may have caused?

Concerning the title of this book, I feel some responsibility, having suggested the word atoms with which the editor and publisher have coupled the word *thoughts;* and certainly if the word *atoms* is taken logically and the word *thoughts* psychologically, the two are incompatible. But now-a-days we speak of split atoms, that can explode and devastate whole cities; so that evidently in common use, when we call an existing body an atom, we mean only that it seems a dot to the eye, or more technically that it is the smallest body that can preserve the chemical properties of that sort of substance since if broken up it turns into other chemical elements. In this popular sense, every intelligible sentence is an atom of thought, since if you changed its terms you would change its deliverance, or if you remembered half of it, you would not have remembered the whole.

In this sense, the most complex composition ever imagined by a painter or the subtlest and profoundest sentiment ever felt by a moralist would be atoms of thought. No such precise vision or precise emotion would probably recur unchanged in the same man's life, much less in the lives of others. If a painter attempted to put his vision on canvas or a moralist to put his emotion into words, both would probably feel that they had not succeeded; the old experience, though veiled, would retain a power that no later rendering could exercise over the soul. Nevertheless, imagination, like the senses, though not literally truthful, is enlightening in that it forms a language native to the brain, in which the assaults of the world upon us, and our reactions, may be recorded, recalled, and dramatically recast into what we call law, history, and science.

It is as being a term in this living language that any distinct thought may be called an atom. It is an atom logically, morally, for the spirit, no matter how entangled and profound its roots may be in the past or how manifold its radiations in possible speculation—it is a spark; and the brighter and briefer it is, the more sharply it breaks through the smoke-screen of mechanical habit, with its intellectual slackness and blur. But the spark at once dies out, and if another succeeds it, the psyche is less quick to ignite; the flash seems less original, less interesting; and in an indefinite series they soon cease to be sparks and become pin-pricks. A thick album of moral pin-pricks is soon closed: you must go for a country walk or a commonplace conversation. Yet the flash of those rockets, each apart in a clear sky, might be a point of departure for a new vision of the world. Even if only momentary and delusive, that flash would have liberated us from the burden of private and public cares; spirit in us would have entered an intelligible world. The natural world would remain, for all that, exactly as it was; yet in granting to intelligence these atomic insights, it would virtually and ideally have reversed its domination over them and confessed that to be so transfigured was the supreme triumph of its own life.

Rome, 1950.

G. Santayana

Introduction to the Second Edition

THE FIRST EDITION of Santayana's "Atoms" was published in 1950, while the philosopher was still living and working. The following year he finished his last book, *Dominations and Powers*. Dr. Santayana's death, at age 88, occurred a year later; therefore the present edition is brought up to date by including thoughts from *Dominations and Powers* as well as from *My Host the World,* a posthumous third volume of Santayana's autobiography. Also included are atoms reformulated by himself from some of his earlier thinking and published earlier under the title *Little Essays.*

It is with considerable diffidence and misgiving that one attempts to lift certain ideas and "atoms" of thought from the discourse of a great philosopher and impeccable writer. With great humility, the editor of these atoms (so named by Mr. Santayana), selected them from the author's thirty books—his careful thinking over a period of three-fourths of a century. As soon as the first printing was available from the original edition, it was examined carefully by Mr. Santayana who was asked by the editor to indicate any atoms which should be omitted, or any overlooked which should be included. He indicated neither.

Introduction

ONE OFTEN WONDERS with what the human species occupied its mind during the million years previous to the advent of the printed page. Today, the book and the magazine seem as necessary to life as food. To be able to enjoy the thoughts of the great and near great of present and past by means of the printed page is a priceless boon—the major contributing factor to popular education.

Probably foremost of my incessant and omnivorous reading have been the writings of George Santayana, my choice doubtless as much for their lucidity and beauty as their philosophical content. "His work is many colored, like a drop of water in the sun, and shifts without due notice from one aspect or interest to another."*

After living with, or upon, Santayana's ideas for many years, I became impressed with one feature regarding them—they are too little known.

The wisdom, the sound philosophy, the exquisite language, the brilliant aphorisms, the charm and subtle humor of George Santayana should not be buried in a mausoleum of philosophical literature—magnificent and imposing as this repository might be. Thus disposed of, they will be available to the few —*very few*—primarily to those technically interested in philosophy. Such an end to this work of art and education would be a calamity of the first order. These gems should be available to the common man who normally sees all too little of the finer productions of the race.

Bertrand Russell has said that Santayana, like Spinoza, is to be read not so much on account of his theoretical doctrines as on account of his views as to what constitutes the good life,

*Baker Brownell.

and of his standard of values in art and morals. According to Corliss Lamont, he "writes philosophy more beautifully than any other thinker since Plato."

One of Santayana's students and admirers says, "To many Americans, Santayana is the Mona Lisa of philosophy. Though eloquent and penetrating, he finally brings forth what seems to them only an enigmatic smile."* It might be added that in spite of their enigmatic character, like the masterpiece of the famous Leonardo, Santayana's sayings and ideas furnish a thrill and an inspiration rarely found elsewhere in recondite philosophical discussions. The Mona Lisa illustration might be carried still further: "Perhaps of all ancient pictures, time has chilled it least."** So with the sayings of Santayana: they are so fundamental and far-reaching that four centuries from now many of them will be as fresh and inspirational as we find Mona Lisa today. Like the great Florentine, Santayana portrays the best of human thought. His ideas, his sayings, his humor will animate and exhilarate men for ages to come.

Some of his statements will be puzzling to the layman, as in his "Poetry and Religion" he attempts to show that religion is but sublimated poetry, then includes in his book a chapter on "The Absence of Religion in Shakespeare", the greatest of our poets. Also great are Shelley, Byron, Omar Khayyám, Lucretius, Villon, Goethe, Heine, Burns, Whitman et alia, a long procession of the greatest—all irreligious or at least highly unorthodox and some of them definitely anti-religious. Even Santayana himself succumbs to the muse in unorthodox form, see O. 13, and his illustrious fellow countryman, the immortal Cervantes, likewise is *unorthodox*. Two other great come to mind, Confucius and Mark Twain—technically not poets, yet very poetical—and anything but religious, as religion is popularly understood.

"In attempting to capture the spirit of antiquity, he (Santayana) does not discuss the truth or falsehood of any religious dogma; indeed he takes it for granted that none is literally

*Baker Brownell
**Walter Pater.

[xiv]

true. Religion, to him, is essentially myth, which may be useful or harmful, noble or ignoble, beautiful or ugly, but which is somewhat Philistine to regard as true or false."*

Even though dealing with recondite subjects, his style is pleasing and non-technical, while discussing religious topics he is urbane and free from dogmatism or fanaticism.

Santayana says, "The only belief that I myself entertain, because I find it irresistible, is the belief in a realm of matter, the expectation of persistence and order in a natural world; and this is a belief which I am confident the reader shares."

His religion (if he may be said to possess such) is doubtless somewhat akin to Henry Seidel Canby's middle-class religion of the nineties: "We went to church from that most primitive of all fears, an instinctive dread of a broken habit."

Santayana, though born in Spain and living more than half his life in England, France, Spain and Italy, considers himself an American. Notwithstanding the fact that he has sojourned in Europe for many years, he spent his later boyhood in Boston and was a professor in Harvard for near a quarter of a century. He chooses the English language for recording his thoughts, and his score or more of books are published in America. While America is honored thus, Santayana nevertheless is a citizen of the world in thought and sympathy. His citizenship status reminds us of our other great American by adoption, Thomas Paine, whose brilliant writings accomplished so much for humanity, for American independence, and for much of the human freedom in the world today. Paine declared "the world is my country, to do good is my religion." Lovers of liberty of France and America have honored Paine for his magnificent work as they doubtless eventually will honor Santayana whose grasp of the great universal truths of the race make him likewise a citizen of the world, as well as its benefactor.

Santayana, writing his soliloquies in England, just at the close of World War I, makes a number of prophetic observa-

*Bertrand Russell

tions on war. (See Soliloquy on Tipperary). Considered in the light of our 1948-49 warmongering, his forecast is almost eerie, see T. 104 and 105.

Many of Santayana's gems of wisdom are too long to quote, e.g. the Soliloquy on "Liberalism and Culture." It will bear frequent reading, but like many a luscious fruit, loses much by cutting. The article must be taken as a whole to derive therefrom the greatest enjoyment and benefit.

In discussing with Dr. Santayana the publication of the quotations, his chief misgiving was the danger of their loss of force in appearing out of context, as some of them do. On the other hand, there is a still greater loss from the impossibility of including the many more lengthy gems—whole paragraphs or more—which would be widely enjoyed. His soliloquies on "The British Character," "The Lion and the Unicorn," "On Leaving Church," and "Death Bed Manners," while of too great length in an anthology of this type, would and should be enjoyed by all.

Santayana's crystal-clear and forceful statements in behalf of science and human experience as foundation stones in philosophical thought are much needed in these days of hysterical propaganda and ballyhoo over conflicting ideologies. His unequivocal support of a materialistic and naturalistic viewpoint of life and the cosmos is welcomed by all sound thinkers as fundamental in the evolution of our educational and cultural life. The lay reader has little opportunity to obtain even an inkling that such a philosophy exists, much less to become acquainted with its details and values. It is hoped this collection may in a measure correct this situation. "The sole advantage in possessing great works of literature lies in what they can help us to become."

Foreword

THIS COLLECTION of paragraphs from the writings of George Santayana has been made over a period of many years. For me they constituted oases of pleasure and inspiration in fields of mental activity and necessity less attractive and edifying. Most of the quotations were made with no thought of publication.

A couple of years ago, the idea of sharing them with others occurred to me, and Professor Santayana kindly gave me permission to publish the thoughts. Later, while visiting with Dr. Corliss Lamont, I found he also had been making a collection of Santayana's sayings, though considerably less extensive than my own. He at once generously offered them to me for inclusion with mine. For these I am very grateful to Dr. Lamont, as a substantial number were not among those I had selected.

An effort has been made to render the quotations more useful by a rather complete index, not only of the paragraph titles, but also of salient and expressive words in the text. For the titles or paragraph headings, I alone am responsible. They were supplied with the idea of easing the introduction of the non-technical reader to philosophical thought; also to aid those who enjoy browsing for mental recreation and refreshment, likewise to facilitate reference by writers and speakers.

Acknowledgment is made to Scribner's, Northwestern University, Herbert S. Stone & Co., The Atlantic Monthly, Modern Monthly, American Mercury, and the New Republic, from whose publications most of the thoughts have been quoted.

I must likewise express my grateful acknowledgment to my secretary Robert Wilson for his careful and efficient typing, re-typing and proof reading, also to Mrs. Frank Hughes for valued assistance in proof reading.

Immediately preceding the index will be found a complete list of the publications, arranged in the order in which they are quoted.

IRA D. CARDIFF

THE WISDOM OF GEORGE SANTAYANA

Sources of Quotations

(Following each quotation will be found a letter and a number.
The letter refers to the volume from which the quotation was
taken, as shown by the list below; the number refers to the
page in that volume where the passage quoted may be found.
There is no significance to the order of arrangement.)

Luc.

Fate

No one is truly happy. Evil things
Fate lays upon us. Yet she makes amends,
Bringing us daily comfort on the wings
Of sleep, and by the willing hands of friends.—Luc-17

Wisest mind

The wisest mind hath something yet to learn.—Luc-18

Truth and the profound

To tune the soul to truth and the profound.—Luc-20

Virtue

O generous soul, that in the lost in hell
Still makes a virtue!—Luc-29

Thought, doubt

O let us shut the future out,
Lest thought should poison with the shaft of doubt
The happy now!—Luc-31

Friends

Yet friends will follow friends to any doom.—Luc-44

Reason, sorrows of the universe

O poisonous alloy
Of reason in me, quickening the heart
With all the sorrow of the universe
To futile anger!—Luc-54

God, unforgiving

Nay, God himself, who saith he died for all,
Remembers not his myriad unforgiven

Children in hell, nor all the worms that crawl
Through suffering to death.—Luc-56

Loyalty of fools

No, but he reigns. That's argument enough
For loyalty of fools.—Luc-64

Noble blood

"These men of noble blood
  When their ambition makes them serve the mob
Sink to their master's level, heart and soul."—Luc-66

Metaphysical air

Metaphysical air
Has ever been the pasture of his soul.
The braying conclave of the saints will grant him
A doctor's title, if his logic prove
How erring Nature is fulfilled by Grace,
With thrice three hundred clinching arguments.—Luc-67

Cruel, who is

He and none else is cruel who began
The fatal work of life, and in each breast
Bade some blind passion torture all the rest,
To die unsatisfied.—Luc-76

Fools who live by rule

. . . my soul hates the fool
Whose only passion is to live by rule.—Luc-77

Master

For every spirit born to breathe the air
Is his own master and himself his doom.—Luc-77

Truth

To suffer for the truth is to succeed.—Luc-83

Reason

Why did I e'er seduce them, trustful fool,
To follow reason? Heaven was their place.—Luc-89

God and the churches

. . . sure I am
God receives many that the churches damn.—Luc-99

Priests and pedants

Prescriptions bind
These priests and pedants.—Luc-100

Throne

Thou art a Greek
Unused to kiss the ground before the throne
Of the Great King.—Luc-101

Priest

Talk meantime to the priest. He is a sage
Of pleasant wit when he forgets his rôle,
And when not bent on catching any soul
Enjoys the fancies of this naughty age.—Luc-101

Believe

CHRIST

He should first believe.

LUCIFER

Believe? Full well thou knowest, as I know,
He never can believe. It is too gross
And palpable a fiction, fit for those
Who dream awake.—Luc-134

Truth and falsehood

And firm beneath the ruins of the sky,
I live by truth, as ye by falsehood die.
The wreck of worlds is my supreme release,
The death of gods mine immortality.—Luc-142

Bondage

O heavy bondage, though a silver chain
Fetter the exile to a golden throne.

[3]

I would go forth, I would be free again
Unwatched, uncensured, unbeloved, alone.—Luc-146

Unhappy lovers

ATHENA

If happy love so sighs,
How shall unhappy lovers breathe their woes?

APHRODITE

They say there is a thorn in every rose,
But that is false; for see, these roses here
Prick not my fingers as I weave the crown.
I cut the thorns off first. Look, sister dear,
And in thy book of wisdom set that down.—Luc-147

Worst

Ay, my lips are dumb,
But my heart saith, the worst is yet to come.—Luc-139

Today

Today the world is fair.
Tomorrow, if dark clouds rebellious run
In flaming rack athwart the seas of heaven,
I shall not less have lived.—Luc-177

Death

We also thought we should not taste of death,
But it is fated. Fleeting is the breath
That saith: I am eternal! We were born
And we must therefore die. Such is the wage
Of being.—Luc-177-178

Time

But the stars are cold.
Fool, fool, to chide his soul with ancient crime,
Nor mark how earth and sky, together rolled,
His loves, his labours, and the gods sublime
He deemed immortal, slowly yield to time.—Luc-179

Death

Ha! What a blessed end it is for all
To die. The flowers of sweetest breath
Are nearest to the blessedness of death,
For as their sweetness is ephemeral
So is their life.—Luc-182

A

The serious vs. the tragic and comic

I cannot take every phase of art or religion or philosophy seriously, simply because it takes itself so. These things seem to me less tragic than they did, and more comic; and I am less eager to choose and to judge among them, as if only one form could be right. When our architecture is too pretentious, before we have set the cross on the spire, the foundations are apt to give way.—A-vi

Myth and sophistry

It had seemed to me that myth and sophistry there spoilt a very fine subject. The subject was the history of human ideas: the sophistry was imposed on Hegel by his ambition to show that the episodes he happened to review formed a dialectical chain: and the myth sprang from the constant suggestion that this history of human ideas made up the whole of cosmic evolution, and that those episodes were the scattered syllables of a single eternal oracle. It occurred to me that a more honest criticism of progress might be based on tracing the distracted efforts of man to satisfy his natural impulses in his natural environment.—A-x-xi

The critic

The critic himself should have a determinate character and a sane capacity for happiness.—A-xi

Universe, opinion of

No conceited postulates need be made about the universe, commanding it to be exceptionally friendly, or to preserve us or those like us forever, or to "conserve values," as if the duration or the multiplication of instances had anything to do with excellence. The wisdom of Socrates was enough for living and judging rightly in any world, the most magical or the most mechanical, the best or the worst.—A-xi-xii

Healthy life

In order to discern this healthy life, for the soul no less than for the body, not much learning is required; only a little experience, a little reflection, and a little candour.—A-xii

Moral philosophy

Moral philosophy is not a science. It moves exclusively in the realm of familiar discourse. The units it distinguishes are dramatic units, like those of literary psychology and historical fiction: ideas, persons, passions, destinies such as imagination presents to me when I survey my own past, or conceive the adventures of another.—A-xii

Uses of science

Nevertheless, the uses of science remain human, in that it employs the mind nobly, chastens the feelings, or increases the safety and comfort of life.—A-xiii

History of progress

The entire history of progress is a moral drama, a tale man might unfold in a great autobiography, could his myriad heads and countless scintillas of consciousness conspire, like the seventy Alexandrian sages, in a single version of the truth committed to each for interpretation.—A-1

Philosopher's ambition

A philosopher could hardly have a higher ambition than to make himself a mouth-piece for the memory and judgment of his race.—A-2

Rational life

Man's rational life consists in those moments in which reflection not only occurs but proves efficacious.—A-2

Life of Reason

We may say with Aristotle that life is reason in operation. The LIFE OF REASON will then be a name for that part of experience which perceives and pursues ideals—all conduct so controlled and all sense so interpreted as to perfect natural happiness.—A-3

Moral being

Man, without the ideal continuity given by memory and reason, would have no moral being.—A-4

Life of Reason is human progress

The Life of Reason is accordingly neither a mere means nor a mere incident in human progress; it is the total and embodied progress itself, in which the pleasures of sense are included in so far as they can be intelligently enjoyed and pursued.—A-4

Reason and humanity, beginnings of

Reason and humanity begin with the union of instinct and ideation, when instinct becomes enlightened, establishes values in its objects, and is turned from a process into an art, while at the same time consciousness becomes practical and cognitive, beginning to contain some symbol or record of the coordinate realities among which it arises.—A-5

To decipher the Life of Reason

To decipher the Life of Reason nothing is needed but an analytic spirit and a judicious love of man, a love quick to distinguish success from failure in his great and confused experiment of living.—A-8

Myths in Christianity

The profound and pathetic ideas which inspired Christianity were attached in the beginning to ancient myths and soon crystallised into many new ones. The mythical manner pervades Christian philosophy; but myth succeeds in expressing ideal life only by misrepresenting its history and conditions.—A-10

Democritus, debt to

We owe to Democritus this ideal of practical intelligibility; and he is accordingly an eternal spokesman of reason. His system, long buried with other glories of the world, has been partly revived; and although it cannot be verified in haste, for it represents an ultimate ideal, every advance in science reconstitutes it in some particular.—A-17

Aristotle's influence on thought

Aristotle, for all his scientific temper and studies, built his natural philosophy on a lamentable misunderstanding, and condemned thought to confusion for two thousand years.—A-18

Aristotle and human nature

In Aristotle the conception of human nature is perfectly sound; everything ideal has a natural basis and everything natural an ideal development. His ethics, when thoroughly digested and weighed, especially when the meagre outlines are filled in with Plato's more discursive expositions, will seem therefore entirely final. The Life of Reason finds there its classic explication.—A-21

Aristotle and the Life of Reason

It might seem vain, therefore, to try to do afresh what has been done before with unapproachable success; and instead of writing inferior things at great length about the Life of Reason, it might be simpler to read and to propagate what Aristotle wrote with such immortal justness and masterly brevity.—A-21

Creative thought, its passing in Greece

That creative breath which had stirred the founders and legislators of Greece no longer inspired their descendants. Helpless to control the course of events, they took refuge in abstention or in conformity, and their ethics became a matter of private economy and sentiment, no longer aspiring to mould the state or give any positive aim to existence. The time was approaching when both speculation and morals were to regard the other world; reason had abdicated the throne, and religion, after that brief interregnum, resumed it for long ages.—A-28

[9]

Morals vs. religion

They attach morals to religion rather than to politics, and this religion unhappily long ago ceased to be wisdom expressed in fancy in order to become superstition overlaid with reasoning.—A-30

Primordial feeling

We may accordingly dispense ourselves from preliminary courtesies to the real universal order, nature, the absolute, and the gods. We shall make their acquaintance in due season and better appreciate their moral status, if we strive merely to recall our own experience, and to retrace the visions and reflections out of which those apparitions have grown.

To revert to primordial feeling is an exercise in mental disintegration, not a feat of science.—A-40

Birth of Reason

Reason was born, as it has since discovered, into a world already wonderfully organised, in which it found its precursor in what is called life, its seat in an animal body of unusual plasticity, and its function in rendering that body's volatile instincts and sensations harmonious with one another and with the outer world on which they depend.—A-40

Conventional history's intelligent man

The intelligent man known to history flourishes within a dullard and holds a lunatic in leash. He is encased in a protective shell of ignorance and insensibility which keeps him from being exhausted and confused by this too complicated world; but that integument blinds him at the same time to many of his nearest and highest interests. He is amused by the antics of the brute dreaming within his breast; he gloats on his passionate reveries, an amusement which sometimes costs him very dear. Thus the best human intelligence is still decidedly barbarous; it fights in heavy armour and keeps a fool at court.—A-50-51

Pleasure and pain

To deny that pleasure is good and pain an evil is a grotesque affectation: it amounts to giving "good" and "evil" artificial definitions and thereby reducing ethics to arbitrary verbiage.—A-55

Superstition

There is nothing people will not maintain when they are slaves to superstition; and candour and a sense of justice are, in such a case, the first things lost.—A-56

Courtesy in scepticism

There is a kind of courtesy in scepticism. It would be an offense against polite conventions to press our doubts too far. —A-93

Kant's mysticism

Kant, like Berkeley, had a private mysticism in reserve to raise upon the ruins of science and common-sense. Knowledge was to be removed to make way for faith. This task is ambiguous, and the equivocation involved in it is perhaps the deepest of those confusions with which German metaphysics has since struggled, and which have made it waver between the deepest introspection and the dreariest mythology.—A-94

Nature and mind

Nature is then the sum total of its own conditions; the whole object, the parts observed *plus* the parts interpolated, is the self-existent fact. The mind, in its empirical flux, is a part of this complex; to say it is its own condition or that of the other objects is a grotesque falsehood.—A-103-104.

The true and the practical

Those spirits in whom the pursuit of the true and the practical never leads to possession of the good, but loses itself, like a river in sand, amid irrational habits and passions.— A-110

Berkeley

Of the moral field he (Berkeley) had, it need hardly be added, a quite childish and perfunctory conception. There the prayer-book and the catechism could solve every problem. He lacked the feeling, possessed by all large and matured minds, that there would be no intelligibility or value in things divine were they not interpretations and sublimations of things natural. To master the real world was an ancient and not too promising ambition: it suited his youthful radicalism better to exorcise or to cajole it. He sought to refresh the world with a water-spout of idealism, as if to change the names of things could change their values. Away with all arid investigation, away with the cold algebra of sense and reason, and let us have instead a direct conversation with heaven, an unclouded vision of the purposes and goodness of God; as if there were any other way of understanding the sources of human happiness than to study the ways of nature and man.— A-110-111

Truism and sophism

In the melodramatic fashion so common in what is called philosophy we may delight ourselves with such flashes of lightning as this: *esse est percipi.*—A-112

Philosophic foible

To confuse the instrument with its function and the operation with its meaning has been a persistent foible in modern philosophy.—A-113

Soliloquy of Berkeley

Let us imagine Berkeley addressing himself to that infant or animal consciousness which first used the category of substance and passed from its perceptions to the notion of an independent thing. "Beware, my child," he would have said, "you are taking a dangerous step, one which may hereafter produce a multitude of mathematical atheists, not to speak of cloisterfuls of scholastic triflers. Your ideas can exist only in your mind; if you suffer yourself to imagine them materialised in mid-air and subsisting when you do not perceive them, you will commit a great impiety. If you unthinkingly believe that when you shut your eyes the world continues to exist until you open them again, you will inevitably be hurried into an infinity of metaphysical quibbles about the discrete and the continuous, and you will be so bewildered and deafened by perpetual controversies that the clear light of the gospel will be extinguished in your soul." "But," that tender Peripatetic might answer, "I cannot forget the things about me when I shut my eyes: I know and almost feel their persistent presence, and I always find them again, upon trial, just as they were before, or just in that condition to which the operation of natural causes would have brought them in my absence. If I believe they remain and suffer steady and imperceptible transformation, I know what to expect, and the event does not deceive me; but if I had to resolve upon action before knowing whether the conditions for action were to exist or no, I should never understand what sort of a world I lived in."

"Ah, my child," the good Bishop would reply, "you misunderstand me. You may indeed, nay, you must, live and think *as if* everything remained independently real. That is part of your education for heaven, which God in his goodness provides for you in this life. He will send into your soul at every moment the impressions needed to verify your necessary hypotheses and support your humble and prudent expectations. Only you must not attribute that constancy to the things themselves which is due to steadfastness in the designs of Providence. *Think and act* as if a material world existed, but do not for a moment *believe* it to exist."—A-115

Moral laws

Vague dramatic and moral laws, when they find any causal application, seem to such dreaming minds more notable truths, deeper revelations of efficacious reality, than the mechanical necessities of the case, which they scarcely conceive of; and in this primordial prejudice they are confirmed by superstitious affinities often surviving in their religion and philosophy.—A-119-120

Indeterminism

Belief in indeterminism is a sign of indetermination. No commanding or steady intellect flirts with so miserable a possibility, which in so far as it actually prevailed would make virtue impotent and experience, in its pregnant sense, impossible.—A-124

Practical thinking

The idea of the physical world is the first flower or thick cream of practical thinking. Being skimmed off first and proving so nutritious, it leaves the liquid below somewhat thin and unsavoury.—A-127

The world and modern minds

The material world, as conceived in the first instance, had not that clear abstractness, nor the spiritual world that wealth and interest, which they have acquired for modern minds.—A-128

The world and early mind

Mind then dwelt in the world, not only in the warmth and beauty with which it literally clothed material objects, as it still does in poetic perception, but in a literal animistic way; for human passion and reflection were attributed to every object and made a fairy-land of the world.—A-128

Inner world evolution

The inner world was all the more ghostly because the outer world was so much alive. This movement of thought, which clothed external objects in all the wealth of undeciphered dreams, has long lost its momentum and yielded to a contrary tendency.—A-128

External world, changing view of

An age of mythology yields to an age of subjectivity; reason being equally neglected and exceeded in both. The reaction against imagination has left the external world, as represented in many minds, stark and bare. All the interesting and vital qualities which matter had once been endowed with have been attributed instead to an irresponsible sensibility in man. And as habits of ideation change slowly and yield only piece-meal to criticism or to fresh intuitions, such a revolution has not been carried out consistently, but instead of a thorough renaming of things and a new organization of thought it has produced chiefly distress and confusion.—A-129

Intelligence and the ultimate

Intelligence is most at home in the ultimate, which is the object of intent. Those realities which it can trust and continually recover are its familiar and beloved companions.—A-130

Ideal world

The brain, though mobile, is subject to habit; its formations, while they lapse instantly, return again and again. These ideal objects may accordingly be in a way more real and enduring than things external. Hence no primitive mind puts all reality, or what is most real in reality, in an abstract material universe. It finds, rather, ideal points of reference by which material mutation itself seems to be controlled. An ideal world is recognized from the beginning and placed, not in the immediate foreground, nearer than material things, but much farther off. It has greater substantiality and independence than material objects are credited with. It is divine.—A-131

Nature, knowledge of

When agriculture, commerce, or manual crafts have given men some knowledge of nature, the world thus recognised and dominated is far from seeming ultimate.—A-132

World, spiritual

The spiritual world is, on the other hand, a constant theme for poetry and speculation. In the absence of ideal science, it can be conceived only in myths, which are naturally as shifting and self-contradictory as they are persistent. They acquire no fixed character until, in dogmatic religion, they are defined with reference to natural events, foretold or reported.—A-133

Spirit

It has been common, for instance, to treat the spiritual as a remote or finer form of the natural. Beyond the moon everything seemed permanent; it was therefore called divine and declared to preside over the rest. The breath that escaped from the lips at death, since it took away with it the spiritual control and miraculous life that had quickened the flesh, was itself the spirit.—A-133

Spirit and nature

What is called spirit would be the ideal in so far as it obtained expression in nature; and the power attributed to spirit would be the part of nature's fertility by which such expression was secured.—A-136

Divine mind

The divine mind has therefore always constituted in philosophy either the alternative to nature or her other name: it is *par excellence* the seat of all potentiality and, as Spinoza said, the refuge of all ignorance.—A-138

Education's effect

Only a long and still unfinished education has taught men to separate emotions from things and ideas from their objects. —A-141

Reality and experience

The qualities attributed to reality must be qualities found in experience, and if we deny their presence in ourselves (e.g. in the case of omniscience), that is only because the idea of self, like that of matter, has already become special and the region of ideals (in which omniscience lies) has been formed into a third sphere.—A-142

The mythologist or poet

The mythologist or poet, before science exists, is accordingly the man of truest and most adequate vision. His persuasion that he knows the heart and soul of things is no fancy reached by artificial inference or analogy, but is a direct report of his own experience and honest contemplation.—A-144

Criticism, effect of

Criticism will tend to clear the world of such poetic distortion; and what vestiges of it may linger will be avowed fables, metaphors employed merely in conventional expression. In the end even poetic power will forsake a discredited falsehood: the poet himself will soon prefer to describe nature in natural terms and to represent human emotions in their pathetic humility, not extended beyond their actual sphere nor fantastically uprooted from their necessary soil and occasions. He will sing the power of nature over the soul, the joy of the soul in the bosom of nature, the beauty visible in things, and the steady march of natural processes, so rich in momentous incidents and collocations. The precision of such a picture will accentuate its majesty, as precision does in the poems of Lucretius and Dante, while its pathos and dramatic interest will be redoubled by its truth.—A-149

Mutual understanding

The limits of mutual understanding coincide with the limits of similar structure and common occupation, so that the distortion of insight begins very near home. It is hard to understand the minds of children unless we retain unusual plasticity and capacity to play; men and women do not really understand each other, what rules between them being not so much sympathy as habitual trust, idealisation, or satire; foreigners' minds are pure enigmas, and those attributed to animals are a grotesque compound of Aesop and physiology.—A-153

Dying language

Even the most inspired verse, which boasts not without a relative justification to be immortal, becomes in the course of ages a scarcely legible hieroglyphic; the language it was written in dies, a learned education and an imaginative effort are requisite to catch even a vestige of its original force. Nothing is so irrevocable as mind.—A-154

Wise governor

When the mind is irrational no practical purpose is served by stopping to understand it, because such a mind is irrelevant to practice, and the principles that guide the man's practice can be as well understood by eliminating his mind altogether. So a wise governor ignores his subjects' religion or concerns himself only with its economic and temperamental aspects; if the real forces that control life are understood, the symbols that represent those forces in the mind may be disregarded. —A-156-157

Sympathy

There is nothing sweeter than to be sympathised with, while nothing requires a rarer intellectual heroism than willingness to see one's equation written out.

Nevertheless this same algebraic sense for character plays a large part in human friendship.—A-157

Society, true

True society, then, is limited to similar beings living similar lives and enabled by the contagion of their common habits and arts to attribute to one another, each out of his own experience, what the other actually endures.—A-159

Ideas and conceived things

A conceived thing is doubly a product of mind, more a product of mind, if you will, than an idea, since ideas arise, so to speak, by the mind's inertia and conceptions of things by its activity. Ideas are mental sediment; conceived things are mental growths.—A-169

Reason with reference to life

Reason is indeed not indispensable to life, nor needful if living anyhow be the sole and indeterminate aim; as the existence of animals and of most men sufficiently proves. In so far as man is not a rational being and does not live in and by the mind, in so far as his chance volitions and dreamful ideas roll by without mutual representation or adjustment, in so far as his body takes the lead and even his galvanised action is a form of passivity, we may truly say that his life is not intellectual and not dependent on the application of general concepts to experience; for he lives by instinct.—A-176

Reason, persistence of

Reason has the indomitable persistence of all natural tendencies; it returns to the attack as waves beat on the shore. To observe its defeat is already to give it a new embodiment. Prudence itself is a vague science, and science, when it contains real knowledge, is but a clarified prudence, a description of experience and a guide to life. Speculative reason, if it is not also practical, is not reason at all. Propositions irrelevant to experience may be correct in form, the method they are reached by may parody scientific method, but they cannot be true in substance, because they refer to nothing. Like music, they have no object. They merely flow, and please those whose unattached sensibility they somehow flatter.—A-176

Substance of things hoped for

Those who look back upon the history of opinion for many centuries commonly feel, by a vague but profound instinct, that certain consecrated doctrines have an inherent dignity and spirituality, while other speculative tendencies and other vocabularies seem wedded to all that is ignoble and shallow. So fundamental is this moral tone in philosophy that people are usually more firmly convinced that their opinions are precious than that they are true. They may avow, in reflective moments, that they may be in error, seeing that thinkers of no less repute have maintained opposite opinions, but they are commonly absolutely sure that if their own views could be generally accepted, it would be a boon to mankind, that in fact the moral interests of the race are bound up, not with discovering what may chance to be true, but with discovering the truth to have a particular complexion. This predominant trust in moral judgments is in some cases conscious and avowed, so that philosophers invite the world to embrace tenets for which no evidence is offered but that they chime in with current aspirations or traditional bias. Thus the substance of things hoped for becomes, even in philosophy, the evidence of things not seen.—A-184-185

Ignorant mind

An ignorant mind believes itself omniscient and omnipotent; those impulses in itself which really represent the inertia and unspent momentum of its last dream it regards as the creative forces of nature.—A-187

Religion of melancholy

It is a remarkable fact, which may easily be misinterpreted, that while all the benefits and pleasures of life seem to be associated with external things, and all certain knowledge seems to describe material laws, yet a deified nature has generally inspired a religion of melancholy.—A-189

Nature's language

The truth is, however, that nature's language is too rich for man; and the discomfort he feels when he is compelled to use it merely marks his lack of education.—A-192

Cheap idealism

There is nothing cheaper than idealism. It can be had by merely not observing the ineptitude of our chance prejudices, and by declaring that the first rhymes that have struck our ear are the eternal and necessary harmonies of the world.—A-193

Reflective man

The thinker's bias is naturally favourable to logical ideas. The man of reflection will attribute, as far as possible, validity and reality to these alone.—A-193

The supernatural, its value

In an original thinker, in one who really thinks and does not merely argue, to call a thing supernatural, or spiritual, or intelligible is to declare that it is no *thing* at all, no existence actual or possible, but a value, a term of thought, a merely ideal principle.—A-194

Plato's religion

Plato ... inherited a religion still plastic and conscious of its poetic essence, and did not have to struggle, like his modern disciples, with the arrested childishness of minds that for a hundred generations have learned their metaphysics in the cradle.—A-194

The historian's work

The mathematician develops the import of given ideas; the psychologist investigates their origin and describes their relation to the rest of human experience. So the prophet develops the import of his trance, and the theologian the import of the prophecy: which prevents not the historian from coming later and showing the origin, the growth, and the possible function of that maniacal sort of wisdom.—A-197

Theological dread

True, the theologian commonly dreads a critic more than does the geometer, but this happens only because the theologian has probably not developed the import of his facts with any austerity or clearness, but has distorted that ideal interpretation with all sorts of concessions and side-glances at other tenets to which he is already pledged, so that he justly fears, when his methods are exposed, that the religious heart will be alienated from him and his conclusions be left with no foothold in human nature. If he had not been guilty of much misrepresentation, no history or criticism that reviewed his construction would do anything but recommend it to all those who found in themselves the primary religious facts and religious faculties which that construction had faithfully interpreted in its ideal deductions and extensions.—A-197

Metaphysical passion

To ask man, in the satisfaction of a metaphysical passion, to forego every other good is to render him fanatical and to shut his eyes daily to the sun in order that he may see better by the star-light.—A-200

Qualities required for intelligence

To be nourished and employed, intelligence must have developed such structure and habits as will enable it to assimilate what food comes in its way; so that the persistence of any intellectual habit is a proof that it has some applicability, however partial, to the facts of sentience.—A-202

Function of reason

The function of reason is to dominate experience; and obviously openness to new impressions is no less necessary to that end than is the possession of principles by which new impressions may be interpreted.—A-204

Reason, origin and evolution of

Nothing is more natural or more congruous with all the analogies of experience than that animals should feel and think. The relation of mind to body, of reason to nature seems to be actually this: when bodies have reached a certain complexity and vital equilibrium, a sense begins to inhabit them which is focused upon the preservation of that body and on its reproduction. This sense, as it becomes reflective and expressive of physical welfare, points more and more to its own persistence and harmony, and generates the Life of Reason. Nature is reason's basis and theme; reason is nature's consciousness; and, from the point of view of that consciousness when it has arisen, reason is also nature's justification and goal.—A-205

The mind

Now the body is an instrument, the mind its function, the witness and reward of its operation.—A.206

Mind and consciousness, character of

That matter cannot by transposition of its particles, *become* what we call consciousness, is an admitted truth; that mind cannot *become* its own occasions or determine its own march, though it be a truth not recognised by all philosophers, is in itself no less obvious.—A-206

Thought, physical conditions of

When the exact physical conditions of thought are discovered in man, we may infer how far thought is diffused through the universe, for it will be coextensive with the conditions it will have been shown to have. Now, in a very rough way, we know already what these conditions are. They are first the existence of an organic body and then its possession of adaptable instincts, of instincts that can be modified by experience.—A-209

Satisfaction and goodness

Satisfaction is the touchstone of value; without reference to it all talk about good and evil, progress or decay, is merely confused verbiage, pure sophistry in which the juggler adroitly withdraws attention from what works the wonder—namely, that human and moral colouring to which the terms he plays with owe whatever efficacy they have. Metaphysicians sometimes so define the good as to make it a matter of no importance; not seldom they give that name to the sum of all evils. A good, absolute in the sense of being divorced from all natural demand and all possible satisfaction, would be as remote as possible from goodness: to call it good is mere disloyalty to morals, brought about by some fantastic or dialectical passion.—A-222-223

Character and happiness

Character is the basis of happiness and happiness the sanction of character.—A-223

Hatred of own condition

A man's hatred of his own condition no more helps to improve it than hatred of other people tends to improve them. —A-225

Ethics of pleasure and pain

To put value in pleasure and pain, regarding a given quantity of pain as balancing a given quantity of pleasure, is to bring to practical ethics a worthy intention to be clear, and, what is more precious, an undoubted honesty not always found in those moralists who maintain the opposite opinion and care more for edification than for truth. For in spite of all logical and psychological scruples, conduct that should not justify itself somehow by the satisfactions secured and the pains avoided would not justify itself at all.—A-236

Ideals vs. demands of living beings

An ideal out of relation to the actual demands of living beings is so far from being an ideal that it is not even a good. The pursuit of it would be not the acme but the atrophy of moral endeavour.—A-260

Flux and constancy in human nature

A conception of something called human nature arises not unnaturally on observing the passions of men, passions which under various disguises seem to reappear in all ages and countries. The tendency of Greek philosphy, with its insistence on general concepts, was to define this idea of human nature still further and to encourage the belief that a single and identical essence, present in all men, determined their powers and ideal destiny. Christianity, while it transposed the human ideal and dwelt on the super-human affinities of man, did not abandon the notion of a specific humanity. On the contrary, such a notion was implied in the Fall and Redemption, in the Sacraments, and in the universal validity of Christian doctrine and precept. For if human nature were not one, there would be no propriety in requiring all men to preserve unanimity in faith or conformity in conduct. Human nature was likewise the entity which the English psychologists set themselves to describe; and Kant was so entirely dominated by the notion of a fixed and universal human nature that its constancy, in his opinion, was the source of all natural as well as moral laws. Had he doubted for a moment the stability of human nature, the foundations of his system would have fallen out; the forms of perception and thought would at once have lost their boasted necessity, since tomorrow might dawn upon new categories and a modified *a priori* intuition of space or time; and the avenue would also have been closed by which man was led, through his unalterable moral sentiments, to assumptions about metaphysical truths.

The force of this long tradition has been broken, however, by two influences of great weight in recent times, the theory of evolution and the revival of pantheism. The first has re-introduced flux into the conception of existence and the second into the conception of values. If natural species are fluid and pass into one another, human nature is merely a name for a group of qualities found by chance in certain tribes of animals, a group to which new qualities are constantly tending to attach themselves while other faculties become extinct, now in whole races, now in sporadic individuals. Human nature is therefore a variable, and its ideal cannot have a greater constancy than the demands to which it gives expression. Nor can the ideal of one man or one age have any authority over another, since the harmony existing in their nature and interests is accidental and each is a transitional phase in an indefinite evolution.—A-269-270-271

Thinkers, variation in

Thinkers of different experience and organisation have *pro tanto* different logics and different moral laws. There are limits to communication even among beings of the same race, and the faculties and ideals of one intelligence are not transferable without change to any other.—A-278

The philosopher's life

The true philosopher, who is not one chiefly by profession, must be prepared to tread the wine-press alone. He may indeed flourish like the bay-tree in a grateful environment, but more often he will rather resemble a reed shaken by the wind. Whether starved or fed by the accidents of fortune he must find his essential life in his own ideal.—A-279

Idolatry

The living mind cannot surrender its rights to any physical power or subordinate itself to any figment of its own art without falling into manifest idolatry.—A-279

Mortality

Mortality has its compensations: one is that all evils are transitory, another that better times may come.—A-289

B

Reproduction

For though the instrumentalities of reproduction may seem gross and trivial from a conventional point of view, its essence is really ideal, the perfect type, indeed, of ideality, since form and an identical life are therein sustained successfully by a more rhythmical flux of matter.—B-6

Anomalies of love

These anomalies (of love) show us how nature is built up and, far from being inexplicable, are hints that tend to make everything clear, when once a verbal and mythical philosophy has been abandoned.—B-23

The child's influence

He who is not childless goes down to his grave in peace. —B-43

Home

The sweets of home are balanced not only by its tenderer sorrows, but by a thousand artificial prejudices, enmities, and restrictions.—B-45

Domestic bliss

It takes patience to appreciate domestic bliss; volatile spirits prefer unhappiness.—B-45

"Love levels all"

They say blood is thicker than water; yet similar forces easily compete while dissimilar forces may perhaps cooperate. It is the end that is sacred, not the beginning. A common origin unites reasonable creatures only if it involves common thoughts and purposes; and these may bind together individuals of the most remote races and ages, when once they

have discovered one another. It is difficulties of access, ignorance, and material confinement that shut in the heart to its
narrow loyalties; and perhaps greater mobility, science, and
the mingling of nations will one day reorganize the moral
world.—B-45-46

Caste, prejudices and conventions

People shudder at the system of castes which prevails in
India; but is not every family a little caste? Was a man assigned to his family because he belonged to it in spirit, or
can he choose another? Half the potentialities in the human
race are thus stifled, half its incapacities fostered and made
inveterate. The family, too, is largely responsible for the fierce
prejudices that prevail about women, about religion, about
seemly occupations, about war, death, and honour. In all these
matters men judge in a blind way, inspired by a feminine
passion that has no mercy for anything that eludes the traditional household.—B-46

Best training

For this reason the noblest and happiest children are those
brought up, as in Greece or England, under simple general
conventions by persons trained and hired for the purpose. The
best training in character is found in very large families or in
schools, where boys educate one another.—B-48-49

Real worth

So wealth, religion, military victory have more rhetorical
than efficacious worth.—B-49

Individualism

While a desirable form of society entirely without the family
is hard to conceive, yet the general tendency in periods of
ripe development, has been toward individualism. Individualism is in one sense the only possible ideal; for whatever social
order may be most valuable can be valuable only for its
effect on conscious individuals. Man is of course a social
animal and needs society first that he may come safely into

being, and then that he may have something interesting to do. But society itself is no animal and has neither instincts, interests, nor ideals. To talk of such things is either to speak metaphorically or to think mythically; and myths, the more currency they acquire, pass the more easily into superstitions. It would be a gross and pedantic superstition to venerate any form of society in itself, apart from the safety, breadth, or sweetness which it lent to individual happiness.—B-53

Individualism vs. social order

Individualism is therefore the only ideal possible. The excellence of societies is measured by what they provide for their members. A cumbrous and sanctified social order manifests dullness, and cannot subsist without it. It immerses man in instrumentalities, weighs him down with atrophied organs, and by subjecting him eternally to fruitless sacrifices renders him stupid and superstitious and ready to be himself tyrannical when the opportunity occurs.—B-53-54

Family, evolution of

The family in a barbarous age remains sacrosanct and traditional; nothing in its law, manners, or ritual is open to amendment. The unhappiness which may consequently overtake individuals is hushed up or positively blamed, with no thought of tinkering with the holy institutions which are its cause. Civilised men think more and cannot endure objectless tyrannies. It is inevitable, therefore, that as barbarism recedes the family should become more sensitive to its members' personal interests. Husband and wife, when they are happily matched, are in liberal communities more truly united than before, because such closer friendship expresses their personal inclination. Children are still cared for, because love of them is natural, but they are ruled less and sooner suffered to choose their own associations. They are more largely given in charge to persons not belonging to the family, especially fitted to supply their education. The whole, in a word, exists more and more for the sake of the parts, and the closeness, duration, and scope of family ties comes to vary greatly in different households. Barbaric custom, imposed in all cases alike without respect of persons, yields to a regimen that dares to be elastic and will take pains to be just.—B-54-55

Political liberty

Political liberty is a sign of moral and economic independence.—B-55

Children

Again, many possessions, if they do not make a man better, are at least expected to make his children happier; and this pathetic hope is behind many exertions.—B-68

The irrational

The irrational in the human has something about it altogether repulsive and terrible, as we see in the maniac, the miser, the drunkard, or the ape.—B-69

Orientals

It suffices to watch an Oriental rabble at prayer, or listening in profound immobility to some wandering story-teller or musician, to feel how much such a people may have to ruminate upon, and how truly Arabian days and Arabian Nights go together.—B-74

Militarism

Tyranny not only protects the subject against his kinsmen, thus taking on the functions of law and police, but it also protects him against military invasion, and thus takes on the function of an army. An army, considered ideally, is an organ for the state's protection; but it is far from being such in its origin, since at first an army is nothing but a ravenous and lusty horde quartered in a conquered country; yet the cost of such an incubus may come to be regarded as an insurance against further attack, and so what is in its real basis an inevitable burden resulting from a chance balance of forces may be justified in after-thought as a rational device for defensive purposes. Such an ulterior justification has nothing to do, however, with the causes that maintain armies or military policies; and accordingly those virginal minds that think things originated in the uses they may have acquired, have frequent cause to be pained and perplexed at the abuses and over-development of militarism. An insurance capitalised may exceed the value of the property insured, and the drain caused by armies and navies may be much greater than the havoc they prevent. The evils against which they are supposed to be directed are often evils only in a cant and conventional sense, since the events deprecated (like absorption by a neighboring state) might be in themselves no misfortune to the people, but perhaps a singular blessing. And those dreaded possibilities, even if really evil, may well be less so than is the hateful actuality of military taxes, military service, and military arrogance. Nor is this all: the military classes, since they inherit the blood and habits of conquerors, naturally love war and their irrational combativeness is reinforced by interest; for in war officers can shine and rise, while the danger of death, to a brave man, is rather a spur and a pleasing excitement than a terror. A military class is therefore always recalling, foretelling, and meditating war; it fosters artificial and senseless jealousies toward other governments that possess armies; and finally, as often as not, it precipitates disaster by bringing about the object-less struggle on which it has set its heart.—B-80-81

The warrior's attitude

To fight is a radical instinct; if men have nothing else to fight over they will fight over words, fancies, or women, or they will fight because they dislike each other's looks, or because they have met walking in opposite directions. To knock a thing down, especially if it is cocked at an arrogant angle, is a deep delight to the blood. To fight for a reason and in a calculating spirit is something your true warrior despises.—B-82

War, character of

To call war the soil of courage and virtue is like calling debauchery the soil of love.—B-83

Blind courage

Blind courage is an animal virtue indispensable in a world full of dangers and evils where a certain insensibility and dash are requisite to skirt the precipice without vertigo. Such animal courage seems therefore beautiful rather than desperate or cruel, and being the lowest and most instinctive of virtues it is the one most widely and sincerely admired.—B-84

War

To delight in war is a merit in the soldier, a dangerous quality in the captain, and a positive crime in the statesman.—B-84

Discipline

Discipline, or the habit of obedience, is a better sort of courage which military life also requires. Discipline is the acquired faculty of surrendering an immediate personal good for the sake of a remote and impersonal one of greater value. This difficult wisdom is made easier by training in an army, because the great forces of habit, example, and social suasion are there enlisted in its service. But these natural aids make it lose its conscious rationality, so that it ceases to be a virtue except potentially; for to resist an impulse by force of habit or external command may or may not be to follow the better course.—B-84

War

Nevertheless the panegyrist of war places himself on the lowest level on which a moralist or patriot can stand and shows as great a want of refined feeling as of right reason. For the glories of war are all blood-stained, delirious, and infected with crime; the combative instinct is a savage prompting by which one man's good is found in another's evil.—B-85

Governments, character of

On account of their irrational basis all governments largely misrepresent the true interests of those who live under them. —B-87

Liberty and leaders

It is no loss of liberty to subordinate ourselves to a natural leader.—B-89

Variety

Variety in the world is an unmixed blessing so long as each distinct function can be exercised without hindrance to any other. There is no greater stupidity or meanness than to take uniformity for an ideal, as if it were not a benefit and joy to a man, being what he is, to know that many are, have been, and will be better than he. Grant that no one is positively degraded by the great man's greatness and it follows that everyone is exalted by it.—B-90

Variety, value of

It is the presence of variety and a nearer approach somewhere to just and ideal achievement that gives men perspective in their judgments and opens vistas from the dull foreground of their lives to sea, mountain, and stars.—B-91

Men and their vocations

It is not society's fault that most men seem to miss their vocation.—B-100

Justification for a god

If all unfortunate people could be proved to be unconscious automata, what a brilliant justification that would be for the ways of both God and man!—B-108

Culture

Great thoughts require a great mind and pure beauties a profound sensibility. To attempt to give such things a wide currency is to be willing to denaturalize them in order to boast that they have been propagated. Culture is on the horns of this dilemma; if profound and noble it must remain rare, if common it must become mean. These alternatives can never be eluded until some purified and high-bred race succeeds the promiscuous bipeds that now blacken the planet.—B-110-111

Representative government

A government is not made representative or just by the mechanical expedient of electing its members by universal suffrage. It becomes representative only by embodying in its policy, whether by instinct or high intelligence, the people's conscious and unconscious interests.—B-121

Work, motives for

The motives for work which have hitherto prevailed in the world have been want, ambition, and love of occupation: in a social democracy, after the first was eliminated, the last alone would remain efficacious. Love of occupation, although it occasionally accompanies and cheers every sort of labour, could never induce men originally to undertake arduous and uninteresting tasks, nor to persevere in them if by chance or waywardness such tasks had been once undertaken. Inclination can never be the general motive for the work now imposed on the masses.—B-124

Culture, source of

To abolish aristocracy, in the sense of social privilege and sanctified authority, would be to cut off the source from which all culture has hitherto flowed.—B-125

Civilization

Civilisation, however, although we are wont to speak the word with a certain unction, is a thing whose value may be questioned.—B-125

Anonymous tyranny

There is no tyranny so hateful as a vulgar and anonymous tyranny. It is all-permeating, all-thwarting; it blasts every budding novelty and sprig of genius with its omnipresent and fierce stupidity.—B-127

[34]

Social democracy

Social democracy at high pressure would leave no room for liberty. The only freeman in it would be one whose whole ideal was to be an average man.—B-128

Selfishness
Public spirit

Where public spirit has held best, as at Sparta or (to take a very different type of communal passion) among the Jesuits, it has been paid for by a notable lack of spontaneity and wisdom; such inhuman devotion to an arbitrary end has made these societies odious. We may say, therefore, that a zeal sufficient to destroy selfishness is, as men are now constituted, worse than selfishness itself.—B-134

Indoctrinated virtue
Fanaticism

It is doubtful whether a society which offered no personal prizes would inspire effort; and it is still more doubtful whether that effort, if actually stimulated by education, would be beneficent. For an indoctrinated and collective virtue turns easily to fanaticism.—B-134

Intellectual and artistic greatness
Sympathy

Intellectual and artistic greatness does not need prizes, but it sorely needs sympathy and a propitious environment.—B-135

Virtue and democracy
Montesquieu

We see therefore how justly flattering and profound, and at the same time how ominous, was Montesquieu's saying that the principle of democracy is virtue.—B-136

Women vs. men

When men and women agree, it is only in their conclusions; their reasons are always different.—B-148

Friendship

The necessity of backing personal attachment with ideal interests is what makes true friendship so rare.—B-155

Heroes and gods, how created

It is in this way that heroes and gods have been created. A legend or fable lying in the mind and continually repeated gained insensibly at each recurrence some new eloquence, some fresh congruity with the emotion it had already awakened, and was destined to awake again. To measure the importance of this truth the reader need only conceive the distance traversed from the Achilles that may have existed to the hero in Homer, or from Jesus as he might have been in real life, or even as he is in the gospels, to Christ in the Church.—B-159

Patriotism

A man's feet must be planted in his country, but his eyes should survey the world.—B-176

Society

Society is like the air, necessary to breathe but insufficient to live on.—B-185

Emotions, transformations of

It is accordingly no paradox that there should be honour among thieves, kindness among harlots, and probity among fanatics. They have not lost their conscience; they have merely introduced a flattering heresy into the conventional code, to make room for the particular passion indulged in their little world.—B-187

What God thinks about the world

Occidental philosophers, in their less simple and less eloquent manner, have often repeated that arrogant Hebraic cry: they have told us in their systems what God thinks about the world. Such pretensions would be surprising did we not remind ourselves of the obvious truth that what men attribute to God is nothing but the ideal they value and grope for in themselves, and that the commandments, mythically said to come from the Most High, flow in fact from common reason and local experience.—B-188

Religious extensions of society

The religious extensions of society should therefore be carefully watched; for while sometimes, as with the Hebrew prophets, religion gives dramatic expression to actual social forces and helps to intensify moral feeling, it often, as in mystics of all creeds and ages, deadens the consciousness of real ties by feigning ties which are purely imaginary.—B-191

Discovery

To discover a law may meantime be the most interesting of events, and the image or formula that expresses a principle may be the most welcome of intellectual presences.—B-191

Spiritual tyrannies
World's conventions

Common men accept these spiritual tyrannies, weak men repine at them, and great men break them down. But to defy the world is a serious business, and requires the greatest courage, even if the defiance touch in the first place only the world's ideals. Most men's conscience, habits, and opinions are borrowed from convention and gather continual comforting assurances from the same social consensus that originally suggested them. To reverse this process, to consult one's own experience and elicit one's own judgment, challenging those in vogue, seems too often audacious and futile; but there are impetuous minds born to disregard the chances against them, even to the extent of denying that they are taking chances at all.—B-194

Religious enthusiasts, their methods and results

Thus, if the innovator be a religious soul, grown conscious of some new spiritual principle, he will try to find support for his inspiration in some lost book of the law or in some early divine revelation corrupted, as he will assert, by wicked men, or even in some direct voice from heaven; no delusion will be too obvious, no re-interpretation too forced, if it can help him to find external support somewhere for his spontaneous conviction.—B-194

Human experiences

A conception not reducible to the small change of daily experience is like a currency not exchangeable for articles of consumption; it is not a symbol, but a fraud.—B-196

C

Contradiction in religion

Each religion, so dear to those whose life it sanctifies, and fulfilling so necessary a function in the society that has adopted it, necessarily contradicts every other religion, and probably contradicts itself.—C-5

What religion

What religion a man shall have is a historical accident, quite as much as what language he shall speak. In the rare circumstances where a choice is possible, he may, with some difficulty, make an exchange; but even then he is only adopting a new convention which may be more agreeable to his personal temper but which is essentially as arbitrary as the old.—C-5

Vestiges

Yet a moment's probing of the conceptions surviving in such minds will show them to be nothing but vestiges of old beliefs, creases which thought, even if emptied of all dogmatic tenets, has not been able to smooth away at its first unfolding.—C-5-6

Ultimate values

The Life of Reason is the seat of all ultimate values.—C-6

Right vs. wrong. Life of Reason

Moreover, the Life of Reason is an ideal to which everything in the world should be subordinated; it establishes lines of moral cleavage everywhere and makes right eternally different from wrong.—C-7

Religion vs. reason. Various religions compared
Imaginary remedies. Betterment of life

Nevertheless, we must confess that this religious pursuit

of the Life of Reason has been singularly abortive. Those within the pale of each religion may prevail upon themselves to express satisfaction with its results, thanks to a fond partiality in reading the past and generous draughts of hope for the future; but any one regarding the various religions at once and comparing their achievements with what reason requires, must feel how terrible is the disappointment which they have one and all prepared for mankind. Their chief anxiety has been to offer imaginary remedies for mortal ills, some of which are incurable essentially, while others might have been really cured by well-directed effort. The Greek oracles, for instance, pretended to heal our natural ignorance, which has its appropriate though difficult cure, while the Christian vision of heaven pretended to be an antidote to our natural death, the inevitable correlate of birth and of a changing and continued existence. By methods of this sort little can be done for the real betterment of life. To confuse intelligence and dislocate sentiment by gratuitous fictions is a short-sighted way of pursuing happiness. Nature is soon avenged.—C-9-10

Morality debauched

Religion too often debauches the morality it comes to sanction, and impedes the science it ought to fulfill.—C-10

Aims of life

The conditions and the aims of life are both represented in religion poetically, but this poetry tends to arrogate to itself literal truth and moral authority, neither of which it possesses. —C-10

Abuse

The poetic value of religion would initially be greater than that of poetry itself, because religion deals with higher and more practical themes, with sides of life which are in greater need of some imaginative touch and ideal interpretation than are those pleasant or pompous things which ordinary poetry dwells upon. But this initial advantage is neutralized in part by the abuse to which religion is subject, whenever its symbolic rightness is taken for scientific truth. Like poetry, it improves the world only by imagining it improved, but not content with making this addition to the mind's furniture—an addition which might be useful and ennobling—it thinks to confer a more radical benefit by persuading mankind that, in spite of appearances, the world is really such as that rather arbitrary idealisation has painted it.—C-11-12

Imaginative achievements. Deception

Religion remains an imaginative achievement, a symbolic representation of moral reality which may have a most important function in vitalising the mind and in transmitting, by way of parables, the lessons of experience. But it becomes at the same time a continuous incidental deception; and this deception, in proportion as it is strenuously denied to be such, can work indefinite harm in the world and in the conscience. —C-12

Reverence and truth

The feeling of reverence should itself be treated with reverence, although not at a sacrifice of truth, with which alone, in the end, reverence is compatible.—C-13

Intolerance

If we hope to gain any understanding of these matters we must begin by taking them out of that heated and fanatical atmosphere in which the Hebrew tradition has enveloped them. The Jews had no philosophy, and when their national traditions came to be theoretically explicated and justified, they were made to issue in a puerile scholasticism, and a rabid intolerance. The question of monotheism, for instance, was a terrible question to the Jews. Idolatry did not consist in worshipping a god, who, not being ideal, might be unworthy of worship, but rather in recognising other gods than the one worshipped in Jerusalem.—C-14

Careless reasoning

In his impotence and laziness the natural man unites any notion with any other in a loose causal relation.—C-15

Experience

We do not ordinarily expect virgins to bear children nor prophets to be fed by ravens nor prayers to remove mountains; but we may believe any of these things at the merest suggestion of fancy or report, without any warrant from experience, so loose is the bond and so external the relation between the terms most commonly associated. A quite unprecedented occurrence will seem natural and intelligible enough if it falls in happily with the current of our thoughts. —C-16-17

Superstition

Hence superstition and the magical function of religion; hence the deceptions men fall into by cogitating on things they are ignorant of and arrogating to themselves powers which they have never learned to exercise.—C-25

Creation of gods. Fear

That fear first created the gods is perhaps as true as anything so brief could be on so great a subject.—C-28

The supernatural

As theoretical superstition stops at any cause, so practical superstition seizes on any means. Religion arises under high pressure: in the last extremity, every one appeals to God. But in the last extremity all known methods of action have proved futile; when resources are exhausted and ideas fail, if there is still vitality in the will it sends a supreme appeal to the supernatural. This appeal is necessarily made in the dark: it is the appeal of a conscious impotence, of an avowed perplexity. What a man in such case may come to do to propitiate the deity, or to produce by magic a result he cannot produce by art, will obviously be some random action. He will be driven back to the place where instinct and reason begin. His movement will be absolutely experimental, altogether spontaneous. He will have no reason for what he does, save that he must do something.—C-33

Pleasing the gods

A man wondering what will please heaven can ultimately light on nothing but what might please himself. It is pathetic to observe how lowly the motives are that religion, even the highest, attributes to the deity, and from what a hard-pressed and bitter existence they have been drawn. To be given the best morsel, to be remembered, to be praised, to be obeyed blindly and punctiliously—these have been thought points of honour with the gods, for which they would dispense favours and punishments on the most exorbitant scale.—C-34

Rites and ceremonies

Sacrifice is a rite, and rites can seldom be made to embody ideas exclusively moral. Something dramatic or mystical will cling to the performance, and, even when the effect of it is to purify, it will bring about an emotional catharsis rather than a moral improvement. The mass is a ritual sacrifice, and the communion is a part of it, having the closest resemblance to what sacrifices have always been. Among the devout these ceremonies, and the lyric emotions they awaken, have a quite visible influence; but the spell is mystic, the god soon recedes, and it would be purely fanciful to maintain that any permanent moral effect comes from such an exercise.—C-38

Prayer

No unsophisticated man prays to have that done for him which he knows how to do for himself.—C-40

Prayer

Prayer, like every other act, becomes in a providential world altogether perfunctory and histrionic; we are compelled to go through it, it is set down for us in the play, but it lacks altogether that moral value which we assign to it. When our prayers fail, it must be better than if they had succeeded, so that prayer, with all free preference whatsoever, becomes an absurdity.—C-41

Mortal man

Man, for instance, is mortal, and his whole animal and

[43]

social economy is built on that fact, so that his practical ideal must start on that basis, and make the best of it.—C-45

Pagan devotion. Prayer

This use of prayer has not been conspicuous in Christian times, because, instead of assimilating the temporal to the eternal, men have assimilated the eternal to the temporal, being perturbed fanatics in religion rather than poets and idealists. Pagan devotion, on the other hand, was full of this calmer spirit.—C-46

Primitive thought. Poetry and prose

Primitive thought has the form of poetry and the function of prose.—C-49

Rational philosophy

The Hebrews, denying themselves a rich mythology, remained without science and plastic art; the Chinese, who seem to have attained legality and domestic arts and a tutored sentiment without passing through such imaginative tempests as have harassed us, remain at the same time without a serious science or philosophy. The Greeks, on the contrary, precisely the people with the richest and most irresponsible myths, first conceived the cosmos scientifically, and first wrote rational history and philosophy.—C-51

Prayer vs. reality

Prayer, among sane people, has never superseded practical efforts to secure the desired end; a proof that the sphere of expression was never really confused with that of reality. Indeed, such a confusion, if it had passed from theory to practice, would have changed mythology into madness. With rare exceptions this declension has not occurred and myths have been taken with a grain of salt which not only made them digestible, but heightened their savour.—C-52

Mythology vs. science

But the most adequate mythology is mythology still; it does not, like science, set things before us in the very terms they

will wear when they are gradually revealed to experience.
—C-54

Scientific formulas

Scientific formulas, on the contrary, cry aloud for retranslation into perceptual terms; they are like tight-ropes, on which a man may walk but on which he cannot stand still. These unstable symbols lead, however, to real facts and define their experimental relations; while the mind reposing contentedly in a myth needs to have all observation and experience behind it, for it will not be driven to gather more.—C-55

Dante

Thus Dante's bad cosmography and worse history do not detract from the spiritual penetration of his thought, though they detract from its direct applicability.—C-56

Apollo. True religion

The religion of Apollo is therefore a true religion, as religions may be true.—C-57

Myths. India. Sacraments

Pythagorean mysteries and hypnotisations, although periodically fashionable, have soon shrivelled in our too salubrious and biting air. Even such charming exotics as Plato's myths have not been able to flourish without changing their nature and passing into ordinary dramatic mythology—into a magic system in which all the forces, once terms in moral experience, became personal angels and demons. Similarly with the Christian sacraments: these magic rites, had they been established in India among a people theosophically minded, might have furnished cues to high transcendental mysteries. Baptism might have been interpreted as a symbol for the purged and abolished will, and Communion as a symbol for the escape from personality. But European races, though credulous enough, are naturally positivistic, so that, when they were called upon to elucidate their ceremonial mysteries, what they lit upon was no metaphysical symbolism but a material and historical drama. Communion became a sentimental interview between the devout soul and the person of Christ; baptism became the legal execution of a mythical contract once entered into between the first and second persons of the Trinity. Thus, instead of a metaphysical interpretation, the extant magic received its needful justification through myths.—C-59

Belief in gods

This pathetic phenomenon is characteristic of religious minds that have outgrown their traditional faith without being able to restate the natural grounds and moral values of that somehow precious system in which they no longer believe. —C-60

Vedas

The gods of the Vedas are unmistakably natural elements. Vulcan is there nothing but fire, Jupiter nothing but the sky. —C-63

Origin of religion

We have need all the more to remember how slowly and reluctantly religion has suffered spiritualisation, how imperfectly as yet its superstitious origin has been outgrown.—C-68

Evolution of Christianity

As the Vedas offer a glimpse into the antecedents of Greek mythology, so Hebrew studies open up vistas into the antecedents of Christian dogma. Christianity in its Patristic form was an adaptation of Hebrew religion to the Greco-Roman world, and later, in the Protestant movement, a readaptation of the same to what we may call the Teutonic spirit. In the first adaptation, Hebrew positivism was wonderfully refined, transformed into a religion of redemption, and endowed with a semi-pagan mythology, a pseudo-Platonic metaphysics, and a quasi-Roman organisation. In the second adaptation, Christianity received a new basis and standard in the spontaneous faith of the individual; and, as the traditions thus undermined in principle gradually dropped away, it was reduced by the German theologians to a romantic and mystical pantheism. Throughout its transformations, however, Christianity remains indebted to the Jews not only for its founder, but for the nucleus of its dogma, cult, and ethical doctrine.—C-69

Jehovah

A wandering tribe, at once oppressed and aggressive, as Israel evidently was from the beginning, is conscious of nothing so much as of its tribal unity. To protect the tribe is accordingly the chief function of its god. Whatever character Jehovah may originally have had, whether a storm-god of Sinai or of Ararat, or a sacred bull, or each of these by affinity and confusion with the other, when the Israelites had once adopted him as their god they could see nothing essential in him but his power to protect them in the lands they had conquered. To this exclusive devotion of Jehovah to Israel, Israel responded by a devotion to Jehovah no less exclusive. They neglected, when at home, the worship of every other divinity, and later even while travelling abroad; and they tended to deny altogether, first the comparable power and finally even the existence of other gods.—C-71

Israel

Israel, like every other nation, thought its traditions divine. —C-74

Dogmas

Dogmas are at their best when nobody denies them, for then their falsehood sleeps, like that of an unconscious metaphor, and their moral function is discharged instinctively. They count and are not defined, and the side of them that is not deceptive is the one that comes forward. What was condemnable in the Jews was not that they asserted the divinity of their law, for that they did with substantial sincerity and truth. Their crime is to have denied the equal prerogative of other nations' laws and deities, for this they did, not from critical insight or intellectual scruples, but out of pure bigotry, conceit, and stupidity. They did not want other nations also to have a god.—C-76-77

[47]

Jewish government

What the moral government (of the Jews) of things meant when it was first asserted was that Jehovah expressly directed the destinies of heathen nations and the course of nature itself for the final glorification of the Jews.—C-77

Jews. Christianity. Mohammedanism. Illusions of religion

No civilised people had ever had such pretensions before. They all recognised one another's religions, if not as literally true (for some familiarity is needed to foster that illusion), certainly as more or less sacred and significant. Had the Jews not rendered themselves odious to mankind by this arrogance, and taught Christians and Moslems the same fanaticism, the nature of religion would not have been falsified among us and we would not now have so much to apologize for and to retract.—C-77

Priests. Bible. Church

Revelation, enigmatically contained in Scripture, found its necessary explication in theology, while the priests, now guardians of the keys of heaven, naturally enlarged their authority over the earth. In fine, the poetic legends and patriarchal worship that had formerly made up the religion of Israel were transformed into two concrete and formidable engines—the Bible and the Church.—C-81-82

Liberality, lack of, among Jews

Among the Jews, there were no liberal interests for the ideal to express. They had only elementary human experience —the perpetual Oriental round of piety and servitude in the bosom of a scorched, exhausted country.—C-85

Hebraic pretensions

Before the rise of those strange and fraudulent Hebraic pretensions there was no question among men about the national, personal and poetic character of religious allegiance. It could never have been a duty to adopt a religion not one's own any more than a language, a coinage, or a costume not current in one's own country. The idea that religion contains a literal, not a symbolic, representation of truth and life is simply an impossible idea.—C-98

Paganism in Christianity

The western intellect, in order to accept the gospel, had to sublimate it into a neo-Platonic system of metaphysics. In like manner the western heart had to render Christianity congenial and adequate by a rich infusion of pagan custom and sentiment. This adaptation was more gentle and facile than might be supposed. We are too much inclined to impute an abstract and ideal Christianity to the polyglot souls of early Christians, and to ignore that mysterious and miraculous side of later paganism from which Christian cultus and ritual are chiefly derived.—C-99

Catholic piety and paganism

The first disciples had been disinherited Jews, with religious habits which men of other races and interests could never have adopted intelligently; the Church was accordingly wise enough to perpetuate in its practice at least an indispensable minimum of popular paganism. How considerable this minimum was a glance at Catholic piety will suffice to convince us.—C-100

Celestial currency. Saints and mysteries

Each religious order and all the laity more or less affiliated to it will cultivate special saints and special mysteries. There are also particular places and days on which graces are granted, as not on others, and the quantity of such graces is measurable by canonic standards. So many days of remitted penance correspond to a work of a certain merit, for there is a celestial currency in which mulcts and remissions may be accurately summed and subtracted by angelic recorders. One man's spiritual earnings may by gift be attributed and imputed to another, a belief which may seem arbitrary and superstitious but which is really a natural corollary to fundamental doctrines

[49]

like the atonement, the communion of saints, and intercession for the dead and living.—C-102

Paganism in Catholicism

Another phase of the same natural religion is seen in frequent festivals, in the consecration of buildings, ships, fields, labours, and seasons; in intercessions by the greater dead for the living and by the living for the lesser dead—a perfect survival of heroes and penates on the one hand and of pagan funeral rites and commemorations on the other. Add Lent with its carnival, ember-days, all saints' and all souls, Christmas with its magi or its Saint Nicholas, Saint Agnes's and Saint Valentine's days with their profane associations, a saint for finding lost objects and another for prospering amourettes, since all great and tragic loves have their inevitable patrons in Christ and the Virgin, in Mary Magdalene, and in the mystics innumerable. This, with what more could easily be rehearsed, makes a complete paganism within Christian tradition, a paganism for which little basis can be found in the gospel, the mass, the breviary, or the theologians.—C-102-103

Paganism and Hebraism, their effect upon Christianity

Nothing is accordingly more patent than that Christianity was paganised by the early Church; indeed, the creation of the Church was itself what to a Hebraising mind must seem a corruption, namely a mixing of pagan philosophy and ritual with the Gospel. But this sort of constitutive corruption would more properly be called an adaption, an absorption, or even a civilisation of Hebraism; for by this marriage with paganism Christianity fitted itself to live and work in the civilised world. By this corruption it was completed and immensely improved, like Anglo-Saxon by its corruption through French and Latin; for it is always an improvement in religion, whose business is to express and inspire spiritual sentiment, that it should learn to express and inspire that sentiment more generously. Paganism was nearer than Hebraism to the Life of Reason because its myths were more transparent and its temper less fanatical; and so a paganised Christianity approached more closely that ideality which constitutes religious truth than a bare and intense Hebraism, in its hostility to human genius, could ever have done if isolated and unqualified.—C-106-107

The Christian story's effect upon other races

To races without experience—that is, without cumulative traditions or a visible past—Christianity could be nothing but a fairy story and a gratuitous hope, as if they had been told about the Sultan of Timbuctoo and promised that they should some day ride on his winged Arabian horses. The tragic meaning of the Christian faith, its immense renunciation of all things earthly and the merely metaphysical glory of its trans-figured life, commonly escaped their apprehension, as it still continues to do. They listened open-mouthed to the missionary and accepted his asseverations with unsuspecting emotion, like the Anglo-Saxon king who likened the soul to a bird fly-ing in and out of a tent at night, about whose further fortunes any account would be interesting to hear. A seed planted in such a virgin and uncultivated soil must needs bring forth fruit of a new savour.—C-111-112

Crusades

The Crusades were not inspired by the Prince of Peace, to whose honour they were fancifully and passionately dedi-cated.—C-113

Fashion

Fashion is something barbarous, for it produces innovation without reason and imitation without benefit.—C-113

Our civilization

To this day we have not achieved a really native civilisa-tion. Our art, morals, and religion, though deeply dyed in native feeling, are still only definable and, indeed, conceiv-able, by reference to classic and alien standards.—C-114

Protestant mistakes

It (Protestantism) accordingly mistakes vitality, both in it-self and in the universe, for spiritual life.—C-116

[51]

Protestantism vs. barbarism

Thus in the Protestant religion the faith natural to barbarism appears clothed, by force of historical accident, in the language of an adapted Christianity.—C-118

Vested illusions
Intellectual development hampered by Christianity

As the Middle Ages advanced the new-born human genius which constituted their culture grew daily more playful, curious, and ornate. It was naturally in the countries formerly pagan that this new paganism principally flourished. Religion began in certain quarters to be taken philosophically; its relation to life began to be understood, that it was a poetic expression of need, hope, and ignorance. Here prodigious vested interests and vested illusions of every sort made dangerous the path of sincerity. Genuine moral and religious impulses could not be easily dissociated from a system of thought and discipline with which for a thousand years they had been intimately interwoven. Scepticism, instead of seeming, what it naturally is, a moral force, a tendency to sincerity, economy, and fine adjustment of life and mind to experience—scepticism seemed a temptation and a danger. This situation, which still prevails in a certain measure, strikingly shows into how artificial a posture Christianity has thrown the mind—C-118-119

The god idea

We may well imagine that lions and porpoises have a more masculine assurance that God is on their side than ever visits the breast of an antelope or jelly-fish.—C-123

Protestantism, character of

It is a part of Protestantism to be austere, energetic, unwearied in some laborious task.—C-124

Negative phase of Protestantism

Hence, in spite of a theoretic optimism, disapproval and proscription play a large part in Protestant sentiment.—C-124

Optimism

Animal optimism is a great renovator and disinfectant in the world.—C-125

Teutonic religion

It was this youthful religion—profound, barbaric, poetical—that the Teutonic races insinuated into Christianity and substituted for that last sigh of two expiring worlds. In the end, with the crumbling away of Christian dogma and tradition, Absolute Egotism appeared openly on the surface in the shape of German speculative philosophy. This form, which Protestantism assumed at a moment of high tension and reckless self-sufficiency, it will doubtless shed in turn and take on new expressions; but that declaration of independence on the part of the Teutonic spirit marks emphatically its exit from Christianity and the end of that series of transformations in which it took the Bible and Patristic dogma for its materials. It now bids fair to apply itself instead to social life and natural science and to attempt to feed its Protean hunger directly from these more Protean sources.—C-125-126

Science

Science is a bridge touching experience at both ends, over which practical thought may travel from act to act, from perception to perception.—C-130

Discredited religions

Religions do not disappear when they are discredited; it is requisite that they should be replaced.—C-131

Pantheism

Pantheism, taken theoretically, is only naturalism poetically expressed.—C-137

Omnipotence

In spite of centuries wasted in preaching God's omnipotence, his omnipotence is contradicted by every Christian judgment and every Christian prayer.—C-142

He (Saint Augustine) is a more genial and complete representative of Christianity than any of the Greek Fathers, in whom the Hebraic and Roman vitality was comparatively absent. Philosophy was only one phase of Augustine's genius; with him it was an instrument of zeal and a stepping-stone to salvation. Scarcely had it been born out of rhetoric when it was smothered in authority. Yet even in that precarious and episodic form it acquired a wonderful sweep, depth, and technical elaboration. He stands at the watershed of history, looking over either land; his invectives teach us almost as much of paganism and heresy as his exhortations do of Catholicism. To Greek subtlety he joins Hebrew fervour and monkish intolerance; he has a Latin amplitude and (it must be confessed) coarseness of feeling; but above all he is the illumined, enraptured, forgiven saint. In him theology, however speculative, remains a vehicle for living piety; and while he has, perhaps, done more than any other man to materialise Christianity, no one was ever more truly filled with its spirit. —C-152

St. Augustine's effect upon Luther and Calvin

It was Saint Augustine, as we know, who, in spite of his fervid Catholicism, was the favourite master of both Luther and Calvin. They emphasised, however, his more fanatical side, and this very predestinarian and absolutist doctrine which he had prevailed on himself to accept.—C-171

Soul

A soul is but the last bubble of a long fermentation in the world.—C-179

Piety

Piety is more closely linked with custom than with thought. It exercises an irrational suasion, moralises by contagion, and brings an emotional peace.—C-186

Morality vs. piety

The object most commonly associated with piety is the

gods. Popular philosophy, inverting the natural order of ideas, thinks piety to the gods the source of morality. But piety, when genuine, is rather an incidental expression of morality.—C-187

Is humanity religious?

Mankind at large is also, to some minds, an object of piety. But this religion of humanity is rather a desideratum than a fact: humanity does not actually appear to anybody in a religious light.—C-189

Simple life—reward

A simple life is its own reward, and continually realises its function. Though a spiritual man may perfectly well go through intricate processes of thought and attend to very complex affairs, his single eye, fixed on a rational purpose, will simplify morally the natural chaos it looks upon and will remain free.—C-194

Spirituality of animals

But it hardly follows that animal feelings are not spiritual in their nature and, on their narrow basis, perfectly ideal. The most ideal human passion is love, which is also the most absolute and animal and one of the most ephemeral.—C-196

Sophistication

The spirit's foe in man has not been simplicity, but sophistication.—C-197

Saint

It is easier to make a saint out of a libertine than out of a prig.—C-201

Variety

There is no more critical moment in the life of a man and a nation than that in which they are first conscience-stricken and convicted of vanity.—C-204

Revealed religion

An oracular morality or revealed religion can hope to support its singular claims only by showing its general conformity to natural reason and its perfect beneficence in the world. Where such justification is wanting the system fanatically embraced is simply an epidemic mania, a social disease for the philosopher to study, and, if possible, to cure.—C-206

Justice and charity

Justice and charity are identical. To deny the initial right of any impulse is not morality but fanaticism.—C-216

Primary morality. Secondary morality

Primary morality, inspired by love of something naturally good, is accordingly charitable and ready to forgive; while secondary morality, founded on prejudice, is fanatical and ruthless.—C-217

Charity

Charity is seldom found uncoloured by fables which illustrate it and lend it a motive by which it can justify itself verbally.—C-222

Buddhist ministry

The Buddhists seem to have shown a finer sense in their ministry, knowing how to combine universal sympathy with perfect spirituality.—C-225

Buddhism

But at least Buddhism knew how to sound the heart and pierce to the genuine principles of happiness and misery.—C-225

Worldliness

In destroying worldliness this religion (Buddhism) avoided imposture. The clearing it made in the soul was soon overgrown again by the inexorable Indian jungle; but had a virile intellect been at hand, it would have been free to raise something solid and rational in the space so happily swept clean of all accumulated rubbish.—C-226

Tenderer minds

Against avarice, lust, and rancour, against cruel and vain national ambitions, tenderer and more recollected minds have always sought some asylum; but they have seldom possessed enough knowledge of nature and of human life to distinguish clearly the genuine and innocent goods which they longed for, and their protest against "the world" has too often taken on a mystical and irrational accent.—C-226

Magic cures

So in the magic cures which from time immemorial have been recorded at shrines of all religions, and which have been attributed to wonder-workers of every sect: the one thing certain about them is that they prove neither the truth of whatever myth is capriciously associated with them, nor the goodness or voluntary power of the miracle-worker himself.—C-231

Hell and morality

That hell may have frightened a few villains into omitting a crime is perhaps credible; but the embarrassed silence which the churches, in a more sensitive age, prefer to maintain on that wholesome doctrine, once, as they taught, the only rational basis for virtue—shows how their teaching has to follow the independent progress of morals. . . . What a despicable creature must a man be, and how sunk below the level of most barbaric virtue, if he cannot bear to live for his children, for his art, or for country!—C-247

Ideals vs. experience

To say that an ideal will be inevitably fulfilled simply because it is an ideal is to say something gratuitous and foolish. Pretence cannot in the end avail against experience.—C-249

Death

We need not wait for our total death to experience dying; we need not borrow from observation of others' demise a prophecy of our own extinction. Every moment celebrates obsequies over the virtues of its predecessor; and the possession of memory, by which we somehow survive in representation, is the most unmistakable proof that we are perishing in reality.

In endowing us with memory, nature has revealed to us a truth utterly unimaginable to the unflective creation, the truth of mortality.—C-260

Existence

Existence is essentially temporal and life foredoomed to be mortal, since its basis is a process and an opposition; it floats in the stream of time, never to return, never to be recovered or repossessed.—C-263

Unanimity in men

Yet, in peaceful rivers, though they flow, there is an appreciable degree of translucency. So, from moment to moment, and from man to man, there is an appreciable element of unanimity, of constancy and congruity of intent. On this abstract and perfectly identical function science rests together with every rational formation.—C-265

Reason and ideals

Reason lifts a larger or smaller element in each man to the plane of ideality according as reason more or less thoroughly leavens and permeates the lump.—C-265

Life

If you have seen the world, if you have played your game and won it, what more would you ask for? If you have tasted the sweets of existence, you should be satisfied; if the experience has been bitter, you should be glad that it comes to an end.—C-269

Eternity

In other words, the happy filling of a single hour is so much gained for the universe at large, and to find joy and sufficiency in the flying moment is perhaps the only means open to us for increasing the glory of eternity.—C-270

Perfection

Every attainment of perfection in an art—as for instance in government—makes a return to perfection easier for posterity, since there remains an enlightening example, together with faculties predisposed by discipline to recover the ancient virtue. The better a man evokes and realises the ideal, the more he leads the life that all others, in proportion to their worth, will seek to live after him, and the more he helps them to live in that nobler fashion. His presence in the society of immortals thus becomes, so to speak, more pervasive. He not only vanquishes time by his own rationality, living now in the eternal, but he continually lives again in all rational beings.— C-272

Prayer

It was a prodigious delusion to imagine that work could be done by magic; and the desperate appeal which human weakness has made to prayer, to castigations, to miscellaneous fantastic acts, in the hope of thereby bending nature to greater sympathy with human necessities, is a pathetic spectacle; all the more pathetic in that here the very importunity of evil, which distracted the mind and allowed it no choice or deliberation, prevented very often those practical measures which, if lighted upon, would have instantly relieved the situation. Religion when it has tried to do man's work for him has not only cheated hope, but consumed energy and drawn away attention from the true means of success.—C-274

Mythology

Mythology, in excogitating hidden dramatic causes for natural phenomena, or in attributing events to the human values which they might prevent or secure, has profoundly perverted and confused the intellect; it has delayed and embarrassed the discovery of natural forces, at the same time fostering presumptions which, on being exploded, tended to plunge men, by revulsion, into an artificial despair.—C-275.

True religion

True religion is entirely human and political, as was that of the ancient Hebrews, Romans, and Greeks. Supernatural machinery is either symbolic of natural conditions and moral aims or else is worthless.—C-276-277.

Mysticism

What is called mysticism is a certain genial loosening of convention, whether rational or mythical; the mystic smiles at science and plays with theology, undermining both by force of his insight and inward assurance. He is all faith, all love, all vision, but he is each of these things *in vacuo,* and in the absence of any object.—C-277

Mysticism a disease

Every religion, all science, all art, is, accordingly, subject to incidental mysticism; but in no case can mysticism stand alone and be the body or basis of anything. In the Life of Reason it is, if I may say so, a normal disease, a recurrent manifestation of lost equilibrium and interrupted growth; but in these pauses, when the depths rise to the surface and obliterate what scratches culture may have made there, the rhythm of life may be more powerfully felt, and the very disappearance of intellect may be taken for a revelation.—C-278

Revelations

Revelations are seldom beneficent.—C-279

Life of Reason and mysticism

The Life of Reason, in so far as it is life, contains the mystic's primordial assurances, and his rudimentary joys; but in so far as it is rational it has discovered what those assurances rest on, in what direction they may be trusted to support action and thought; and it has given those joys distinction and connexion, turning a dumb momentary ecstasy into a many-colored and natural happiness.—C-279

$\mathcal{D}$

Poetry and philosophy; Religion, myth, and religious ethics

No instance or institution was ever so absurd as is a large part of human poetry and philosophy, while the margin of ineptitude is much broader in religious myth than in religious ethics.—D-5

Causes

Causes at best are lightly assigned by mortals.—D-5

Will vs. experience

The pure will's impotence is absolute, and it would writhe for ever and consume itself in darkness if perception gave it no light and experience no premonition.—D-6

Genius

All invention is tentative, all art experimental, and to be sought, like salvation, with fear and trembling. There is a painful pregnancy in genius, a long incubation and waiting for the spirit, a thousand rejections and futile birth-pangs, before the wonderful child appears, a gift of the gods, utterly undeserved and inexplicably perfect.—D-8

Life, experimental. Evolution of life

Though life, however, is initially experimental and always remains experimental at bottom, yet experiment fortifies certain tendencies and cancels others, so that a gradual sediment of habit and wisdom is formed in the stream of time. Action then ceases to be merely tentative and spontaneous, and becomes art.—D-35

Art and life

The subject matter of art is life, life as it actually is; but the function of art is to make life better. The depth to which an artist may find current experience to be sunk in discord and confusion is not his special concern; his concern is, in some measure, to lift experience out.—D-66

God

As to the word "God," all mutual understanding is impossible. It is a floating literary symbol, with a value which, if we define it scientifically, becomes quite algebraic. As no experienced object corresponds to it, it is without fixed indicative force, and admits any sense which its context in any mind may happen to give it. In the first sentence of Genesis its meaning, we may safely say, is "a masculine being by whom heaven and earth were created." To fill out this implication other instances of the word would have to be gathered, in each of which, of course, the word would appear with a new and perhaps incompatible meaning.—D-97

Lying

Lying is a privilege of poets because they have not reached the level on which truth and error are discernible. Veracity and significance are not ideals for a primitive mind; we learn to value them as we learn to live, when we discover that the spirit cannot be wholly free and solipsistic. To have to distinguish fact from fancy is so great a violence to the inner man that not only poets, but theologians and philosophers, still protest against such a distinction.—D-100

Poetry vs. prose

As men of action have a better intelligence than poets, if only their action is on a broad enough stage, so the prosaic rendering of experience has the greater value, if only the experience rendered covers enough human interests. Youth and aspiration indulge in poetry; a mature and masterful mind will often despise it, and prefer to express itself laconically in prose.—D-101

Prose vs. poetry

Prose is in that measure a fine art. It might be called poetry that had become pervasively representative, and was altogether faithful to its rational function.—D-104

Truth

Truth is a jewel which should not be painted over; but it may be set to advantage and shown in a good light.—D-105

Man's consonances

The consonances man introduces into nature will follow him wherever he goes.—D-119

Ideals in forms

It is a sign of stupidity in general to stick to physical objects and given forms apart from their ideal functions.— D-120

Unhappiness, its cause

A man remains incorrigibly unhappy and perplexed, cowed, and helpless, because not intelligent enough to readjust his actions; his idol must be the self-same hereditary stock, or at least it must have the old sanctified rigidity and stare. Plastic impulse, as yet sporadic, is overwhelmed by a brute idolatrous awe at mere existence and actuality. What is, what has always been, what chance has associated with one person, alone seems acceptable or conceivable.—D-120

Man's desolation

Irrational hopes, irrational shames, irrational decencies, make man's chief desolation.—D-124

The engineer in art

Of the two approaches which barbaric architecture makes to beauty—one through ornamentation and the other through mass—the latter is in general the more successful. An engineer fights with nature hand to hand; he is less easily extravagant than a decorator; he can hardly ever afford to be absurd. He becomes accordingly more rapidly civilised and his work acquires, in spite of itself, more rationality and a more permanent charm. A self-sustaining structure, in art as in life, is the only possible basis for a vital ideal.—D-126-127

Ideas

An artist may visit a museum, but only a pedant can live there. Ideas that have long been used may be used still, if they remain ideas and have not been congealed into memories.— D-129

Art in religion

What structural elucidation did for church architecture was much like what scholastic elucidation did for church dogma: it insinuated a logic into the traditional edifice which was far from representing its soul or its genuine value.—D-137

Middle Ages, their character

The Middle Ages were, in their way, merry, sturdy, and mischievous.—D-140

Myths and symbols

In spite of the theologians, we know by instinct that in speaking of the gods we are dealing in myths and symbols.— D-175

Heaven and Hell. Beauty in its place

So men have feverishly conceived a heaven only to find it insipid, and a hell to find it ridiculous. Theodicies that were to demonstrate an absolute cosmic harmony have turned the universe into a tyrannous nightmare, from which we are glad to awake again in this unintentional and somewhat tractable world. Thus the fancies of effeminate poets in violating science are false to the highest art, and the products of sheer confusion, instigated by the love of beauty, turn out to be hideous. A rational severity in respect to art simply weeds the garden; it expresses a mature aesthetic choice and opens the way to supreme artistic achievements. To keep beauty in its place is to make all things beautiful.—D-190

Reason, its foundation

Reason, with the order which in every region it imposes on life, is grounded on an animal nature and has no other function than to serve the same.—D-191

Dogmatism

Dogmatism in the thinker is only the speculative side of greed and courage in the brute. The brute cannot surrender his appetites nor abdicate his primary right to dominate his environment. What experience and reason may teach him is merely how to make his self-assertion well balanced and successful.—D-192

Reflection

Reflection refines particular sentiments by bringing them into sympathy with all rational life.—D-192

Our standards

Half our standards come from our first masters, and the other half from our first loves. Never being so deeply stirred again, we remain persuaded that no objects save those we then discovered can have a true sublimity.—D-194

Elementary beauties

Indeed, ability to revert to elementary beauties is a test that judgment remains sound.—D-197

Ideas

Ideas, like men, live in society. Not only has each a will of its own and an inherent ideal, but each finds itself conditioned for its expression by a host of other beings, on whose cooperation it depends. Good taste, besides being inwardly clear, has to be outwardly fit.—D-199

Invariability in human nature

Human nature, for all its margin of variability, has a substantial core which is invariable, as the human body has a structure which it cannot lose without perishing altogether; for as creatures grow more complex a greater number of their organs become vital and indispensable. Advanced forms will rather die than surrender a tittle of their character; a fact which is the physical basis for loyalty and martyrdom. Any deep interpretation of oneself, or indeed of anything, has for that reason a largely representative truth. Other men, if they

[65]

look closely, will make the same discovery for themselves. Hence distinction and profundity, in spite of their rarity, are wont to be largely recognised. The best men in all ages keep classic traditions alive. These men have on their side the weight of superior intelligence, and, though they are few, they might even claim the weight of numbers, since the few of all ages, added together, may be more than the many who in any one age follow a temporary fashion.—D-206

Ignorance of self

The deviations between races and men are not yet so great as is the ignorance of self, the blindness to the native ideal, which prevails in most of them. Hence a great man of a remote epoch is more intelligible than a common man of our own time.—D-206

Citizenship

Citizenship is conferred only on creatures with human and cooperative instincts. A civilised imagination has to understand and to serve the world.—D-207

Harmony in impulses

Morality too often puts up with being a constraint, and even imagines such a disgrace to be its essence. Art, on the contrary, as often hugs unreason for fear of losing its inspiration, and forgets that it is itself a rational principle of creation and order. Morality is thus reduced to a necessary evil and art to a vain good, all for want of harmony among human impulses.
—D-208

Subject material of art

Why art, the most vital and generative of activities, should produce a set of abstract images, monuments to lost intuitions, is a curious mystery. Nature gives her products life, and they are at least equal to their sources in dignity. Why should mind, the actualisation of nature's powers, produce something so inferior to itself, reverting in its expression to material being, so that its witnesses seem so many fossils with which it strews its path? What we call museums—mausoleums, rather, in which a dead art heaps up its remains—are those the places where the Muses intended to dwell? We do not keep in show-cases the coins current in the world. A living art does not produce curiosities to be collected but spiritual necessaries to be diffused.—D-208-209

Emotions vs. necessities

A richer plexus of emotions is concerned in producing or contemplating something humanly necessary than something idly conceived.—D-210

Art and emotions

Any absolute work of art which serves no further purpose than to stimulate an emotion has about it a certain luxurious and visionary taint.—D-212

Art vs. dreams

Art, so long as it needs to be a dream, will never cease to prove a disappointment.—D-212

Art in heart of man. Art in heart of nature

Art springs so completely from the heart of man that it makes everything speak to him in his own language; it reaches, nevertheless, so truly to the heart of nature that it co-operates with her, becomes a parcel of her creative material energy, and builds by her instinctive hand.—D-229-230

E

The past of religion and art

Religion and art have had their day; indeed a part of the faith they usually inspire is to believe that they have long ago revealed their secret.—E-3

Science, its handicaps

Another circumstance that impeded the growth of science was the forensic and rhetorical turn proper to Greek intelligence. This mental habit gave a tremendous advantage in philosophy to the moralist and poet over the naturalist or mathematician. Hence what survived in Greece after the heyday of theoretic achievement was chiefly philosophies of life, and these—at the death of liberty—grew daily more personal and ascetic.—E-4

Socratic philosophy

While the Socratic school bequeathed to posterity a well-developed group of moral sciences, rational in principle, but destined to be soon overlaid with metaphysical and religious accretions, so that the dialectical nerve and reasonableness of them were obliterated, and there survived only miscellaneous conclusions, fragments of wisdom built topsy-turvy into the new mythical edifice. It is the sad task reserved for historical criticism to detach those sculptured stones from the rough mass in which they have been embedded and to rearrange them in their pristine order, thus rediscovering the inner Socratic principle of moral philosophy, which is nothing but self-knowledge—a circumspect, systematic utterance of the speaker's mind, disclosing his implicit meaning and his ultimate preferences.—E-5

Verification in science

The true contrast between science and myth is more nearly touched when we say that science alone is capable of verification.—E-10

Gods as hypotheses

The gods are demonstrable only as hypotheses, but as hypotheses they are not gods.—E-13

Fiat of Jehovah

The fiat of a vehement Jehovah swimming about in a chaos.—E-14

Ecstasy

Disembodied and timeless ecstasy.—E-14

Amusement in thought

Mere amusement in thought as in sportive action is tedious and illiberal; it marks a temperament so imperfectly educated that it prefers idle to significant play and a flimsy to a solid idea.—E-18

Science and common knowledge

Science differs from common knowledge in scope only, not in nature.—E-18

Science, its merits and defects

The defect of science is that it is inadequate or abstract, that the account it gives of things is not full and sensuous enough; but its merit is that, like sense, it makes external being present to a creature that is concerned in adjusting itself to its environment, and informs that creature about things other than itself.—E-22

Comparison of sciences and languages

Languages and religions are necessarily rivals, but sciences are necessarily allies.—E-24

Science as a disciplinarian

Science is a great disciplinarian, and misses much of the sport which the absolute is free to indulge in.—E-25

Hope of science

But the hope of science, a hope which is supported by every success it scores, is that a simpler law than has yet been discovered will be found to connect units subtler than those yet known; and that in these finer terms the universal mechanism may be exhaustively rendered.—E-33

Dialectic

Dialectic is a human pursuit and has, at bottom, a moral function; otherwise, at bottom, it would have no value. And the moral function and ultimate justification of dialectic is to further the Life of Reason, in which human thought has the maximum practical validity, and may enjoy in consequence the richest ideal development.—E-34

Dialectic vs. Science

As musicians are an honour to society, so are dialecticians that have a single heart and an exquisite patience. But somehow the benefit must redound to society and to practical knowledge, or these abstracted hermits will seem at first use-less and at last mad. The logic of nonsense has a subtle charm only because it can so easily be turned into the logic of common sense. Empty dialectic is, as it were, the ballet of science: it runs most neatly after nothing at all.—E-35

Respect for science

If science deserves respect, it is not for being oracular but for being useful and delightful, as seeing is.—E-35

Science and experience

Science, then, is the attentive consideration of common experience; it is common knowledge extended and refined. Its validity is of the same order as that of ordinary perception, memory, and understanding. Its test is found, like theirs, in actual intuition, which sometimes consists in perception and sometimes in intent. The flight of science is merely longer from perception to perception, and its deduction more accurate of meaning from meaning and purpose from purpose. It generates in the mind, for each vulgar observation, a whole brood of suggestions, hypotheses, and inferences. The sciences bestow, as is right and fitting, infinite pains upon that experience which in their absence would drift by unchallenged or misunderstood. They take note, infer, and prophesy. They compare prophecy with event; and altogether they supply— so intent are they on reality—every imaginable background and extension for the present dream.—E-38

Poets

The innocent poet believes his own lies.—E-43

Trash in historical record

The recorder of verbal tradition religiously sets down its inconsistencies and leaves in the transfigured chronicles many tell-tale incidents and remarks which, like atrophied organs in an animal body, reveal its gradual formation. Art and a deliberate pursuit of unction or beauty would have thrown over this baggage. The automatic and pious minstrel carries it with him to the end.—E-44

History

History is always written wrong, and so always needs to be rewritten.—E-45

Partisan history

Some historians, indeed, are so frankly partisan or cynical that they avowedly write history with a view to effect, either political or literary.—E-47

Investigation, historical. Reconstruction of history

Historical investigation is the natural science of the past. The circumstance that its documents are usually literary may somewhat disguise the physical character and the physical principles of this science; but when a man wishes to discover what really happened at a given moment, even if the event were somebody's thought, he has to read his sources, not for what they say, but for what they imply. In other words, the witnesses cannot be allowed merely to speak for themselves, after the gossiping fashion familiar in Herodotus; their testimony has to be interpreted according to the laws of evidence. The past needs to be reconstructed out of reports, as in geology or archaeology it needs to be reconstructed out of stratifications and ruins.—E-49

Thoughts to be forgotten. Aristotle

There are many things which, as Aristotle says, it is better not to know than to know—namely, those things which do not count in controlling the mind's fortunes nor enter into its ideal expression. Such is the whole flux of immediate experience in other minds or in one's own past; and just as it is better to forget than to remember a nightmare or the by-gone sensations of seasickness, so it is better not to conceive the sensuous pulp of alien experience, something infinite in amount and insignificant in character.—E-52

Physical causes and moral units

In fine, historical terms mark merely rhetorical unities, which have no dynamic cohesion, and there are no historical laws which are not at bottom physical, like the laws of habit —those expressions of Newton's first law of motion. An essayist may play with historical apperception as long as he will and always find something new to say, discovering the ideal nerve and issue of a movement in a different aspect of the facts. The truly proportionate, constant, efficacious relations between things will remain material. Physical causes traverse the moral units at which history stops, determining their force and duration, and the order, so irrelevant to intent, in which they succeed one another.—E-54

Fuzzy thinking

Or was it (as has been seriously maintained) in order that the converted Indians of South America might console Saint Peter for the defection of the British and Germans? Or was America, as Hegel believed, ideally superfluous, the absolute having become self-conscious enough already in Prussia?—E-56

In truth, whatever plausibility the providential view of a given occurrence may have is dependent on the curious limitation and selfishness of the observer's estimations. Sheep are providentially designed for men; but why not also for wolves, and men for worms and microbes? If the historian is willing to accept such a suggestion, and to become a blind worshipper of success, applauding every issue, however lamentable for humanity, and calling it admirable tragedy, he may seem for a while to save his theory by making it mystical; yet presently this last illusion will be dissipated when he loses his way in the maze and finds that all victors perish in their turn and everything, if you look far enough, falls back into the inexorable vortex. This is the sort of observation that the Indian sages made long ago; it is what renders their philosophy, for all its practical impotence, such an irrefragable record of experience, such a superior, definitive perception of the flux. Beside it, our progresses of two centuries and our philosophies of history, embracing one-quarter of the earth for three thousand years, seem puerile vistas indeed. Shall all eternity and all existence be for the sake of what is happening here to-day, and to me? Shall we strive manfully to the top of this particular wave, on the ground that its foam is the culmination of all things for ever? —E-56-57

Rhetorical mentalities pollute historical record

Every "historical force" pompously appealed to breaks up on inspection into a cataract of miscellaneous natural processes and minute particular causes. It breaks into its mechanical constituents and proves to have been nothing but an *effet d'ensemble* produced on a mind whose habits and categories are essentially rhetorical.—E-57

Improvement

However good or however bad the universe may be it is always worth while to make it better.—E-61

"Function of history"

The function of history is to lend materials to politics and to poetry.—E-66

Experience. Personal failures

The whole dignity of human endeavor is thus bound up with historic issues; and as conscience needs to be controlled by experience if it is to become rational, so personal experience itself needs to be enlarged ideally if the failure and successes it reports are to touch impersonal interests.*—E-68

Abstraction

The scepticism which comes from distrust of abstraction and disgust with reckoning of any sort is not a scientific force; it is an intellectual weakness.—E-70

Prejudices

Prejudices, however refractory to new evidence, evolve inwardly of themselves.—E-71

Optimism. Self-indulgent minds

Any chance conjunction, any incidental harmony, will start a hypothesis about the nature of the universe and be the parent image of a whole system of philosophy. In self-indulgent minds most of these standard images are dramatic, and the cue men follow in unravelling experience is that offered by some success or failure of their own. The sanguine, having once found a pearl in a dunghill, feel a glorious assurance that the world's true secret is that everything in the end is ordered for everybody's benefit—and that is optimism. —E-73

---

*Many of these quotations lose much of their force and beauty where separated from the context of the thesis as a whole.

World, how ruled

Any one who can at all catch the drift of experience—moral no less than physical—must feel that mechanism rules the whole world.—E-76

Parasitical minds

Thus the parasitical human mind, finding what clear knowledge it has laughably insufficient to interpret its destiny, takes to neglecting knowledge altogether and to hugging instead various irrational ideas. On the one hand it lapses into dreams which, while obviously irrelevant to practice, express the mind's vegetative instincts; hence art and mythology, which substitute playworlds for the real one on correlation with which human prosperity and dignity depend.—E-80

Courageous thinking vs. miscellaneous habits
Public sentiment vs. enlightenment
Aristotle. Democritus

Thus even Aristotle felt that good judgment and the dramatic habit of things altogether excluded the simple physics of Democritus. Indeed, as things then stood, Democritus had no right to his simplicity, except that divine right which comes of inspiration. His was an indefensible faith in a single radical insight, which happened nevertheless to be true. To justify that insight forensically it would have been necessary to change the range of human vision, making it telescopic in one region and microscopic in another; whereby the objects so transfigured would have lost their familiar aspect and their habitual context in discourse. Without such a startling change of focus nature can never seem everywhere mechanical. Hence, even to this day, people with broad human interests are apt to discredit a mechanical philosophy. Seldom can penetration and courage in thinking hold their own against the miscellaneous habits of discourse; and nobody remembers that moral values must remain captious, and imaginative life ignoble and dark, so long as the whole basis and application of them is falsely conceived. Discoveries in science are made only by near-sighted specialists, while the influence of public sentiment and policy still works systematically against enlightenment.—E-83.

Material engines vs. ideal spirits

It is doubtless better to find material engines—not necessarily inanimate, either—which may really serve to bring order, security and progress into our lives, than to find impassioned or ideal spirits, that can do nothing for us except, at best, assure us that they are perfectly happy.—E-85

Social inertia
Mechanism, prejudice against

The artificial prejudice against mechanism is a fruit of party spirit. When a myth has become the centre or sanction for habits and institutions, these habits and institutions stand against any conception incompatible with that myth. It matters nothing that the values the myth was designed to express may remain standing without it, or may be transferred to its successor. Social and intellectual inertia is too great to tolerate so simple an evolution.—E-87

Materialism. Democritus

Materialism has its distinct aesthetic and emotional colour, though this may be strangely affected and even reversed by contrast with systems of an incongruous hue, jostling it accidentally in a confused and amphibious mind. If you are in the habit of believing in special providences, or of expecting to continue your romantic adventures in a second life, materialism will dash your hopes most unpleasantly, and you may think for a year or two that you have nothing left to live for. But a thorough materialist, one born to the faith and not half plunged into it by an unexpected christening in cold water, will be like the superb Democritus, a laughing philosopher. His delight in a mechanism that can fall into so many marvellous and beautiful shapes, and can generate so many exciting passions, should be of the same intellectual quality as that which the visitor feels in a museum of natural history.—E-90

Vanity. Don Quixote

But against evils born of pure vanity and self-deception, against the verbiage by which man persuades himself that he is the goal and acme of the universe, laughter is the proper defence. Laughter also has this subtle advantage, that it need not remain without an overtone of sympathy and brotherly understanding; as the laughter that greets Don Quixote's absurdities and misadventures does not mock the hero's intent. His ardour was admirable, but the world must be known before it can be reformed pertinently, and happiness, to be attained, must be placed in reason.—E-91

Reflection. Materialism

It is true that materialism prophesies an ultimate extinction for man and all his works. The horror which this prospect inspires in the natural man might be mitigated by reflection. —E-92

Natural existence. Saint Augustine

The panic which seems to seize some minds at the thought of a merely natural existence is something truly hysterical; and yet one wonders why ultimate peace should seem so intolerable to people who not so many years ago found a stern religious satisfaction in consigning almost the whole human race to perpetual torture, the Creator, as Saint Augustine tells us, having in his infinite wisdom and justice devised a special kind of material fire that might avail to burn resurrected bodies for ever without consuming them.—E-93

Population control

The passion for a large and permanent population in the universe is not obviously rational.—E-93-94

Man of science vs. philosopher
Darwin. Newton. Mechanism

Not to be a philosopher is even an advantage for a man of science, because he is then more willing to adapt his methods to the state of knowledge in his particular subject, without insisting on ultimate intelligibility; and he has perhaps more joy of his discoveries than he might have if he had discounted them in his speculations. Darwin, for instance, did more than any one since Newton to prove that mechanism is universal.—E-9

The scientific army. Scientific methods

This cautious peripheral attack, which does so much honour to the scientific army and has won it so many useful victories, is another proof that science is nothing but common knowledge extended. It is willing to reckon in any terms and to study any subject-matter; where it cannot see necessity it will notice law; where laws cannot be stated it will describe habits; where habits fail it will classify types; and where types even are indiscernible, it will not despise statistics.—E-98

Morals. Life. Evolution

All that is scientific or Darwinian in the theory of evolution is accordingly an application of mechanism, a proof that mechanism lies at the basis of life and morals.—E-108

Critique of science

A moral and truly transcendental critique of science, as of common sense, is never out of place, since all such a critique does is to assign to each conception or discovery its place and importance in the Life of Reason.—E-124

Social imagination

If psychology is a science, many things that books of psychology contain should be excluded from it. One is social imagination.—E-126

Psychology

Psychology then remains what it was in Aristotle's *De Anima*—an ill-developed branch of natural science, pieced out with literary terms and perhaps enriched by occasional dramatic interpretations.—E-141

Thought in nature

Thought's place in nature is exiguous, however broad the

landscape it represents; it touches the world tangentially only, in some ferment of the brain.—E-146

Mental world

There is indeed a strange half-assumption afloat, a sort of reserved faith which every one seems to respect but nobody utters, to the effect that the mental world has a mechanism of its own, and that ideas intelligently produce and sustain one another. Systematic idealists, to be sure, have generally given a dialectical or moral texture to the cosmos, so that the passage from idea to idea in experience need not be due, in their physics, to any intrinsic or proportionate efficacy in these ideas themselves. The march of experience is not explained at all by such high cosmogonies. They abandon that practical calculation to some science of illusion that has to be tolerated in this provisional life. Their own understanding is of things merely in the gross, because they fall in with some divine plan and produce, unaccountably enough, some interesting harmony.—E-150

Thoughts, material

We are not plainly aware (in spite of headaches, fatigue, sleep, love, intoxication, and madness) that the course of our thoughts is as directly dependent on the body as is their inception.—E-153

Natural history

Much natural history has been written and studied with the idea of finding curious facts. The demand has not been for constant laws or intelligibility, but for any circumstance that could arrest attention or divert the fancy.—E-154

Psychology, its limitations

What scientific psychology has to attempt—for little has been accomplished—may be reduced to this: To develop physiology and anthropology until the mechanism of life becomes clear, at least in its general method, and then to determine, by experiment and by well-sifted testimony, what conscious sublimation each of those material situations attains, if indeed it attains any. There will always remain, no doubt, many a region where the machinery of nature is too fine for us to trace or eludes us by involving agencies that we lack senses to perceive. In these regions where science is denied we shall have to be satisfied with landscape-painting. The more obvious results and superficial harmonies perceived in those regions will receive names and physics will be arrested at natural history. Where these unexplained facts are mental it will not be hard to do more systematically what common sense has done already, and to attach them, as we attach love or patriotism, to the natural crises that subtend them.—E-158-159

Psychology and literature

Where psychology depends on literature, where both its units and its method are poetical, there can be no talk of science. We may as justly, or as absurdly, speak of the spirit of an age or of a religion as of a man's character or a river's god. Particulars in illustration may have good historic warrant, but the unities superimposed are ideal. Such metaphors may be very useful, for a man may ordinarily be trusted to continue his practices and a river its beneficent or disastrous floods; and since those rhetorical forms have no existence in nature we may continue to frame them as may be most convenient for discourse.—E-160

Moral energy

Moral energy, so closely analogous to physical interplay, is of course not without a material basis. Spiritual sublimation does not consist in not using matter but in using it up, in making it all useful.—E-175

Intelligence

Intelligence is not a substance; it is a principle of order and of art; it requires a given situation and some particular natural interest to bring it into play. In fact, it is nothing but a name for the empire which conscious, but at bottom irrational, interests attain over the field in which they operate; it

is the fruition of life, the token of successful operation.—
E-177

Thought and physical nature

No thought is found without an organ; none is conceivable
without an expression which is that organ's visible emanation;
and none would be significant without a subject-matter lying
in the world of which that organ is a part.—E-179

Matter and form, a fable

A fable about matter and form.

In order to live—if such a myth may be allowed—the Titan
Matter was eager to disguise his incorrigible vagueness and
pretend to be something. He accordingly addressed himself
to the beautiful company of Forms, sisters whom he thought
all equally beautiful, though their number was endless, and
equally fit to satisfy his heart. He wooed them hypocritically,
with no intention of wedding them; yet he uttered their names
in such seductive accents (called by mortals intelligence and
toil) that the virgin goddesses offered no resistance—at least
such of them as happened to be near or of a facile disposition.
They were presently deserted by their unworthy lover; yet
they, too, in that moment's union, had tasted the sweetness of
life. The heaven to which they returned was no longer an
infinite mathematical paradise. It was crossed by memories of
earth, and a warmer breath lingered in some of its lanes and
grottoes. Henceforth its nymphs could not forget that they
had awakened a passion and that, unmoved themselves, they
had moved a strange indomitable giant to art and love.—
E-185-186

Artifices of languages

The most obvious artifices of language are often the most
deceptive and bring on epidemic prejudices.—E-188

Number and measure. Human perception

At the same time number and measure are the grammar of
sense; and the more this inner logic is cultivated and refined

the greater subtlety and sweep can be given to human perception.—E-193

Meanings. Hegel

The effort to explain meanings is in most cases abortive because these meanings melt in our hands—a defeat which Hegel would fain have consecrated, together with all other evils, into necessity and law.—E-195

Physics and dialectic
Matter and God

It would not occur to a geometer to ask with trepidation what difference it would make to the Pythagorean proposition if the hypothenuse were said to be wise and good. Yet metaphysicians, confounding dialectic with physics and thereby corrupting both, will discuss for ever the difference it makes to substance whether you call it matter or God.—E-202-203

Theology

The romance of an unstable and groping theology, full of warm intentions and impossible ideas, he took to be typical of all experience and of all science.—E-205

Virtue

With maturity comes the recognition that the authorized precepts of morality were essentially not arbitrary; that they expressed the genuine aims and interests of a practised will; that their alleged alien and supernatural basis (which if real would have deprived them of all moral authority) was but a mythical cover for their forgotten natural springs. Virtue is then seen to be admirable essentially, and not merely by conventional imputation.—E-218

Conscience

Men know better what is right and wrong than what is ultimately good or evil; their conscience is more vividly present to them than the fruits which obedience to conscience might bear; so that the logical relation of means to ends, of methods to activities, eludes them altogether.—E-227

Poetry vs. science

The fortunate instincts of a race destined to long life and rationality express themselves in significant poetry before they express themselves in science.—E-229

Conscience, reason

And so soon as the conscience summons its own dicta for revision in the light of experience and of universal sympathy, it is no longer called conscience, but reason. So, too, when the spirit summons its traditional faiths, to subject them to a similar examination, that exercise is not called religion, but philosophy.—E-232

Antipathies

The physical repulsion, however, which everybody feels to habits and interests which he is incapable of sharing is no part of rational estimation, large as its share may be in the fierce prejudices and superstitions which pre-rational morality abounds in. The strongest feelings assigned to the conscience are not moral feelings at all; they express merely physical antipathies.—E-234-235

Science in society

Perhaps the art of politics, if it were practised scientifically, might obviate war, religious enmities, industrial competition, and human slavery; but it would certainly not leave a free field for all animals nor for all monstrosities in men. Even while admitting the claims of monsters to be treated humanely, reason could not suffer them to absorb those material resources which might be needed to maintain rational society at its highest efficiency. We cannot, at this immense distance from a rational social order, judge what concessions individual genius would be called upon to make in a system of education and government in which all attainable goods should be pursued scientifically.—E-237

Rational morality

A truly rational morality, or social regimen, has never existed in the world and is hardly to be looked for. What guides men and nations in their practice is always some partial interest or some partial disillusion.—E-239

Science and virtue

True science, then, was that which enabled a man to disentangle and attain his natural good; and such a science is also the art of life and the whole of virtue.—E-243

Rational ethics

Rational ethics is an embodiment of volition, not a description of it. It is the expression of living interest, preference, and categorical choice. It leaves to psychology and history a free field for the description of moral phenomena. It has no interest in slipping far-fetched and incredible myths beneath the facts of nature, so as to lend a non-natural origin to human aspirations. It even recognises, as an emanation of its own force, that uncompromising truthfulness with which science assigns all forms of moral life to their place in the mechanical system of nature.—E-244

Natural morality
Rational ethics

Rational ethics, then, resembles pre-rational precepts and half-systems in being founded on impulse. It formulates a natural morality. It is a settled method of achieving ends to which man is drawn by virtue of his physical and rational constitution. By this circumstance rational ethics is removed from the bad company of all artificial, verbal, and unjust systems of morality, which in absolving themselves from relevance to man's endowment and experience merely show how completely irrelevant they are to life.—E-248-249

Discipline

It is discipline that renders men rational and capable of happiness, by suppressing without hatred what needs to be suppressed to attain a beautiful naturalness. Discipline discredits the random pleasures of illusion, hope, and triumph, and substitutes those which are self-reproductive, perennial, and serene, because they express an equilibrium maintained with reality.—E-253

Wisdom

Wisdom and happiness consist in having recast natural energies in the furnace of experience.—E-253

Politics

Politics is expected to be sophistical; and in the soberest parliaments hardly an argument is used or an ideal invoked which is not an insult to reason. Majorities work by a system of bribes offered to the more barren interests of men and to their more blatant prejudices. The higher direction of their lives is relegated to religion, which, unhappily, is apt to suffer from hereditary blindness to natural needs and to possible progress.—E-255

Sympathy

It is a noble thing to be sensitive to others' hardships, and happy in their happiness; but it is noble because it refines the natural will without enfeebling it, offering it rather a new and congenial development, one entirely predetermined by the fundamental structure of human nature. Were man not gregarious, were he not made to be child, friend, husband, and father by turns, his morality would not be social, but, like that of some silk-worm or some seraph, wholly industrious or wholly contemplative. Parental and sexual instincts, social life and the gift of co-operation carry sympathy implicitly with them, as they carry the very faculty to recognise a fellow-being.—E-259

Statesmen

A statesman entrusted with power should regard nothing but his country's interests; to regard anything else would be treason. He cannot allow foreign sentiment or private hobbies to make him misapply the resources of his fellow-countrymen to their own injury. But he may well have an enlightened view of the interests which he serves; he might indeed be expected to take a more profound and enlightened view of them than his countrymen were commonly capable of, else he would have no right to his eminent station. He should be the first to feel that to inflict injury or foster hatred among other populations should not be a portion of a people's happiness. A nation, like a man, is something ideal. Indestructible mountains and valleys, crawled over by any sort of race, do not constitute its identity. Its essence is a certain spirit, and only what enters into this spirit can bind it morally, or preserve it. —E-260

Conscience

The true conscience is rather an integrated natural will, chastened by clear knowledge of what it pursues and may attain.—E-261

Morality

What morality has to consider is the form of life, not its quantity.—E-261

Socrates. Ethics, of Greece

When Socrates and his two great disciples composed a system of rational ethics they were hardly proposing practical legislation for mankind. One by his irony, another by his frank idealism, and the third by his preponderating interest in history and analysis, showed clearly enough how little they dared to hope. They were merely writing an eloquent epitaph on their country. They were publishing the principles of what had been its life, gathering piously its broken ideals, and interpreting its momentary achievement.—E-262

Mohammed

Had Mohammed spoken only of the dynamic unity in things, the omnipresence of destiny, and the actual conditions of success and failure in the world, he would not have been called a prophet or have had more than a dozen intelligent followers, scattered over as many centuries; but the weakness

[86]

of his intellect, and his ignorance of nature, made the success of his mission. It is easier to kindle righteous indignation against abuses when, by abating them, we further our personal interests.—E-277

Prayers and dreams

Out of the play of notions carried on in a prayerful dream wonderful mysteries can be constructed, to be presently announced to the people and made the core of sacramental injunctions. When the tide of vulgar superstition is at the flood and every form of quackery is welcome, we need not wonder that a theosophy having so respectable a core—something, indeed, like a true logic misunderstood—should gain many adherents.—E-281

Buddhism compared with Christianity

Christianity persecuted, tortured, and burned. Like a hound it tracked the very scent of heresy. It kindled wars, and nursed furious hatreds and ambitions. It sanctified, quite like Mohammedanism, extermination and tyranny. All this would have been impossible if, like Buddhism, it had looked only to peace and the liberation of souls. It looked beyond; it dreamt of infinite blisses and crowns it should be crowned with before an electrified universe and an applauding God. These were rival baits to those which the world fishes with, and were snapped at, when seen, with no less avidity. Man, far from being freed from his natural passions, was plunged into artificial ones quite as violent and more disappointing. Buddhism had tried to quiet a sick world with anaesthetics; Christianity sought to purge it with fire.—E-286

Trappist and Calvinist

Trappist or Calvinist may be practising a heroic and metaphysical self-surrender while the busy-bodies of their respective creeds are fostering, in God's name, all their hot and miscellaneous passions.—E-287

The notion that every sin must be expiated does not carry with it any information about what acts are sins.—E-292

Mythical consolations

This is the heavy price paid for mythical consolations, that they invalidate the moral values they are intended to emphasise. Nature has allowed the innocent to suffer for the guilty, and the guilty, perhaps, to die in some measure unpunished. To correct this imperfection we feign a closed circle of personal retributions, exactly proportionate to personal deserts. But thereby, without perceiving it, we have invalidated all political and social responsibility, and denied that any man can be benefited or injured by any other. Our moral ambition has overleaped itself and carried us into a non-natural world where morality is impotent and unmeaning.—E-297

Faith in the supernatural

Faith in the supernatural is a desperate wager made by man at the lowest ebb of his fortunes; it is as far as possible from being the source of that normal vitality which subsequently, if his fortunes mend, he may gradually recover. Under the same religion, with the same posthumous alternatives and mystic harmonies hanging about them, different races or the same race at different periods, will manifest the most opposite moral characteristics. Belief in a thousand hells and heavens will not lift the apathetic out of apathy or hold back the passionate from passion; while a newly planted and ungalled community, in blessed forgetfulness of rewards or punishments, of cosmic needs or celestial sanctions, will know how to live cheerily and virtuously for life's own sake, putting to shame those thin vaticinations. To hope for a second life, to be had gratis, merely because this life has lost its savour, or to dream of a different world, because nature seems too intricate and unfriendly, is in the end merely to play with words; since the supernatural has no permanent aspect or charm except in so far as it expresses man's natural situation and points to the satisfaction of his earthly interests. What keeps super-natural morality, in its better forms, within the limits of sanity is the fact that it reinstates in practice, under novel associations and for motives ostensibly different, the very natural virtues and hopes which, when seen to be merely natural, it had thrown over with contempt. The new dispensation itself, if treated in the same spirit, would be no less contemptible; and what makes it genuinely esteemed is the restored authority of those human ideals which it expresses in a fable.—E-298

Life of Reason

Life of Reason which science crowns, and justifies to re-flection.—E-301

Science

Science, purged of all needless realism and seen in its rela-tion to human life, would continue to offer the only concep-tion of reality which is pertinent or possible to the practical mind.—E-302

Science and philosophy

The curse of modern philosophy is only that it has not drawn its inspiration from science; as the misfortune of science is that it has not yet saturated the mind of philosophers and recast the moral world.—E-304

Revelations

Revelations are necessarily mythical and subrational; they express natural forces and human interests in a groping way, before the advent of science. To stick in them, when some-thing more honest and explicit is available, is inconsistent with caring for attainable welfare or understanding the situation. It is to be stubborn and negligent under the cloak of religion. These prejudices are a drag on progress, moral no less than material; and the sensitive conservatism that fears they may be indispensable is entangled in a pathetic delusion. It is conser-vatism in a ship-wreck. It has not the insight to embrace the fertile principles of life, which are always ready to renew life after no matter what natural catastrophe. The good laggards have no courage to strip for the race. Rather than live otherwise, and live better, they prefer to nurse the memories of youth and to die with a retrospective smile upon their countenance.—E-307

Science

Science is nothing but developed perception, interpreted intent, common sense rounded out and minutely articulated. —E-307

Reason's danger

What has reason to tremble at a demand for its credentials is surely not natural science: it is rather those mystical theologies or romantic philosophies of history which aspire to take its place.—E-314

Task of science

But there remain unexplored jungles and monster-breeding lairs within our nominal jurisdiction which it is the immediate task of science to clear. The darkest spots are in man himself, in his fitful, irrational disposition. Could a better system prevail in our lives a better order would establish itself in our thinking. It has not been for want of keen senses, or personal genius, or a constant order in the outer world, that mankind have fallen back repeatedly into barbarism and superstition. It has been for want of good character, good example, and good government. There is a pathetic capacity in men to live nobly, if only they would give one another the chance. —E-320

F

Philosophical odor

But it was not of their soft bodies that I was speaking, but of their rotten minds. Did you never hear that a philosophy can be smelt?—F-1

Dual minds

Almost always, in the sensitive life of animals, there is an element of true art and knowledge, together with an element of madness.—F-3

Odor

A single skunk, by emitting a little fluid, will qualify space further than a herd of elephants, and one he-goat browsing amid the crags of the acropolis will neutralise from certain quarters the whole agora full of voting democrats.—F-6

Nature vs. man

The vapours of vanity exuding from the brain if blown away here must gather there into some new phantom for fools to worship; and it requires courage to stand alone, smiling at those inevitable follies, and recognising the immense disproportion between nature and man, and her reptilian indifference to her creatures.—F-22

Reason's severity

The severity of reason in disabusing us of these vain passions shows true kindness to the soul; nor is it a morose severity, but paternal and indulgent towards every amiable pleasure.—F-23

Lusty core in man

There is a lusty core in the human animal that survives all revolutions.—F-25

[91]

Wit

Human wit is seldom to be trusted in prophecy. The mind thinks in gaudy images and nature moves in dark currents of molecular change.—F-25

Truth

There is indeed no wisdom like that of the atoms, which, being compelled to move by fate, move without caring whither. But when by this very motion life and will have arisen, and the foolish heart must be set on something, it is the part of a relative wisdom to set it on the truth.—F-26

Dreams

The dreamer can know no truth, not even about his dream, except by awaking out of it. If you spin one dream to explain another, as do your talking philosophers, how will you ever come out of the labyrinth?—F-27

Thoughts

Man is a fighting animal, his thoughts are his banners, and it is a failure of nerve in him if they are only thoughts.—F-31

Crazy world

If you bravely make the best of a crazy world, eternity is full of champions that will defend you.—F-32

Honest humanity
Greeks, their day

How simple it was once to be a Greek and ingenuously human; yet nature suffered that honest humanity to exist only for a few doubtful years. It peeped once into being, like a weed amid the crevices of those Aegean mountains, and all the revolving aeons will not bring it back.—F-38

Sweetness vs. long life

The fly that prefers sweetness to a long life may drown in honey; nor is an agony of sweetness forbidden by nature to those inclined to sing or to love.—F-38

Fancy

Indeed fancy as if aware of its vanity, makes holiday as long as it can; its joy is in fiction, and it would soon fade and grow weary if it had to tell the truth.—F-41

Mortals' stupidity

This divine simplicity of nature is ill understood by mortals, who address everything to their mean uses and vain advantage; whereby in the struggle to lengthen their days a little they fill them with distraction.—F-43

Mind, illusion of

As the chief endeavour of the animal body is to defend and propagate itself at all costs, so the chief and most lasting illusion of the mind is the illusion of its own importance.—F-44

Madness vs. sanity

Meantime, in the interests of human life, without inquiring into its ultimate vanity, a conventional distinction may be drawn between madness and sanity. Belief in the imaginary and desire for the impossible will justly be called madness; but those habits and ideas will be conventionally called sane which are sanctioned by tradition and which, when followed, do not lead directly to the destruction of oneself or of one's country. Such conventional sanity is a normal madness like that of images in sense, love in youth, and religion among nations.—F-36

Virginity. Soul

The soul, too, has her virginity and must bleed a little before bearing fruit.—F-56

Weeping and laughing

The young man who has not wept is a savage, and the old man who will not laugh is a fool.—F-57

Tails. Fickleness

All living souls welcome whatsoever they are ready to cope with; all else they ignore, or pronounce to be monstrous and wrong, or deny to be possible. So the mother of the first tailless child—for men formerly had tails—wept bitterly and consulted the soothsayers, elders conspicuous for their long and honourable tails, who gave out oracles from the hollow of ancient trees; and she asked what unwitting impiety she or her husband could have committed, that the just gods should condemn their innocent child to such eternal disgrace. When, however, other tailless births began to occur, at first the legislators had the little monsters put rigorously to death; but soon, as the parents began to offer resistance, they suffered a scape-goat to be sacrificed instead; and persons without a tail were merely condemned to pass their lives in slavery, or at least without the rights of citizenship; because the philosophers, who all belonged to the elder generation with ample tails, declared that without a tail no man was really human or could be admitted after death into the company of the gods. Yet later, when that hinder ornament had become rare, opinion was reversed, until the priests, legislators, and sages gathered in council and decreed, by a majority vote, that a tail in man was unnatural, and that the tradition that such things had existed was an invention of ignorant poets, and absurd When, however, by a casual reversion, and sport of nature, a child with a tail was born here and there, not only was the infant instantly despatched, but the mother was burned alive for having had commerce with a devil.—F-63

Vanity, consciousness of

The consciousness of vanity is a great disinfectant: it fills religion, as it fills life, with fortitude, dignity, and kindness. —F-65

Fancy. Illusions

Fancy can conceive only a kindred fancy, such as might spring from organs similar to its own; but if life is lavish in illusion here, why not also there? A prudent man will not blaspheme against any god.—F-68-69

Latest thing

There is nothing that recommends any opinion or custom to us more than to hear that it is the latest thing, that everybody is adopting it, and that it is universal nowadays in the leading circles.—F-94

Cooks, religion and government

Every sturdy race stews its home-made dishes, to which its stomach is hardened and which it fondly relishes as incomparably the best. Few cooks anywhere are inventive—a fact which saves many lives; and our traditional government, like our home religion, though there is no science in it, is not too poisonous. The sun rises in spite of it, and our children have red cheeks.—F-98-99

Government, good

If the god had spoken in prose, without wishing to be oracular, he would have said that there is no right government except good government; that good government is that which benefits the governed; that the good of the governed is determined not by their topmost wishes or their ruling passions, but by their hidden nature and their real opportunities; and that only knowledge, discovering this hidden nature and these real opportunities, and speaking in their name, has a right to rule in the state or in the private conscience.—F-106

Natural man. Sanctified idiots

Man is a natural being; if he is ill at ease in the world, it is only because he is ignorant of the world and of his own good; and the discord between man and nature would be wholly resolved if man would practise the true arts of medicine and politics. But your Prophet seems to have delivered precepts which, if ever his disciples had obeyed them, would have turned them into sanctified idiots, contemptible in his own eyes.—F-144

Greek vs. Christian

Better the cup of hemlock in time. Why nurse disease or deformity? Death is not an evil, but vileness is; and when vileness is cultivated for the sake of life it renders life vile also. I thanked the gods when I was alive for having been born a Greek and not a barbarian, and now that I am dead I thank them that I died in time, lest I should have become a Christian.—F-158

Time and eternity

If time bred nothing, eternity would have nothing to embalm.—F-174

Fact and fable

Many voyages have been made since your day, and many discoveries; and the ruin of empires and religions has repeatedly admonished mankind, if they have any wit at all, to distinguish fact from fable.—F-174-175

G

"Winds of Doctrine"

This book belongs to another age; it was written before the war. To bring it up to date would hardly be possible; a revision would destroy whatever quiet justice or sympathetic insight those observations may have had in the past, without availing to measure the force or direction of the much rougher winds that are now blowing.—G-v

Russell

In Mr. Russell's analysis of facts, whether physical or historical, I confess I have little confidence; it is when he derides the existent or plays with the non-existent that I find him admirable.—G-v

Spirit

Spirit is not the pursuit of this good or that beauty, but of the beautiful and good.—G-vi

Present age

The present age is a critical one and interesting to live in. —G-1

Monarchy and aristocracy

We still love monarchy and aristocracy.—G-1

Christendom. New spirit

On the other hand the shell of Christendom is broken. The unconquerable mind of the East, the pagan past, the industrial socialistic future confront it with their equal authority. Our whole life and mind is saturated with the slow upward filtration of a new spirit—that of an emancipated, atheistic, international democracy.—G-1

[97]

Prelates. Missionaries

Even prelates and missionaries are hardly sincere or conscious of an honest function, save as they devote themselves to social work.—G-2

The world

Meantime our bodies in this generation are generally safe, and often comfortable; and for those who can suspend their irrational labours long enough to look about them, the spectacle of the world, if not particularly beautiful or touching, presents a rapid and crowded drama and (what here concerns me most) one unusually intelligible.—G-2

Time's change

We are not condemned, as most generations have been, to fight and believe without an inkling of the cause.—G-2

Comedy of the times

The whole drift of things presents a huge, good-natured comedy to the observer. It stirs not unpleasantly a certain sturdy animality and hearty self-trust which lie at the base of human nature.—G-2-3

Vagary in human nature

Who can tell what vagary or what compromise may not be calling itself Christianity? A bishop may be a modernist, a chemist may be a mystical theologian, a psychologist may be a believer in ghosts.—G-4

Liberalism vs. control. Marriage

Liberalism had been supposed to advocate liberty; but what the advanced parties that still call themselves liberal now advocate is control, control over property, trade, wages, hours of work, meat and drink, amusements, and in a truly advanced country like France control over education and religion; and it is only on the subject of marriage (if we ignore eugenics) that liberalism is growing more and more liberal.—G-4-5

Quality vs. quantity

Those who speak most of progress measure it by quantity and not by quality; how many people read and write, or how many people there are, or what is the annual value of their trade; whereas true progress would rather lie in reading or writing fewer and better things, and being fewer and better men, and enjoying life more.—G-5

Majorities

But the philanthropists are now preparing an absolute subjection of the individual, in soul and body, to the instincts of the majority—the most cruel and unprogressive of masters; and I am not sure that the liberal maxim, "the greatest happiness of the greatest number," has not lost whatever was just or generous in its intent and come to mean the greatest idleness of the largest possible population.—G-5

International brotherhood

The idea of solidarity is indeed often invoked in speeches, and there is an extreme socialistic party that—when a wave of national passion does not carry it the other way—believes in international brotherhood. But even here, black men and yellow men are generally excluded.—G-5

Materialism. Mind

Anomalies of this sort will never be properly understood until people accustom themselves to a theory to which they have always turned a deaf ear, because, though simple and true, it is materialistic: namely, that mind is not the cause of our actions but an effect, collateral with our actions, of bodily growth and organisation.—G-7

Manners

So that (to speak geologically) our practice may be historic, our manners glacial, and our religion palaeozoic.—G-7

Anomalies of present time

The ideals of the nineteenth century may be said to have

been all belated; the age still yearned with Rousseau or speculated with Kant, while it moved with Darwin, Bismarck, and Nietzsche: and to-day, in the half-educated classes, among the religious or revolutionary acts, we may observe quite modern methods of work allied with a somewhat antiquated mentality.—G-7

Reform

Reform! This magic word itself covers a great equivocation. —G-8

Life's dilemma

It is a terrible dilemma in the life of reason whether it will sacrifice natural abundance to moral order, or moral order to natural abundance.—G-9-10

Social and intellectual trends

Perhaps in the century that has elapsed since the French Revolution the pendulum has had time to swing as far as it will in the direction of negative reform, and may now begin to move towards that sort of reform which is integrating and creative. The veering of the advanced political parties from liberalism to socialism would seem to be a clear indication of this new tendency. It is manifest also in the love of nature, in athletics, in the new woman, and in a friendly medical attitude towards all the passions.—G-10

Art trends

In the fine arts, however, and in religion and philosophy, we are still in full career towards disintegration. It might have been thought that a germ of rational order would by this time have penetrated into fine art and speculation from the prosperous constructive arts that touch the one, and the prosperous natural and mathematical sciences that touch the other. But as yet there is little sign of it. Since the beginning of the nineteenth century painting and sculpture have passed through several phases, representatives of each naturally surviving after the next had appeared. Romanticism, half lurid, half effeminate, yielded to a brutal pursuit of material truth, and a pious preference for modern and humble sentiment. This realism had a romantic vein in it, and studied vice and crime, tedium and despair, with a very genuine horrified sympathy. Some went in for a display of archaeological lore or for exotic *motifs;* others gave all their attention to rediscovering and emphasising abstract problems of execution, the highway of technical tradition having long been abandoned. Beginners are still supposed to study their art, but have no masters from whom to learn it. Thus, when there seemed to be some danger that art should be drowned in science and history, the artists deftly eluded it by becoming amateurs. One gave himself to religious archaism, another to Japanese composition, a third to barbaric symphonies of colour; sculptors tried to express dramatic climaxes, or inarticulate lyrical passion, such as music might better convey; and the latest whims are apparently to abandon painful observation altogether, to be merely decorative or frankly mystical, and to be satisfied with the childishness of hieroglyphics or the crudity of caricature. The arts are like truant children who think their life will be glorious if they only run away and play for ever; no need is felt of a dominant ideal passion and theme, nor of any moral interest in the interpretation of nature. Artists have no less talent than ever; their taste, their vision, their sentiment are often interesting; they are mighty in their independence and feeble only in their works.—G-10-11

Experience

Immediate feeling, pure experience, is the only reality, the only *fact.*—G-12

Life

Life, like the porcupine when not ruffled by practical alarms, can let its fretful quills subside.—G-13

Mystic

The Mystic can live happy in the droning consciousness of his own heart-beats and those of the universe.—G-13

Intelligence, its difficulties

Human intelligence is certainly a product, and a late and highly organised product, of evolution; it ought apparently to be as much admired as the eyes of molluscs or the antennae of ants. And if life is better the more intense and concentrated it is, intelligence would seem to be the best form of life. But the degree of intelligence which this age possesses makes it so very uncomfortable that, in this instance, it asks for something less vital, and sighs for what evolution has left behind. In the presence of such cruelly distinct things as astronomy or such cruelly confused things as theology it feels *la nostalgie de la boue.*—G-18

Passions

Small half-borrowed passions which we clothe in a mean rhetoric and dot with vulgar pleasures.—G-18

The primitive

Not free enough themselves morally, but bound to the world partly by piety and partly by industrialism, they (our contemporaries) cannot think of rising to a detached contemplation of earthly things, and of life itself and evolution; they revert rather to sensibility, and seek some by-path of instinct or dramatic sympathy in which to wander. Having no stomach for the ultimate, they burrow downwards towards the primitive. But the longing to be primitive is a disease of culture; it is archaism in morals.—G-19

Low vitality

Only when vitality is low do people find material things oppressive and ideal things unsubstantial.—G-19

Chaos. Great men

When chaos has penetrated so far into the moral being of nations they can hardly be expected to produce great men. —G-20

First man

The first man was a great man for this latter reason; having been an ape perplexed and corrupted by his multiplying instincts, he suddenly found a new way of being decent, by harnessing all those instincts together, through memory and imagination, and giving each in turn a measure of its due; which is what we call being rational.—G-20-21

Greatness

Greatness is spontaneous.—G-21

This age

Without great men and without clear convictions this age is nevertheless very active intellectually; it is studious, empirical, inventive, sympathetic. Its wisdom consists in a certain contrite openness of mind; it flounders, but at least in floundering it has gained a sense of possible depths in all directions. Under these circumstances, some triviality and great confusion in its positive achievements are not unpromising things, nor even unamiable.—G-23

Liberal Catholicism

In more recent times we have heard of liberal Catholicism, the attitude assumed by some generous but divided minds, too much attached to their traditional religion to abandon it, but too weak and too hopeful not to glow also with enthusiasm for modern liberty and progress.—G-26

Christian requisites

To believe this in our day may require courage, even a certain childish simplicity; but were not courage and a certain childish simplicity always requisite for Christian faith? It never was a religion for the rationalist and the worldling; it was based on alienation from the world, from the intellectual world no less than from the economic and political. It flourished in the Oriental imagination that is able to treat all existence with disdain and to hold it superbly at arm's length, and at the same time is subject to visions and false memories, is swayed by the eloquence of private passion, and raises confidently to heaven the cry of the poor, the bereaved, and the distressed. Its daily bread, from the beginning, was hope for a miraculous change of scene, for prison-walls falling to the ground about it, for a heart inwardly comforted, and a shower of good things from the sky.—G-35

Conversion to Christianity

It is clear that a supernaturalistic faith of this sort, which might wholly inspire some revolutionary sect, can never wholy inspire human society. Whenever a nation is converted to Christianity, its Christianity, in practice, must be largely converted into paganism.—G-35

"Ages of Faith". Thirteenth century

The ages of faith, the age of Christian unity, were such only superficially. When all men are Christians only a small element can be Christian in the average man. The thirteenth century, for instance, is supposed to be the golden age of Catholicism; but what seems to have filled it, if we may judge by the witness of Dante? Little but bitter conflicts, racial and religious; faithless rebellions, both in states and in individuals, against the Christian regimen; worldliness in the church, barbarism in the people, and a dawning of all sorts of scientific and aesthetic passions, in themselves quite pagan and contrary to the spirit of the gospel. Christendom at that time was by no means a kingdom of God on earth; it was a conglomeration of incorrigible rascals, intellectually more or less Christian.—G-36

Renaissance, The

In every age in which a supernaturalistic system is preached we must accordingly expect to find the world standing up stubbornly against it, essentially unconverted and hostile, whatever name it may have been christened with; and we may expect the spirit of the world to find expression, not only in overt opposition to the supernaturalistic system, but also in the surviving or supervening worldliness of the faithful. Such an insidious revulsion of the natural man against a religion he does not openly discard is what, in modern Christendom, we call the Renaissance. No less than the Revolution (which is the later open rebellion against the same traditions) the Renaissance is radically inimical to Christianity. To say that Christianity survives, even if weakened or disestablished, is to say that the Renaissance and the Revolution are still incomplete. Far from being past events they are living programmes. The ideal of the Renaissance is to restore pagan standards in polite learning, in philosophy, in sentiment, and in morals. It is to abandon and exactly reverse one's baptismal vows.—G-38

Modernists

A scrupulous honesty in admitting the probable facts of history, and a fresh up-welling of mystical experience, these are the motives, creditable to any spiritual man, that have made modernists of so many.—G-41

Modernism
Pius X, his encyclical

Rationalistic history and criticism are therefore based, as Pius X most accurately observed in his Encyclical on modernism, on rationalistic philosophy; and we might add that rationalistic philosophy is based on practical art, and that practical art, by which we help ourselves, like Prometheus, and make instruments of what religion worships, when this art is carried beyond the narrowest bounds, is the essence of pride and irreligion. Miners, machinists, and artisans are irreligious by trade. Religion is the love of life in the consciousness of impotence.—G-43

Non-Christian criterion in history

But what is remarkable and well-nigh incredible is that even for a moment they should have supposed this non-Christian criterion in history and this non-Christian direction in metaphysics compatible with adherence to the Catholic church. That seems to pre-suppose, in men who in fact are particularly thoughtful and learned, an inexplicable ignorance of history, of theology, and of the world.—G-43

The Catholic seminary

In a Catholic seminary, as the modernists bitterly complain, very little is heard of the views held in the learned world outside. It is not taught there that the Christian religion is only one of many, some of them older and superior to it in certain respects; that it itself is eclectic and contains inward contradictions; that it is and always has been divided into rancorous sects; that its position in the world is precarious and its future hopeless. On the contrary, everything is so presented as to persuade the innocent student that all that is good or true anywhere is founded on the faith he is preparing to preach, that the historical evidences of its truth are ir-refragable, that it is logically perfect and spiritually all-sufficing.—G-44

Catholic teaching

In the routine of Catholic teaching and worship there is notoriously a deal of mummery: phrases and ceremonies abound that have lost their meaning, and that people run through without even that general devout attitude and unction, which, after all, is all that can be asked for in the presence of mysteries.—G-48

Modernism. Fable. Paganism

Modernism is accordingly an ambiguous and unstable thing. It is the love of all Christianity in those who perceive that it is all a fable. It is the historic attachment to his church of a Catholic who has discovered that he is a pagan.

The gospel

The gospel has been encased in theology, in ritual, in ecclesiastical authority, in conventional forms of charity, like some small bone of a saint in a gilded reliquary; but the relic for once is genuine, and the gospel has been preserved by those thick incrustations.—G-53

Hope of the church

In a frank supernaturalism, in a tight clericalism, not in a pleasant secularisation, lies the sole hope of the church. Its sole dignity also lies there. It will not convert the world; it never did and it never could. It will remain a voice crying in the wilderness; but it will believe what it cries, and there will be some to listen to it in the future, as there have been many in the past.—G-56

Modernism

As to modernism, it is suicide. It is the last of those concessions to the spirit of the world which half-believers and double-minded prophets have always been found making; but it is a mortal concession. It concedes everything; for it concedes that everything in Christianity, as Christians hold it, is an illusion.—G-57

Ideas in mind. Locke. English psychology

The one blunder was that of the English malicious psychology which had maintained since the time of Locke that the ideas in the mind are the only objects of knowledge, instead of being the knowledge of objects.—G-62

Blunder of Protestantism

The other blunder was that of Protestantism that, in groping after that moral freedom which is so ineradicable a need of a pure spirit, thought to find it in a revision of revelation, tradition, and prejudice, so as to be able to cling to these a little longer.—G-62

Bergson

But with regard to his (Bergson's) own philosophy I am afraid he thinks that all previous systems empty into it, which is hardly true, and that all future systems must flow out of it, which is hardly necessary.—G-62

Human prejudices. Illusions. Bergson

M. Bergson is at bottom an apologist for very old human prejudices, an apologist for animal illusion. His whole labour is a plea for some vague but comfortable faith which he dreads to have stolen from him by the progress of art and knowledge.—G-63

Fears of Bergson

M. Bergson is afraid of space, of mathematics, and of necessity, and of eternity; he is afraid of the intellect and the possible discoveries of science; he is afraid of nothingness and death.—G-63

Timidity and illusion

Animal timidity and animal illusion are deep in the heart of all of us.—G-63

Jesuit. Protestant theology

Yet with a certain irritation and haste to be done with it, somewhat as a Jesuit might study Protestant theology.—G-64

Bergson

He little knows the pleasures of a liberal mind, ranging over the congenial realm of internal accuracy and ideal truth, where it can possess itself of what treasures it likes in perfect security and freedom.—G-66

Of Bergson

Aristotle at least could refer particulars to their specific types, as medicine and social science are still glad enough to it can possess itself of what treasures it likes in perfect security and freedom.—G-66

Hume, Mill, Huxley, Bergson

Hume, Mill, and Huxley were scientific at heart, and full of the intelligence they dissected; they seemed to cry to nature: Though thou dost not exist, yet will I trust in thee. Their idealism was a theoretical scruple rather than a passionate superstition. Not so M. Bergson; he is not so simple as to invoke the malicious criticism of knowledge in order to go on thinking rationalistically. Reason and science make him uncomfortable. His point accordingly is not merely that mechanism is a hypothesis, but that it is a wrong hypothesis. Events do not come as if mechanism brought them about; they come, at least in the organic world, as if a magic destiny, and inscrutable ungovernable effort, were driving them on.—G-70

Psychological illusions

The psychological illusion that our ideas and purposes are original facts and forces (instead of expressions in consciousness of facts and forces which are material) and the practical and optical illusion that everything wheels about us in this world—these are the primitive persuasions which the enemies of naturalism have always been concerned to protect.—G-72

Ghostly madness

M. Bergson thus introduces his metaphysical force as a peculiar requirement of biology; he breaks the continuity of nature; he loses the poetic justification of a metaphysical vitalism; he asks us to believe that life is not a natural expression of material being, but an alien and ghostly madness descending into it—I say a ghostly madness, for why should disembodied life wish that the body should live?—G-73

Israel. Bergson

M. Bergson would have us believe that mankind is what nature has set her heart on and the best she can do, for whose sake she has been long making very special efforts. We are fortunate that at least her darling is all mankind and not merely Israel.—G-73

Paul. Peter. Spinoza

The idea Paul has of Peter, Spinoza observes, expresses the nature of Peter less than it betrays that of Paul; and so an idea framed by a man of the consciousness of things in general reveals the mind of that man rather than the mind of the universe.—G-77

Day-dream, its result

In a sensuous day-dream past feelings survive in the present, images of the long ago are shuffled together with present sensations, the roving imagination leaves a bright wake behind it like a comet, and pushes a rising wave before it, like the bow of a ship; all is fluidity, continuity without identity, novelty without surprise.—G-78

Bergson

So immediate consciousness yields the two factors of Bergsonian freedom, continuity and indetermination.—G-79

Philosophers vs. scientists

Poor guileless reader! If philosophers were straight-forward men of science, adding each his mite to the general store of knowledge, they would all substantially agree, and while they might make interesting discoveries, they would not herald each his new transformation of the whole universe.—G-82

Philosophers

But philosophers are either revolutionists or apologists, and some of them, like M. Bergson, are revolutionists in the interests of apologetics. Their art is to create some surprising inversion of things, some system of the universe contrary to common apprehension, or to defend some such inverted system, propounded by poets long ago, and perhaps consecrated by religion.—G-82

Metaphysics—Europe. Fancy—India
Rhetoric—Greece.

The metaphysical abuse of psychology is as extraordinary in modern Europe as that of fancy ever was in India or of rhetoric in Greece.—G-94

Bergson

Elsewhere he says, in a phrase already much quoted and perhaps destined to be famous, that in man the spirit can "spurn every kind of resistance and break through many an obstacle, perhaps even death." Here the tenor has ended on the inevitable high note, and the gallery is delighted. But was that the note set down for him in the music? And has he not sung it in falsetto?—G-107

Bergson

What is this creative purpose, that must wait for sun and

rain to set it in motion? What is this life, that in any individual can be suddenly extinguished by a bullet? What is this *elan vital,* that a little fall in temperature would banish altogether from the universe? The study of death may be out of fashion, but it is never out of season. The omission of this, which is almost the omission of wisdom from philosophy, warns us that in M. Bergson's thought we have something occasional and partial, the work of an astute apologist, a party man, driven to desperate speculation by a timid attachment to prejudice. Like other terrified idealisms, the system of M. Bergson has neither good sense, nor rigour, nor candour, nor solidity. It is a brilliant attempt to confuse the lessons of experience by refining upon its texture, an attempt to make us halt, for the love of primitive illusions, in the path of discipline and reason. It is likely to prove a successful attempt, because it flatters the weaknesses of the moment, expresses them with emotion, and covers them with a feint at scientific speculation.—G-107-108

Critique of Bergson

Instead of telling us, as a stern and contrite philosophy would, that the truth is remote, difficult, and almost undiscoverable by human efforts, that the universe is vast and unfathomable, yet that the knowledge of its ways is precious to our better selves, if we would not live befooled, this philosophy rather tells us that nothing is truer or more precious than our rudimentary consciousness, with its vague instincts and premonitions, that everything ideal is fictitious, and that the universe, at heart, is as palpitating and irrational as ourselves. —G-108

Life

Rather live on; work, it matters little at what, and grow, it matters nothing in what direction. Exert your instinctive powers of vegetation and emotion; let your philosophy itself be a frank expression of this flux, the roar of the ocean in your little sea-shell, a momentary posture of your living soul, not a stark adoration of things reputed eternal.—G-108

Bergson

M. Bergson's philosophy itself is a confession of a certain mystical rebellion and atavism in the contemporary mind.— G-109

Eternal truth

Eternal truth is as disconsolate as it is consoling, and as dreary as it is interesting.—G-118

Santayana quotes William James

'The prince of darkness,' James says, 'may be a gentleman, as we are told he is, but whatever the God of earth and heaven is, he can surely be no gentleman.'—G-125

Man's relation to the world

I myself, for instance, like to look at things from this angle: not that I have ever doubted the reality of the natural world, or been able to take very seriously any philosophy that denied it, but precisely because, when we take the natural world for granted, it becomes a possible and enlightening inquiry to ask how the human animal has come to discover his real environment, in so far as he has done so, and what dreams have intervened or supervened in the course of his rational awakening.—G-128

Pragmatism

Pragmatic "truth," on the contrary, is the relative and provisional justification of fiction; and pragmatism is not a theory of truth at all, but a theory of theory, when theory is instrumental.—G-136

"Theological truth"

Theology has long applied the name truth pre-eminently to fiction. When the conviction first dawned upon pragmatists that there was no absolute or eternal truth, what they evidently were thinking of was that it is folly, in this changing world, to pledge oneself to any final and inflexible creed.—G-137

Habit of Protestantism

It is characteristic of Protestantism that, when it gives up anything, it transfers to what remains the unction, and often the name, proper to what it has abandoned.—G-137

Pleasure

Yet changeless pleasure, without memory or reflection, without the wearisome intermixture of arbitrary images, is just what the mystic, the voluptuary, and perhaps the oyster find to be good.—G-147

Revolutionists

Now the misfortune of revolutionists is that they are disinherited, and their folly is that they wish to be disinherited even more than they are. Hence, in the midst of their passionate and even heroic idealisms, there is commonly a strange poverty in their minds, many an ugly turn in their lives, and an ostentatious vileness in their manners. They wish to be the leaders of mankind, but they are wretched representatives of humanity. In the concert of nature it is hard to keep in tune with oneself if one is out of tune with everything.—G-156

Requisites for art

Substance, sanity, and even a sort of pervasive wisdom are requisite for supreme works of art.—G-157

Rebels. Individualists

On the other hand—who can honestly doubt it?—the rebels and individualists are the men of direct insight and vital hope. —G-157

Shelley

The poetry of Shelley in particular is typically poetical. It is poetry divinely inspired.—G-157

Shelley

It is a fact of capital importance in the development of human genius that the great revolution in Christendom against Christianity, a revolution that began with the Renaissance and is not yet completed, should have found angels to herald it, no less than that other revolution did which began at Bethlehem; and that among these new angels there should have been one so winsome, pure, and rapturous as Shelley.—G-157

Revolutionists

Few revolutionists would be such if they were heirs to a baronetcy.—G-158

Shelley. Finished child of nature
Liberty. Justice

Shelley was one of these spokesmen of the *a priori,* one of these nurslings of the womb, like a bee or a butterfly; a dogmatic, inspired, perfect, and incorrigible creature. He was innocent and cruel, swift and wayward, illuminated and blind. Being a finished child of nature, not a joint product, like most of us, of nature, history, and society, he abounded miraculously in his own clear sense, but was obtuse to the droll, miscellaneous lessons of fortune. The cannonade of hard, inexplicable facts that knocks into most of us what little wisdom we have left Shelley dazed and sore, perhaps, but uninstructed. When the storm was over, he began chirping again his own natural note. If the world continued to confine and obsess him, he hated the world, and gasped for freedom. Being incapable of understanding reality, he revelled in creating world after world in idea. For his nature was not merely pre-determined and obdurate, it was also sensitive, vehement and fertile. With the soul of a bird, he had the senses of a man-child; the instinct of the butterfly was united in him with the instinct of the brooding fowl and of the pelican. This winged spirit had a heart. It darted swiftly on its appointed course, neither expecting nor understanding opposition; but when it met opposition it did not merely flutter and collapse; it was inwardly outraged, it protested proudly against fate, it cried aloud for liberty and justice.—G-158-159

Moral life and judgment. Private ideal

All moral life and moral judgment have this deeply romantic character; they venture to assert a private ideal in the face of an intractable and omnipotent world.—G-160

For his moral feeling was based on suffering and horror at what is actual, no less than on love of a visioned good. His conscience was, to a most unusual degree, at once elevated and sincere.—G-162

Inspiration of Shelley

Hence that extraordinary moral fervour which is the soul of his poetry. His imagination is no playful undirected kaleidoscope; the images, often so tenuous and metaphysical, that crowd upon him, are all sparks thrown off at white heat, embodiments of a fervent, definite, unswerving inspiration.—G-162-163

Need - Shelley

He undoubtedly shatters the world to bits, but only to build it nearer to the heart's desire, only to make out of its coloured fragments some more Elysian home for love, or some more dazzling symbol for that infinite beauty which is the need—the profound, aching, imperative need—of the human soul. —G-163

Good and Shelley

But to exaggerate good is to vivify, to enhance our sense of moral coherence and beautiful naturalness; it is to render things more graceful, intelligible, and congenial to the spirit which they ought to serve.—G-164

Fine illusions

Every modern school of poets, once out of fashion, proves itself to have been sadly romantic and sentimental. None has done better than to spangle a confused sensuous pageant with some sparks of truth, or to give it some symbolic relation to moral experience. And this Shelley has done as well as anybody: all other poets also have been poets of illusion. The distinction of Shelley is that his illusions are wonderfully fine, subtle, and palpitating; that they betray passions and mental habits so singularly generous and pure.—G-169

Quality of Shelley's mind

Shelley's mind was angelic not merely in its purity and fervour, but also in its moral authority, in its prophetic strain.—G-170

The most rational nature

If he had understood universal nature, he would not have so glorified his own. And his own nature was worth glorifying; it was, I think, the purest, tenderest, richest, most rational nature ever poured forth in verse. I have not read in any language such a full expression of the unadulterated instincts of the mind.—G-174

Shelley

He was like a child, like a Platonic soul just fallen from the Empyrean; and the child may be dazed, credulous, and fanciful; but he is not mad.—G-175

Free love. Shelley. Tyranny

From the point of view of a poet, there can be little essential freedom so long as he is forbidden to live with the people he likes, and compelled to live with the people he does not like. This, to Shelley, seemed the most galling of tyrannies; and free love was, to his feeling, the essence and test of freedom. Love must be spontaneous to be a spiritual bond in the beginning and it must remain spontaneous if it is to remain spiritual. To be bound by one's past is as great a tyranny to pure spirit as to be bound by the sin of Adam, or by the laws of Artaxerxes; and those of us who do not believe in the possibility of free love ought to declare frankly that we do not, at bottom, believe in the possibility of freedom.—G-178

Arnold, Matthew. Shelley

I see no reason, in the analogies of the natural world, for supposing that the circumstances of human life are the only circumstances in which the spirit of life can disport itself. Even on this planet, there are sea-animals and air-animals, ephemeral beings and self-centred beings, as well as persons who can grow as old as Matthew Arnold, and be as fond as he was of classifying other people. And beyond this planet, and in the interstices of what our limited senses can perceive, there are probably many forms of life not criticised in any of the books which Matthew Arnold said we should read in order to know the best that has been thought and said in the world. The future, too, even among men, may contain, as Shelley puts it, many "arts, though unimagined, yet to be."—G-183

Singer. Shelley

Being a singer inwardly inspired, Shelley could picture the ideal goals of life, the ultimate joys of experience, better than a discursive critic or observer could have done.—G-183

Cor cordium

So purely ideal and so deeply human are the visions of Shelley. So truly does he deserve the epitaph which a clear-sighted friend wrote upon his tomb: *cor cordium*, the heart of hearts.—G-185

America

America is a young country with an old mentality.—G-187

Calvinistic philosophy
Misery. Jews. Protestants

To be a Calvinist philosophically is to feel a fierce pleasure in the existence of misery, especially of one's own, in that this misery seems to manifest the fact that the Absolute is irresponsible or infinite or holy. Human nature, it feels, is totally depraved: to have the instincts and motives that we necessarily have is a great scandal, and we must suffer for it; but that scandal is requisite, since otherwise the serious importance of being as we ought to be would not have been vindicated.

To those of us who have not an agonised conscience this system may seem fantastic and even unintelligible; yet it is logically and intently thought out from its emotional premises. It can take permanent possession of a deep mind here and there, and under certain conditions it can become epidemic.

Imagine, for instance, a small nation with an intense vitality, but on the verge of ruin, ecstatic and distressful, having a strict and minute code of laws, that paints life in sharp and violent chiaroscuro, all pure righteousness and black abominations, and exaggerating the consequences of both perhaps to infinity. Such a people were the Jews after the exile, and again the early Protestants. If such a people is philosophical at all, it will not improbably be Calvinistic. Even in the early American communities, many of these conditions were fulfilled. The nation was small and isolated; it lived under pressure and constant trial; it was acquainted with but a small range of goods and evils.—G-190

Edwards, Jonathan. God's enemies. Calvinists

How strange to the American now that saying of Jonathan Edwards, that men are naturally God's enemies! Yet that is an axiom to any intelligent Calvinist, though the words he uses may be different. If you told the modern American that he is totally depraved, he would think you were joking, as he himself usually is. He is convinced that he always has been, and always will be, victorious and blameless.

Calvinism thus lost its basis in American life.—G-191

Poe, Hawthorne, Emerson—starved

The three American writers whose personal endowment was perhaps the finest—Poe, Hawthorne, and Emerson—had all a certain starved and abstract quality. They could not retail the genteel tradition; they were too keen, too perceptive, and too independent for that. But life offered them little digestible material, nor were they naturally voracious. They were fastidious, and under the circumstances they were starved.—G-192

Digestion of vacancy. The genteel tradition. Poe, Emerson, Hawthorne

Therefore the genius of Poe and Hawthorne, and even of Emerson, was employed on a sort of inner play, or digestion of vacancy. It was a refined labour, but it was in danger of being morbid, or tinkling, or self-indulgent. It was a play of

[118]

intra-mental rhymes. Their mind was like an old music-box, full of tender echoes and quaint fancies. These fancies expressed their personal genius sincerely, as dreams may; but they were arbitrary fancies in comparison with what a real observer would have said in the premises. Their manner, in a word, was subjective. In their own persons they escaped the mediocrity of the genteel tradition, but they supplied nothing to supplant it in other minds.—G-193

Calvinism. Infant damnation. Hell-fire

The churches, likewise, although they modified their spirit, had no philosophy to offer save a new emphasis on parts of what Calvinism contained. The theology of Calvin, we must remember, had much in it besides philosophical Calvinism. A Christian tenderness, and a hope of grace for the individual, came to mitigate its sardonic optimism; and it was these evangelical elements that the Calvinistic churches now emphasised, seldom and with blushes referring to hell-fire or infant damnation. Yet philosophic Calvinism, with a theory of life that would perfectly justify hell-fire and infant damnation if they happened to exist, still dominates the traditional metaphysics. —G-193

Transcendentalism

Transcendentalism is systematic subjectivism. It studies the perspectives of knowledge as they radiate from the self; it is a plan of those avenues of inference by which our ideas of things must be reached, if they are to afford any systematic or distant vistas. In other words, transcendentalism is the critical logic of science.—G-193-194

Transcendentalism

I regard it (Transcendentalism) as the chief contribution made in modern times to speculation. But it is a method only, an attitude we may always assume if we like and that will always be legitimate. It is no answer, and involves no particular answer, to the question: What exists; in what order is what exists produced; what is to exist in the future? This question must be answered by observing the object and tracing humbly the movement of the object. It cannot be answered at all by harping on the fact that this object, if discovered, must be discovered by somebody, and by somebody who has an interest in discovering it. Yet the Germans who first gained the full transcendental insight were romantic people, they were more or less frankly poets; they were colossal egotists, and wished to make not only their own knowledge but the whole universe centre about themselves.—G-194

Transcendental logic and method

Transcendental logic, the method of discovery for the mind, was to become also the method of evolution in nature and history. Transcendental method, so abused, produced transcendental myth. A conscientious critique of knowledge was turned into a sham system of nature. We must therefore distinguish sharply the transcendental grammar of the intellect, which is significant and potentially correct, from the various transcendental systems of the universe, which are chimeras. —G-195

Emerson

Emerson was a shrewd Yankee, by instinct on the winning side; he was a cheery, child-like soul, impervious to the evidence of evil, as of everything that it did not suit his transcendental individuality to appreciate or to notice. More, perhaps, than anybody that has ever lived, he practised the transcendental method in all its purity.—G-197

Emerson

Yet he never insisted on his notions so as to turn them into settled dogmas; he felt in his bones that they were myths. —G-197

Truth. Philosophers vs. scientists
Bertrand Russell

To covet truth is a very distinguished passion. Every philosopher says he is pursuing the truth, but this is seldom the case. As Mr. Bertrand Russell has observed, one reason why philosophers often fail to reach the truth is that often they do not desire to reach it. Those who are genuinely concerned in discovering what happens to be true are rather the men of science, the naturalists, the historians; and ordinarily they discover it, according to their lights. The truths they find are never complete, and are not always important; but they are integral parts of the truth, facts and circumstances that help to fill in the picture, and that no later interpretation can invalidate or afford to contradict. But professional philosophers are usually only apologists: that is, they are absorbed in defending some vested illusion or some eloquent idea. Like lawyers or detectives, they study the case for which they are retained, to see how much evidence or semblance of evidence they can gather for the defense, and how much prejudice they can raise against the witnesses for the prosecution; for they know they are defending prisoners suspected by the world, and perhaps by their own good sense of falsification.—G-198

Understanding

No doubt the spirit or energy of the world is what is acting in us, as the sea is what rises in every little wave; but it passes through us, and cry out as we may, it will move on. Our privilege is to have perceived it as it moves. Our dignity is not in what we do, but in what we understand.—G-199

Joy of unhappiness

Serious poetry, profound religion (Calvinism, for instance), are the joys of an unhappiness that confesses itself.—G-200

Italian Renaissance. Catholic tradition

Similarly in Italy, during the Renaissance, the Catholic tradition could not be banished from the intellect, since there was nothing articulate to take its place; yet its hold on the heart was singularly relaxed. The consequence was that humorists could regale themselves with the foibles of monks and of cardinals, with the credulity of fools, and the bogus miracles of the saints; not intending to deny the theory of the church, but caring for it so little at heart that they could find it infinitely amusing that it should be contradicted in men's lives and that no harm should come of it.—G-202

Walt Whitman

The one American writer who has left the genteel tradition entirely behind is perhaps Walt Whitman. For this reason educated Americans find him rather an unpalatable person, who they sincerely protest ought not to be taken for a representative of their culture; and he certainly should not, because their culture is so genteel and traditional. But the foreigner may sometimes think otherwise, since he is looking for what may have arisen in America to express, not the polite and conventional American mind, but the spirit and the inarticulate principles that animate the community, on which its own genteel mentality seems to sit rather lightly. —G-202

Theory and intelligence

There is a feeling abroad now, to which biology and Darwinism lend some colour, that theory is simply an instrument for practice, and intelligence merely a help toward material survival. Bears, it is said, have fur and claws, but poor naked man is condemned to be intelligent, or he will perish.—G-206

Profundity vs. sincerity

We need not be afraid of being less profound, for being direct and sincere. The intellectual world may be traversed in many directions; the whole has not been surveyed; there is a great career in it open to talent.—G-211

The bluff of transcendentalism

Natural science, history, the beliefs implied in labour and invention, could not be disregarded altogether; so that the transcendental philosopher was condemned to a double allegiance, and to not letting his left hand know the bluff that his right hand was making.—G-212

Everywhere is beauty and nowhere permanence, everywhere an incipient harmony, nowhere an intention, nor a responsibility, nor a plan. It is the irresistible suasion of this daily spectacle, it is the daily discipline of contact with things, so different from the verbal discipline of the schools, that will, I trust, inspire the philosophy of your children.—G-214

H

Ambiguous German philosophy

During more than twenty years, while I taught philosophy at Harvard College, I had continual occasion to read and discuss German metaphysics. From the beginning it wore in my eyes a rather questionable shape. Under its obscure and fluctuating tenets I felt something sinister at work, something at once hollow and aggressive. It seemed a forced method of speculation producing more confusion than it found, and calculated chiefly to enable practical materialists to call themselves idealists and rationalists to remain theologians.—H-5

Function of history

The function of history or of criticism is not passively to reproduce its subject-matter.—H-6

Egotism. Perversity

Egotism—subjectivity in thought and wilfulness in morals —which is the soul of German philosophy is by no means a gratuitous thing. It is a genuine expression of the pathetic situation in which any animal finds itself upon earth, and any intelligence in the universe. It is an inevitable and initial circumstance in life. But like every material accident, it is a thing to abstract from and to discount as far as possible. The perversity of the Germans, the childishness and sophistry of their position, lies only in glorifying what is an inevitable impediment.—H-7

False religion

It is a terrible thing to have a false religion, all the more terrible the deeper its sources are in the human soul.—H-7

German subjectivism

It has all the qualities that gave early Protestantism its religious force. It is rebellious to external authority, conscious of inward light and of absolute duties. It is full of faith, if by faith we understand not definite beliefs held on inadequate evidence, but a deep trust in instinct and destiny.—H-13

German philosophy

German philosophy is a sort of religion, and like other religions it may be capable of assimilating a great amount of wisdom, while its first foundation is folly. This first folly itself will not lack plausible grounds; there is provocation enough in a single visit to a madhouse for the assertion that the mind can know nothing but the ideas it creates; nevertheless the assertion is false; and such facile scepticism loses sight of the essence of knowledge.—H-18

Fichte. Hegel

The moment we hear Fichte and Hegel mentioning a providential plan of the world, we gather that in their view the history of things is not infinite and endlessly various, but has a closed plot like a drama in which one nation (the very one to which these philosophers belong) has the central place and the chief role; and we perceive at once that theirs is a revealed philosophy. It is the heir of Judaism.—H-22

German philosophy vs. Protestantism

German philosophy has inherited from Protestantism its earnestness and pious intention; also a tendency to retain, for whatever changed views it may put forward, the names of former beliefs.—H-23

Habit of using old names for new delusions

But whether candid or disingenuous, this habit has the advantage of oiling the wheels of progress with a sacred unction. In facilitating change it blurs the consciousness of change, and leads people to associate with their new opinions sentiments which are logically incompatible with them. The attachment of many tender-minded people to German philosophy is due to this circumstance, for German philosophy is not tender.—H-24

Kant, Fichte, Hegel, Schopenhauer, Nietzsche

Kant was a puritan; he revered the rule of right as something immutable and holy, perhaps never obeyed in the world. Fichte was somewhat freer in his Calvinism; the rule of right was the moving power in all life and nature, though it might have been betrayed by a doomed and self-seeking generation. Hegel was a very free and superior Lutheran; he saw that the divine will was necessarily and continuously realised in this world, though we might not recognise the fact in our petty moral judgments. Schopenhauer, speaking again for this human judgment, revolted against that cruel optimism, and was an indignant atheist; and finally, in Nietzsche, this atheism became exultant; he thought it the part of a man to abet the movement of things, however calamitous, in order to appropriate its wild force and be for a moment the very crest of its wave.—H-25

Protestantism

Protestantism was not a reformation by accident, because it happened to find the church corrupt; it is a reformation essentially, in that every individual must reinterpret the Bible and the practices of the church in his own spirit. If he accepted them without renewing them in the light of his personal religious experience, he would never have what Protestantism thinks living religion.—H-25-26

Primitive faith

Faith for the Germans must be a primitive and groundless assurance, not knowledge credibly transmitted by others whose experience may have been greater than our own.—H-27

Intolerance of Protestantism

For favourable as Protestantism is to investigation and learning, it is almost incompatible with clearness of thought and fundamental freedom of attitude.—H-29

German philosophers. Animal will. Experience

The German philosophers have carried on Protestantism beyond itself. They have separated the two ingredients mingled in traditional religions. One of these ingredients— the vital faith or self-trust of the animal will—they have retained. The other—the lessons of experience—they have rejected. To which element the name of religion should still be given, if it is given to either, is a matter of indifference. The important thing is that, call it religion or irreligion, we should know what we are clinging to.—H-31

Locke. Self-analysis. Ego

It was Locke who first thought of looking into his own breast to find there the genuine properties of gold and of an apple; and it is clear that nothing but lack of consecutiveness and courage kept him from finding the whole universe in the same generous receptacle. This method of looking for reality in one's own breast, when practised with due consecutiveness and courage by the Germans, became the transcendental method; but it must be admitted that the German breast was no longer that anatomical region which Locke had intended to probe, but a purely metaphysical point of departure, a migratory ego that could be here, there, and everywhere at once, being present at any point from which thought or volition might be taken to radiate.—H-32

Subjective philosophy

The practice of looking for all things within one's own breast, in the subtler sense of searching for them in one's memory and experience, begat in time the whole romantic and subjective school of philosophy.—H-32-33

Goethe

In his warm pantheistic way Goethe felt the swarming universal life about him; he had no thought of dragooning it all, as sectarians and nationalists would, into vindicating some particular creed or nation. Yet that fertile and impartial universe left each life free and in uncensored competition with every other life.—H-49

Equivocation with conscience

He (Kant), therefore, hastened to adopt a corrective principle of reconstruction, no less fallacious, namely, that conscience bids us assume certain things to be realities which reason and experience know nothing of. This brought him round to a qualified and ambiguous form of his original dogmas, to the effect that although there was no reason to think that God, heaven, and free-will exist, we ought to act as if they existed, and might call that wilful action of ours faith in their existence.—H-59

German religion. Kant. Follies, ancient

Thus it is from Kant, directly or indirectly, that the German egotists draw the conviction which is their most tragic error. Their self-assertion and ambition are ancient follies of the human race; but they think these vulgar passions the creative spirit of the universe. Kant, or that soul within Kant which was still somewhat cramped in its expression, was the prophet and even the founder of the new German religion.—H-64

Fantastic metaphysics

The Germans, in the midst of their fantastic metaphysics, sometimes surprise us by their return to immediate experience; after all, it was in wrestling with the Lord that their philosophy was begotten.—H-66

Fichte

I am not sure how far Fichte, in his romantic and puritan tension of soul, would have relished the present organisation of Germany. He was a man of the people, a radical and an agitator as much as a prophet of nationalism, and the shining armour in which German freedom is now encased might

[128]

have seemed to him too ponderous. He might have discerned in victory the beginning of corruption.—H-69

Transcendentalist and God

We are told that God, when he had made the world, found it very good, and the transcendentalist, when he assumes the Creator's place, follows his example.—H-71

Ego

The ego, particularly in philosophers, is a nebula of words. —H-90

Psychology of German moralists

The Germans are by nature a good stolid people, and it is curious that their moralists, of every school, are so fantastic and bad. The trouble lies perhaps in this, that they are all precipitate. They have not taken the trouble to decipher human nature, which is an *endowment,* something many-sided, unconscious, with a margin of variation, and have started instead with the will, which is only an *attitude,* something casual, conscious, and narrowly absolute. Nor have they learned to respect sufficiently the external conditions under which human nature operates and to which it must conform—God, the material world, the nature and will of other men. Their morality consequently terminates in ideals, casual, conscious, and absolute expressions of the passions, or else expires in a mysticism which renounces all moral judgment. A reasonable morality terminates instead in the arts, by which human ideals and passions are compounded with experience and adapted to the materials they must work in. The immaturity of the German moralists appears in their conception that the good is life, which is what an irrational animal might say; whereas for a rational being the good is only the good part of life, that healthy, stable, wise, kind, and beautiful sort of life which he calls happiness.—H-103

Equivocal religious spirit in Germany. Leibniz

German philosophy has a religious spirit, but its alliance

with Christianity has always been equivocal and external. Even in the speculations of Leibniz, concerned as he was about orthodoxy, there was a spirit of independence and absolutism which was rationalistic, not to say heathen.—H-104

Kant, Fichte, and Hegel—their theology

Kant, Fichte, and Hegel were less punctilious in their theology, but they still intended to be or to seem Christians. They felt that what made the sanctity of traditional religion and its moral force could be recovered in purer form in their systems. This feeling of theirs was not unwarranted; at least, many religious minds, after the first shock of losing their realistic faith, have seen in transcendentalism a means, and perhaps the only safe means, of still maintaining a sort of Christianity which shall not claim any longer to be a miraculous or exceptional revelation, but only a fair enough poetic symbol for the principles found in all moral life.—H-105

Intellectual ignominy

The intellectual ignominy of believing what we believe simply because of the time and place of our birth, escapes many evolutionists.—H-129-130

Ideals

To frame solid ideals, which would, in fact, be better than actual things, is not granted to the merely irritable poet; it is granted only to the master-workman, to the modeller of some given substance to some given use—things which define his aspiration, and separate what is relevant and glorious in his dreams from that large part of them which is merely ignorant and peevish.—H-137

Beautiful life

How life can be fulfilled and made beautiful by reason was never better shown than by the Greeks, both by precept and example.—H-139

Oxford

Oxford, the paradise of dead philosophies.—H-144

Heathen

It conveys, as no other word can, the sense of vast multitudes tossing in darkness, harassed by demons of their own choice.—H-144

Will, religion of

Heathenism is the religion of will, the faith which life has in itself because it is life, and in its aims because it is pursuing them.—H-149

Natural world dethroned

German philosophy does this (ignores the external forces) theoretically, by dethroning the natural world and calling it an idea created by the ego for its own purposes; and it does this practically also by obeying the categorical imperative—no longer the fabled imperative of Sinai or of Königsberg, but the inward and vital imperative which the bull obeys, when trusting absolutely in his own strength, rage, and courage, he follows a little red rag and his destiny this way and that way.—H-153

Religions and philosophies adjusted by their truth
Dead religions and philosophies—their interest

It is customary to judge religions and philosophies by their truth, which is seldom their strong point; yet the application of that unsympathetic criterion is not unjust, since they aspire to be true, maintain that they are so, and forbid any opposed view, no matter how obvious and inevitable, to be called true in their stead. But when religions and philosophies are dead, or when we are so removed from them by time or training that the question of their truth is not a living question for us, they do not on that account lose all their interest; then, in fact, for the first time they manifest their virtues to the unbeliever. He sees that they are expressions of human genius; that however false their subject-matter may

[131]

be, like the conventions of art they are true to the eye and to the spirit that fashioned them. And as nothing in the world, not even the truth, is so interesting as human genius, these incredible or obsolete religions and philosophies become delightful to us. The sting is gone out of their errors, which no longer threaten to delude us, and they have acquired a beauty invisible to the eye of their authors, because of the very refraction which the truth suffered in that vital medium. —H-154-155

The Germans

Consider, in this respect, the pathetic history of the German people. It conquered the Roman empire and it became Roman, or wished to become so. It had had a mythology and a morality of its own (very like in principle to those it has since rediscovered), yet it accepted Christianity with the docility of a child. It began to feel, after some centuries, how alien to its genius this religion was, but it could find relief only in a fresh draught from the same foreign sources, or others more remote. To cease to be Roman it tried to become Hebraic and Greek. In studying these models, however, it came upon a new scent. What passed for revelation or for classical perfection was of human national growth, stratified like the rocks, and not divine or authoritative at all. If you only made hypotheses enough, you could prove how it all arose according to necessary laws, logical, psychological, historical, economical, and aesthetical. Above all, you could prove how nobody had understood anything properly before, and how the key to it all was in your single hand.

Yet the triumphs of theory alone soon seemed unsatisfying. Wine, science, and song once seemed to make Germany happy, but if a prince imposed military discipline, might not that be an even better thing? For a time wistfulness, longing, and the feeling of Titanic loneliness and of a world to be evoked and snuffed out like a dream, seemed to fill the cup of intense living, and the greatest and happiest of Germans could cry—

Nur wer die Sehnsucht kennt
weiss, was ich leide,
allein und abgetrennt
von aller Freude.

But presently true intensity of life appeared to lie rather in being a victorious general or an ironmaster, or a commercial traveller, or a reveller in the Friedrichstrasse, or a spy and conspirator anywhere in the world.

All these turbid and nondescript ambitions are in a sense artificial; the Germans accept them now as a thousand years ago they accepted Christianity, because such things are suddenly thrust upon them. By nature they are simple, honest, kindly, easily pleased. There is no latent irony or disbelief in their souls. The pleasures of sense, plain and copious, they enjoy hugely, long labour does not exasperate them, science fills them with satisfaction, music entrances them. There ought to be no happier or more innocent nation in this world. Unfortunately their very goodness and simplicity render them helpless; they are what they are dragooned to be. There is no social or intellectual disease to which, in spots, they do not succumb, as to an epidemic; their philosophy itself is an example of this. They have the defects of the newly prosperous; they are far too proud of their possessions, esteeming them for being theirs, without knowing whether they are good of their kind. Culture is a thing seldom mentioned by those who have it. The real strength of the Germans lies not in those external achievements of which at this moment they make so much—for they may outgrow this new materialism of theirs—it lies rather in what they have always prized, their *Gemüth* and their music.—H-158-159-160

Egotism

The particular theory of egotism arises from an exorbitant interest in ourselves, in the medium of thought and action rather than in its objects. It is not necessarily incorrect, because the self is actual and indispensable; but the insistence on it is a little abnormal, because the self, like consciousness, ought to be diaphanous. Egotism in philosophy is, therefore, a pretty sure symptom of excessive pedantry and inordinate self-assertion.—H-162-163

Passion and egotism

If the egotist suffers passion to speak in his philosophy, it is perhaps because he has so little passion. Men of frank passions quickly see the folly of them; but the passions of the egotist are muffled, dull, like the miserly passions of old men; they are diffused into sensuality and sentiment, or hardened into maxims.—H-165

Transcendentalism, false. Montaigne
Life a compromise

The whole transcendental philosophy, if made ultimate, is false, and nothing but a private perspective. The will is absolute neither in the individual nor in humanity. Nature is not a product of the mind, but on the contrary there is an external world, ages prior to any idea of it, which the mind recognises and feeds upon. There is a steady human nature within us, which our moods and passions may wrong but cannot annul. There is no categorical imperative but only the operation of instincts and interests more or less subject to discipline and mutual adjustment. Our whole life is a compromise, an incipient loose harmony between the passions of the soul and the forces of nature, forces which likewise generate and protect the souls of other creatures, endowing them with powers of expression and self-assertion comparable with our own, and with aims no less sweet and worthy in their own eyes; so that the quick and honest mind cannot but practise courtesy in the universe, exercising its will without vehemence or forced assurance, judging with serenity, and in everything discarding the word absolute as the most false and the most odious of words. As Montaigne observes, "He who sets before him, as in a picture, this vast image of our mother Nature in her entire majesty; who reads in her aspect such universal and continual variety; who discerns himself therein, and not himself only but a whole kingdom, to be but a most delicate dot—he alone esteems things according to the just measure of their greatness."—H-168

Clannish pride. Ambition. Vanity. Superstition

Now official German philosophy has ceased to be theological and idealistic, without ceasing to be egotistical; for in adopting a kind of vitalistic naturalism, it has retained its trust in prophetic divination, so that the supreme destiny formerly assigned to the German race as chosen vehicles of universal spirit continues to be assigned to that race as being naturally the best, strongest, most prolific, and most artistic of races, bound therefore by natural necessity to dominate the earth.

If this prophecy were a scientific hypothesis based on positive evidence there would be nothing egotistical about it. Quite possibly one human race may be destined to survive or to enslave all the others, and I, for my part, should not be appalled if I learned on good authority that this race was to be the German, rather than the Chinese, Japanese, Jewish or Russian. The big blond beast is an excellent beast, endowed with a first-class intelligence, sensibility, and capacity for steady work. But this is not the real ground for the German claim to supremacy. The real ground is the same that the ancient Hebrews had for proclaiming themselves the chosen people; it is clannish pride, ambition and vanity, with the determination to encourage these passions, when in straits, by the aid of superstition. By this appeal to superstition the natural ignorant confidence that every healthy creature or nation has in itself reacts against discouragement and becomes egotism.—H-175-176

Egotism, its origin

Might not German philosophy, now so realistic in many ways, be satisfied with an honest naturalism, and cease to be egotistical? Might it not stop attributing natural perform-

[135]

ances to magic and turning history into fable? Certainly it might, if philosophy were a disembodied logic, working itself out apart from times, places, traditions, and persons. But in this case circumstances prevent. One of these circumstances, perhaps the most important, is the fact that German religion and philosophy are drawn, by a curious irony, from Jewish sources. It was the ancient Hebrews that first invented egotism, and have transmitted it to the rest of the world. Not that it appears in them at first, for egotism is a secondary thing, but they seem to have possessed from the beginning an extraordinary tenacity and fervour in sticking to life; so that although conquered, enslaved, murdered, and banished more often than any other people, they succeeded in surviving and spreading all over the world. This concentrated vitality, glowing obstinately like a spark buried deep in ashes, produced their monotheism; something quite different from the pantheism into which polytheism melts or rises in other peoples; for the one God remained their special national God; so that the creator of the world and the providence ruling over history was pledged, according to their insane persuasion, to ordain everything solely for their ultimate triumph.—H-178-179

Evolution of German thought

Thus, when the German genius at the Reformation cast off the leading-strings of Rome, and very gradually, like a good apprentice, asserted its own instincts against all borrowed traditions, it reverted from asceticism to manliness and thrift, and from supernaturalism to a conceptual philosophy of history; but up to the present time it has not discarded that original Hebraic egotism which dreamt of a chosen people and a promised land. On the contrary, it stoutly reasserts it with all the craft and patience of Jacob and all the ruthlessness of Joshua.—H-180-181

Conceit of nations

All nations are conceited, and they dare proclaim their conceit on the housetops, because even the most absurd enthusiasm masters the human heart when a group of persons is at hand ready to share it. But this natural boastfulness and false courage lapse on reflection; the true interests at stake are obviously better served by recognising the circumstances, and therefore responsible heads will soon limit their ambition to the possible and their self-praise to the credible.—H-181

Morality, pre-rational. Socrates

Like the animal life which it expresses, pre-rational morality is far from being inwardly wicked or condemnable. On the contrary, it is the soil of all the radical virtues. There spring our primary moral judgments and admirations, our horror at this and our allegiance to that. In maintaining the wholeness and strength of a biological character once achieved, conscience and duty show their true colors. Reason cannot oppose these intuitions but may insinuate itself into them and transform them. Therefore, Socrates, the father of rational ethics, though he had clear moral and political allegiances of his own, never imposed them dogmatically upon his disciples.
—H-184

I

Humanists of Renaissance

The humanists of the Renaissance were lovers of Greek and of good Latin, scornful of all that was crabbed, technical, or fanatical: they were pleasantly learned men, free from any kind of austerity, who, without quarrelling with Christian dogma, treated it humanly, and partly by tolerance and partly by ridicule hoped to neutralise all its metaphysical and moral rigour.—I-4-5

Life demands

Life demands a great insensibility, as well as a great sensibility.—I-8

Three R's of history

The three R's of modern history, the Renaissance, the Reformation, and the Revolution.—I-8

Renaissance. Middle Ages

The Renaissance really tended to emancipate the passions and to exploit nature for fanciful and for practical human uses: it simply continued all that was vivacious and ornate in the Middle Ages. It called those ages barbarous, partly for writing dog Latin and partly for being hard, penitential, warlike, and migratory; one might almost say, for being religious. —I-9-10

Leonardo. Shakespeare. Bacon. Machiavelli

A genius typical of the Renaissance, such as Leonardo or Shakespeare, could not be of that consecrated kind. In his omnivorous intelligence and zest, in his multiform contacts and observations, in so many lights kindled inconclusively, such a genius, except for the intensity of his apprehension, would not have been a master or a poet at all. He would have been, like Bacon and Machiavelli, a prophet of Big Business. There might still be passion and richness in the accents, but the tidings were mean. The Renaissance, for all its poetry, scholarship, and splendour, was a great surrender of the spirit to the flesh, of the essence for the miscellany of human power.—I-10-11

Religion and madness

In religious experience, taken as its own criterion, there is nothing to distinguish religion from moral sentiment or from sheer madness.—I-11

Protestantism

I think we might say of Protestantism something like what Goethe said of Hamlet. Nature had carelessly dropped an acorn into the ancient vase of religion, and the young oak, growing within, shattered the precious vessel.—I-12-13

Modern history. Natural man

So far, then, the gist of modern history would seem to be this: a many-sided insurrection of the unregenerate natural man, with all his physical powers and affinities, against the regimen of Christendom. He has convinced himself that his physical life is not as his ghostly mentors asserted, a life of sin; and why should it be a life of misery? Society has gradually become a rather glorious, if troubled, organisation of matter, and of man for material achievements.—I-18

Private anarchy vs. public order

Either the private anarchy will ruin public order, or the public order will cure private anarchy.—I-19

Big Business

Big Business is an amiable monster, far kindlier and more innocent than anything Machiavelli could have anticipated, and no less lavish in its patronage of experiment, invention, and finery than Bacon could have desired.—I-22

Supernatural

So when native zeal and integrity, either in nations or persons, has given way to fatigue or contagion, a supernatural assurance needing no test may take possession of the mind.—I-44

Milton—his work

That was a confused and insolent ambition in Milton to justify the ways of God to man.—I-46

Platonism. Christianity

Platonism and Christianity, on the contrary, except in a few natural mystics and speculative saints, seem to sacrifice ruthlessly one set of passions merely in order to intensify another set.—I-46

Morality

On the contrary, I think that it is only when he can see the natural origin and limits of the moral sphere that a moralist can be morally sane and just. Blindness to the biological truth about morality is not favourable to purity of moral feeling: it removes all sense of proportion and relativity; it kills charity, humility, and humour; and it shuts the door against that ultimate light which comes to the spirit from the spheres above morality.—I-51

Reason vs. supernaturalism

I think that pure reason in the naturalist may attain, without subterfuge, all the spiritual insights which supernaturalism goes so far out of the way to inspire.—I-64

Happiness

Although happiness, like everything else, can be experienced only in particular moments, it is found in conceiving the total issue and the ultimate fruits of life; and no passing sensation could be enjoyed with a free mind, unless the blessing of reason and of a sustained happiness were felt to hang over it.—I-66

New England conscience

Those who have lived in Boston—and who else should know?—are aware how earnestly the reformed New England conscience now disapproves of its disapprovals.—I-69

Protestant genteel tradition

But can it be that all Latins and Slavs, all Arabs, Chinamen, and Indians, if they were not benighted in mind and degenerate in body, would be model Anglo-Americans? That is what British and American politicians and missionaries seem to believe: all nations are expected gladly to exchange their religion and their customs for the protestant genteel tradition. —I-70

Naturalness. Morality

When therefore a tender conscience extends its maxims beyond their natural basis, it not only ceases to be rational in its deliverances, and becomes fanatical, but it casts the livid colours of its own insanity upon nature at large. A strained holiness, never without its seamy side, ousts honourable virtue, and the fear of so many enemies becomes the greatest enemy of the soul. No true appreciation of anything is possible without a sense of its *naturalness,* of the innocent necessity by which it has assumed its special and perhaps extraordinary form. In a word, the principle of morality is naturalistic. Call it humanism or not, only a morality frankly relative to man's nature is worthy of man, being at once vital and rational, martial and generous; whereas absolutism smells of fustiness as well as of faggots.—I-74

J

Thoughts

I have no axe to grind; only my thoughts to burnish.—J-vi

Romantic Christendom

Romantic Christendom—picturesque, passionate, unhappy episode—may be coming to an end. Such a catastrophe would be no reason for despair.—J-vii

The American

There is much forgetfulness, much callow disrespect for what is past or alien; but there is a fund of vigour, goodness, and hope such as no nation ever possessed before. In what sometimes looks like American greediness and jostling for the front place, all is love of achievement, nothing is unkindness; it is a fearless people, and free from malice, as you might see in their eyes and gestures, even if their conduct did not prove it.—J-viii

New England's Indian Summer of the mind

About the middle of the nineteenth century, in the quiet sunshine of provincial prosperity, New England had an Indian summer of the mind; and an agreeable reflective literature showed how brilliant that russet and yellow season could be. There were poets, historians, orators, preachers, most of whom had studied foreign literatures and had travelled; they demurely kept up with the times; they were universal humanists. But it was all a harvest of leaves; these worthies had an expurgated and barren conception of life; theirs was the purity of sweet old age. Sometimes they made attempts to rejuvenate their minds by broaching native subjects; they wished to prove how much matter for poetry the new world supplied, and they wrote "Rip van Winkle", "Hiawatha", or "Evangeline".—J-2

William James. Free will. Departed spirits
Tutelary gods

Even in William James, spontaneous and stimulating as he was, a certain underlying discomfort was discernible; he had come out into the open, into what should have been the sunshine, but the vast shadow of the temple still stood between him and the sun. He was worried about what *ought* to be believed and the awful deprivations of disbelieving. What he called the cynical view of anything had first to be brushed aside, without stopping to consider whether it was not the true one; and he was bent on finding new and empirical reasons for clinging to free-will, departed spirits, and tutelary gods.—J-6-7

Nineteenth century tradition

Unfortunately, in the nineteenth century, in America as elsewhere, the ruling tradition was not only erratic and far from the highway of truth, but the noonday of this tradition was over, and its classic forms were outgrown.—J-8

Jonathan Edwards

If Jonathan Edwards, for instance, was a Calvinist of pristine force and perhaps the greatest *master* in false philosophy that America has yet produced, he paid the price by being abandoned, even in his lifetime, by his own sect, and seeing the world turn a deaf ear to his logic without so much as attempting to refute it.—J-9

Our predecessors

We do not nowadays refute our predecessors, we pleasantly bid them good-bye.—J-9

Traditional belief in New England

In spite of this profound mutation at the core, and much paring at the edges, traditional belief in New England retained its continuity and its priestly unction; and religious teachers and philosophers could slip away from Calvinism and even from Christianity without any loss of elevation or austerity.—J-13

Orthodoxy among high-brows

There was still an orthodoxy among American high-brows at the end of the nineteenth century, dissent from which was felt to be scandalous; it consisted in holding that the universe exists and is governed for the sake of man or of the human spirit. This persuasion, arrogant as it might seem, is at bottom an expression of impotence rather than of pride.—J-17

Rational animal. Greeks

Hardly anybody, except possibly the Greeks at their best, has realised the sweetness and glory of being a rational animal.—J-18

Materialists. New England

Orthodoxy in New England, even so transformed and attenuated, did not of course hold the field alone. There are materialists by instinct in every age and country; there are always private gentlemen whom the clergy and the professors cannot deceive.—J-23

Intellectual shyness

These men believed in nature, and were materialists at heart and to all practical purposes; but they were shy intellectually, and seemed to think they ran less risk of error in holding a thing covertly than in openly professing it.—J-29

All-inclusiveness

The love of all-inclusiveness is as dangerous in philosophy as in art.—J-30

Dunce

There is no dunce like a mature dunce.—J-60

Morning

It was a fresh morning in the life of reason, cloudy but brightening.—J-63

Illusion vs. truth

To be boosted by an illusion is not to live better than to live in harmony with the truth; it is not nearly so safe, not nearly so sweet, and not nearly so fruitful. These refusals to part with a decayed illusion are really an infection to the mind. Believe, certainly; we cannot help believing; but believe rationally, holding what seems certain for certain, what seems probable for probable, what seems desirable for desirable, and what seems false for false.—J-87

Courage, reasonable

Courage is not a virtue, said Socrates, unless it is also wisdom. Could anything be truer both of courage in doing and courage in believing? But it takes tenacity, it takes *reasonable* courage, to stick to scientific insights such as this of Socrates or that of James about the emotions; it is easier to lapse into the traditional manner, to search natural philosophy for miracles and moral lessons, and in morals proper, in the reasoned expression of preference, to splash about without a philosophy.—J-90

Liberty

Liberty is not an art, liberty must be used to bring some natural art to fruition.—J-91

Love, penetrating

Love is very penetrating, but it penetrates to possibilities rather than to facts.—J-94

Reason

Royce insisted on seeing reason at the bottom of things as well as at the top, so that he could never understand either the root or flower of anything.—J-118

Consistency

Consistency is a jewel; and, as in the case of other jewels, we may marvel at the price that some people will pay for it. In any case, we are led to this curious result: that radical empiricism ought to deny that any idea of the past can be true at all.—J-160

Human mind—facts and principles

Never was the human mind master of so many facts and sure of so few principles. Will this suspense and fluidity of thought crystallise into some great new system?—J-163

Comparison

Comparison is the expedient of those who cannot reach the heart of the things compared.—J-166

Idealization

A man who does not idealise his experiences, but idealises *a priori*, is incapable of true prophecy.—J-178

Politics, marriage, literature—in America

Advanced opinions on politics, marriage, or literature are comparatively rare in America; they are left for the ladies to discuss, and usually to condemn, while the men get on with their work.—J-180

Religion and idealism in America

In music and landscape, in humour and kindness, he touches the ideal more truly, perhaps, than in his ponderous academic idealisms and busy religions; for it is astonishing how much even religion in America (can it possibly be so in England?) is a matter of meetings, building-funds, schools, charities, clubs, and picnics.—J-180

The individual in English liberty compared with the Oriental

English liberty is a method, not a goal. It is related to the value of human life very much as the police are related to public morals or commerce to wealth; and it is no accident that the Anglo-Saxon race excels in commerce and in the commercial as distinguished from the artistic side of industry, and that having policed itself successfully it is beginning to police the world at large. It is all an eminence in temper, good-will, reliability, accommodation. Probably some other races, such as the Jews and Arabs, make individually better merchants, more shrewd, patient, and loving of their art. Englishmen and Americans often seem to miss or force opportunities, to play for quick returns, or to settle down into ponderous corporations; for successful men they are not particularly observant, constant, or economical. But the superiority of the Oriental is confined to his private craft; he has not the spirit of partnership. In English civilisation the individual is neutralised; it does not matter so much even in high places if he is rather stupid or rather cheap; public spirit sustains him, and he becomes its instrument all the more readily, perhaps, for not being very distinguished or clear-headed in himself. The community prospers; comfort and science, good manners and generous feelings are diffused among the people, without the aid of that foresight and cunning direction which sometimes give a temporary advantage to a rival system like the German. In the end, adaptation to the world at large, where so much is hidden and unintelligible, is only possible piecemeal, by groping with a genuine indetermination in one's aims. Its very looseness gives the English method its lien on the future. To dominate the world co-operation is better than policy, and empiricism safer than inspiration. Anglo-Saxon imperialism is unintended; military conquests are incidental to it and often not maintained; it subsists by a mechanical equilibrium of habits and interests, in which every colony, province, or protectorate has a different status. It has a commercial and missionary quality, and is essentially an invitation to pull together—an invitation which many nations may be incapable of accepting or even of understanding, or which they may deeply scorn, because it involves a surrender of absolute liberty on their part; but whether accepted or rejected, it is an offer of co-operation, a project for a limited partnership, not a complete plan of life to be imposed on anybody.—J-199-200-201

[147]

English liberty, assumptions of

The practice of English liberty presupposes two things: that all concerned are fundamentally unanimous, and that each has a plastic nature, which he is willing to modify.—J-205

Free government

Free government works well in proportion as government is superfluous.—J-207

Slavery in America

America is all one prairie, swept by a universal tornado. Although it has always thought itself in an eminent sense the land of freedom, even when it was covered with slaves, there is no country in which people live under more overpowering compulsions.—J-209

Popes and liberty

Even the popes, without thinking to be ironical, have often raised a wail for liberty.—J-217

Absolute liberty vs. English liberty

Absolute liberty and English liberty are incompatible, and mankind must make a painful and a brave choice between them. The necessity of rejecting and destroying some things that are beautiful is the deepest curse of existence.—J-233

K

Monks and nuns

Have you ever talked with monks and nuns? You may admit that some of these good souls may be saints, but their conversation, even on spiritual subjects, very soon becomes arid and stereotyped, always revolving around a few dulcet incorrigible maxims.—K-7-8

Puritanism vs. purity

It's a popular error to suppose that puritanism has anything to do with purity. The old Puritans were legally strict, they were righteous, but they were not particularly chaste. —K-8

Bolshevists and Puritanism

The Bolshies have the one element of Puritanism which was the most important, at least for Oliver: integrity of purpose and scorn of all compromises, practical or theoretical. —K-8-9

Athletics

The need of exercise, he said, was a modern superstition, invented by people who ate too much, and had nothing to think about. Athletics didn't make anybody either long-lived or useful.—K-16

Ministers

People wouldn't become ministers unless they had rather second-hand minds.—K-19

Heaven

It would be so awkward in heaven, after all one had discovered, to have to put on a perfect innocence.—K-22

The male chromosome

The child had been born punctually. This first grave and alarming duty of entering into the world was performed not only unflinchingly but with a flourish: for this thoroughly satisfactory child was a boy. His little organism, long before birth, had put aside the soft and drowsy temptation to be a female. It would have been so simple for the last pair of chromosomes to have doubled up like the rest, and turned out every cell in the future body complete, well-balanced, serene, and feminine. Instead, one intrepid particle decided to live alone, unmated, unsatisfied, restless, and masculine; and it imposed this unstable romantic equilibrium on every atom of the man-child's flesh, and of the man-child's sinews. To be a male means to have chosen the more arduous, though perhaps the less painful adventure, more remote from home, less deeply rooted in one soil and one morality. It means to be pledged to a certain courage, to a certain recklessness about the future: and if these risks are to be run without disaster, there should also be a greater buoyancy, less sensitiveness, less capacity for utter misery than women commonly show. Yet this compensation is sometimes lacking. Mysterious influences may cross and pervade the system, and send through it, as it were, a nostalgia for femininity, for that placid, motherly, comfortable fulness of life proper to the generous female. —K-75

Living in harmony with truth

I mean loving the face of nature, and preferring to live in harmony with the truth, rather than with what people about you think it proper to say.—K-105

Nature

Oliver soon found, as he afterward used to put it, that there was a sunny and a shady side to the road of knowledge. The sunny side was the study of nature, where all exploration was joyful, and free from evil passion and prejudice. The same was true of mathematics which, if not so sunny as geography or astronomy or natural history, at least was pure from human taint. You were honestly challenged by your problem, and could work your way honestly forward until you came to an honest solution or an honest difficulty. Only non-human subjects were fit for the human mind. They alone were open, friendly, and rewarding.—K-113-114

Fables. Human world

The human world was so horrible to the human mind, that it could be made to look at all decent and interesting only by ignoring one half the facts, and putting a false front on the other half. Hence all that brood of fables.—K-114

Mental poison

A man who gives a wrong twist to your mind, meddles with you just as truly as if he hit you in the eye; the mark may be less painful, but it's more lasting.—K-163

Public opinion

What another man may think or even know about you does you no harm, so long as your public standing is unchallenged and you pass for an ordinary person; but your best friend will drop you if he finds you are in bad odour.—K-163

Self-deceit

How can people like to deceive themselves?

They don't do it on purpose. Religion takes hold on them just as drink and women take hold on the rest of us. There's the advantage of being a sailor. The sea was never a Christian and never will be. Your religions can spring up only on dry land, very dry land, all rocks and pits and sand deserts and burning sun, except for an occasional terrific thunder-storm from nowhere. That's what that blasted Palestine is like— I've seen it—and that infernal blighted Arabia. People discover God only where he has cursed them. If poor old Wetherbee weren't humped as he is, he wouldn't think as he does. You can't see straight if you are crooked, and it's only your deuced lucky chaps that can get on without illusions.

[151]

Your father, for instance; and I'm not sure that he's much the happier for it. My own father too, although he's a parson, gets on without them, and being poor, it's all the more remarkable. But then he's no hunchback: a well set-up old Englishman or Scot—I don't know which—and a philosopher by nature who honestly doesn't care a fig for money or position. Besides, he knows the secret of theology and of Christian piety and is at home in the English liturgy: lovely, sweet channel through which to pour out your feelings, not personal enough to be blushy and not committing you to a single damned dogma: because nobody nowadays is expected to take the Bible seriously or the catechism or the thirty-nine articles. But I tell you, it's a rare thing for a man to strip himself clean like that of every rag of false comfort. It makes the deuce of a hard life.

Goethe didn't have a hard life, yet I don't believe he had any illusions.

He was one of your lucky dogs, wasn't he? Still had a glad eye for the gals at seventy-two.—K-201-202

Goethe

Here Goethe had been in the right, in spite of Cousin Caleb: he had breathed in the ether freely, and had breathed it out again warmed; breathed it out completely, fearlessly, joyously. He had obeyed every vital impulse; had shaken off every chain not forged by nature in putting us together, every bond not itself a fibre in our vital organism.—K-202

Clergymen

As for the clergymen, he thinks they are simply the ladies' oracles, putting their delusions into words for them, and painting the universe all pink and blue for them to be comfy in. —K-213-214

Crying

Half the pleasure of crying is missed if there's nobody by to pity and comfort you.—K-217

The world and its people

Better not travel, if you wished to admire the world; if you wished to think highly of your fellow men, better not hug them too close.—K-227

Mob spirit

I suppose people aren't ashamed of doing or feeling anything, no matter what, if only they can do it together. And sometimes two people are enough.—K-232

Reformers

Nothing seemed to him more odious in this world than the people bent on reforming it. The truly sweet fruits of existence were to be picked by the way: they were amusement, kindness, and beauty. But reformers blindly pursued something else, which if realised would probably be worthless; and meantime they screamed with the fanatical hatred of everything human.—K-244

Thought and reality

Thought is never sure of its contacts with reality; action must intervene to render the rhetoric of thought harmless and its emotions sane.—K-284

England—her metamorphoses

Look at England. England is always dying gently, cheerfully, the executioner succeeding to the government. Catholic England—the England that was a part of Europe—died at the Reformation. Romantic England died with the Stuarts. Commercial, naval, Protestant England died the other day with Queen Victoria. Yet something survives—something inferior, but for the moment capable of existing. We may now have another England that is a part of America. Why drag the weight of those vain affections? Let the dead bury their dead.—K-287

Twentieth century. Democracy, dominance of

The twentieth (century)—what little there was yet of it—betrayed a frightened retreat before democracy, and the dominance of athletics. What the dominance of democracy and athletics could mean, Oliver knew by experience. It was a double tyranny which he took for granted without protest, like that of sunshine and rain.—K-311

Compromising England

"England," he said, "is an easy enough country to live in, but very hard to understand. It never has understood itself: it exists by a living compromise between incompatible tendencies."—K-313

Humorous view of world

Learning again to look at this poor world with humour and at passions without passion.—K-321

Smiles. Scientific advertising

Merely by smiling, you could neutralise all the indecent assaults on the mind committed by scientific advertising and professional humbug.—K-382

Conversation, its use

The primary use of conversation is to satisfy the impulse to talk.—K-385

Longfellow. Literary critics

"As to my worthy cousin," he observed, "Brother Oliver Alden, you mustn't be surprised if you see him nowadays walking about abstracted and Hamlet-like, with his mouth open and his tie loose. He is not in love; he hasn't seen a ghost: but he is secretly engaged in composing his thesis for a Ph.D—fortunately in the German language—on the secret significance of Longfellow's poetry. It will be a revolutionary work and epoch-making. People will say Before Alden and After Alden as we say B.C. and A.D. He has already half-reconstructed the lost document Q from which that rogue Longfellow drew his best-sellers. It was a mediaeval collection of Milesian tales of a—well—most unpleasant character. The originals of Evangeline and Priscilla—though Oliver's ancestresses—were no better than white slaves. All uplift will be gone from the cry, Excelsior. It will no longer echo in every Christian home. Hotels called by that name will be avoided by self-respecting financiers. Banished, too, will be those household words:

> She stirs, she moves, she seems to feel
> The thrill of life along her keel;

and the sands of time, flowing faster than ever through the hour-glass of progress, will erase the footprints of Hiawatha and of the good man Friday."—K-405-406

Religions, compared. Good women

"I was never enthusiastic about being a Jew, but the first drop of baptismal water washed me of all desire to be a Christian. One religion is as good as another when good people practise it and believe they believe it. It's a play they like to act; they compose a part for themselves in it much more important than the role that falls to them in real life. It's a great safety valve; it reconciles them with existence. As for me, I find religion enough in the love of beautiful things. Jewels and flowers seem to me different forms of the same beauty: Jewels are flowers petrified and become luminous: while flowers are jewels become sensitive and frail, swaying in the wind, and dying young. And there's a third form of beauty, combining the other two, and that's a good woman; because a good woman is like a flower in her body and like a jewel in her mind. Keep to good women, my boy, and you'll be all right."—K-434-435

Life levels

"Don't think you've done your duty if you distribute your money in pennies, one for every beggar, and leave the world as flat and desolate as if there were no wealth in it at all. The use of riches isn't to disperse riches, but to cultivate the art of living, to produce beautiful houses, beautiful manners, beautiful speech, beautiful charities. You individually can't raise the lowest level of human life, but you may raise the highest level."—K-459

[155]

Those Mediterranean countries where the Church is so paganised.—K-466

Romanism, Protestantism and Anglican traditions compared

Originally, Christianity was partly poetry and partly delusion. The Roman Church clings to both parts equally; Protestantism has kept the delusion and destroyed the poetry; and only the Anglican tradition is capable of preserving the poetry, while sweeping the delusion away.—K-475

Vulgarity and the press

The first news every day had been from the London or New York Stock Exchange; and the home newspapers had reported the stale catastrophes of weeks before with a ghastly crudity. There was no private space any longer in the world, and no freedom: every chink and cranny was choked with the same vulgarity.—K-507

Pretension of first magnitude

In Rome he had even seen greatness of a sort actually surviving, when the Pope was carried into St. Peter's to the sound of silver trumpets. Here was still a man who believed he was the Vice-regent of God. Could such a pretension suffice to raise people to the top of the world?—K-512

Old customs. Fearless reason

Curious old customs were pleasant if they were honoured without superstition; and so was fearless reason, if you were loyal at heart to your traditions.—K-513

War compared with football
Moronic psychology

When a private at first in the ranks, and soon in various more responsible posts, he realised how exactly war was like football. He remembered all the false reasons which his mother and other high-minded people used to give to justify that game: that it was good for the health, or for young men's morals, or for testing and strengthening character; whereas he knew by experience that after the playing season every blackguard was as much, or twice as much, a blackguard as before, every sneak a sneak and every rake a rake. So now the same outsiders apologised for this war, saying that poor Serbia had been outraged, or poor Belgium invaded, or the *Lusitania* sunk; all of which might be grounds for resentment. Yet the soldier feels no resentment—except perhaps against his own officers—and has suffered no wrong. He simply hears the bugle, as it were for the chase; endures discipline, when once he is caught in the mesh, because he can't help it; and fights keenly on occasion, because war is the greatest excitement, the greatest adventure in human life. Just so, in little, football had been an outlet for instinct, and a mock war. The howling crowds were stirred vicariously by the same craving for rush and rivalry, and were exactly like the public in time of war, cheering each its own side. Oliver, in his secret mind, perfectly perceived all those pathetic but normal necessities; and he could acquiesce in them with a smile, because the physical man in him was engaged healthily, and seemed to move in unison with the world. It was a comfort to run in harness, and to wear blinkers, fatigue shutting out the irrelevant prospect on one side, and public opinion shutting it off on the other.—K-541

Old ladies

All old ladies, unless they were lachrymose pacifists, were furious patriots.—K-542

All religions false

But Christianity and all the other religions are so childishly false that I wonder how some people can put up with them.—K-570

Triumphs and contentment

We must be satisfied to catch our triumphs on the wing, to die continually, and to die content.—K-584

L

Accidents

Accidents are accidents only to ignorance; in reality all physical events flow out of one another by a continuous intertwined derivation.—L-2

Snobs. Caste

An unprejudiced man will be ready and happy to live in any class of society; he will find there occasions enough for merriment, pleasure, and kindness. Only snobs are troubled by inequality, or by exclusion from something accidental, as all particular stations are. Why should I think it unjust that I am not an applauded singer nor a field-marshal nor a puppet king? I am rather sorry for them; I mean, for the spirit in them. Success and failure in the world are sprinkled over it like dew: it does not depend on the species of plant that receives it, save that the plant must exist and must spread its living texture to the elements. That is a great privilege, and a great danger. I would not multiply or inflate myself of my own accord. Even the punctilious honour of the Spanish gentleman is only an eloquent vanity, disdaining many advantages for the sake of a pose. Why assume so much dignity, if you have it not? And if you have it, what need have you of parading it? The base and sordid side of life must be confessed and endured humbly; the confession and the endurance will raise you enough above it.—L-13

Newman. Santayana's father

Speaking once of Newman, he said he wondered why Newman broke with the Anglican establishment. Was it so as to wear a trailing red silk gown? I had some difficulty in making him admit that Newman could have been sincere; perhaps it was possible, if, as I said, Newman had never doubted the supernatural authority of the Church. But of inner unrest or faith suddenly born out of despair my father had absolutely no notion. Could he ever have read the Confessions of his patron saint, Saint Augustine? Was that not a natural sequel to the tragedies of Seneca?—L-15

Soldier vs. hangman

I am glad that our son has no inclination to be a soldier. No career displeases me more, and if I were a man it would repel me less to be a hangman than a soldier, because the one is obliged to put to death only criminals sentenced by the law, but the other kills honest men who like himself bathe in innocent blood at the bidding of some superior. Barbarous customs that I hope will disappear when there are no Kings and no desire for conquest and when man has the world for his country and all his fellow-beings for brothers. You will say that I am dreaming. It may be so. Adieu.—L-22

Malays. Primitive people

We had lived among the Malays in the Philippines, the most blameless of primitive peoples, and he spoke kindly of them; but the only Malays he respected were those that had become Mohammedan and warlike—pirates if you like—and had kept their independence.—L-23

Servants in Spain

Going to the fountain (as it was called) was a chief occupation for servants in Avila, whether girls or men, and also a chief amusement as were the innumerable errands they were sent on; it gave them a breath of air, a little freedom from the mistress's eye, and a lovely occasion for gossip and for lovemaking. Without going to the fountain and without errands (since all messages were sent by word of mouth, never by written notes) the life of domestic servants would have been prison-labor. As it was they knew everybody, heard everything, and saw wonderful things.—L-27

Reason vs. religion

It was not religion that made people safely good, it was reason.—L-35

Natural love. Virtue

Are those blameless children of nature (natives of Batang) for instance, promiscuous in their loves? Instead of crying, How shocking! the moralist has only to familiarize himself with their view, sanctioned by the experience of ages, in order to recognize that promiscuity may be virtuous no less than a fidelity imposed by oaths and fertile in jealousy and discord.—L-36

Tropical climate, its effects

A tropical climate is fatal to the white race. The white race must live in the temperate zone, it must invent arts and governments, it must be warlike and industrious, or it cannot survive. This fatality of course is not absolute or immediate; white men may live in the tropics, protecting themselves by a special regimen, and returning home occasionally to recover their tone; but if they leave children in those torrid regions, the children will die out or be assimilated, in aspect and temperament, and probably also in blood, to the natives.—L-37

Boston, moral nursery

Boston was a nice place with very nice people in it; but it was an excellent point of vantage from which to start out, if you belonged there, rather than a desirable point to arrive at if you were born in some other place. It was a moral and intellectual nursery, always busy applying first principles to trifles.—L-53

Solitude

I doubt whether this practice is altogether wholesome in youth. Animals are born and bred in litters. Solitude grows blessed and peaceful only in old age.—L-61

Beards, appropriate types

Nevertheless I didn't like him. He had a full round beard, and I cannot like that. A long white, or gray, or even yellow beard, especially if clean, forked or blown into strands, is suitable for Michelangelo's Moses or Charon in his bark, or even for God the Father; but a round short full beard like Saint Peter's is vulgar.—L-69

Religion to be omitted

Everything happens, and we had better take it all as easily or as resignedly as possible. But this without a shadow of religion.—L-74

Poland. Nationality and religion. Paderewski

I remember speaking there with the prima donnas Sembrich and Emma Eames and with Madame Paderewska. I asked the latter about the fidelity of the men in Poland to the Church; and she said that they all *had* to remain good Catholics, because a soul lost to the Church means a soul lost to Poland. This Eastern way of identifying religion with nationality gave me a useful hint for the interpretation of both.—L-83

Religion and philosophy

Now I was aware, at first instinctively and soon quite clearly on historical and psychological grounds, that religion and all philosophy of that kind was *invented*.—L-85

Modernist. Catholic priests

In a word, I was a spontaneous modernist in theology and philosophy: but not being pledged, either socially or superstitiously, to any sect or tradition, I was spared the torments of those poor Catholic priests or those limping Anglicans who think they can be at once modernists and believers. They can be only amateurs, at best connoisseurs, in religion. The rest for them will only be a belated masquerade.—L-86

American humor

There is a curious cruelty mixed sometimes with American shrewdness and humor. The sharp mind finds things queer, crooked, perverse; it puns about them; and it doesn't see why they shouldn't be expected and commanded to be quite other than they are; but all this without much hope of mending

them, and a sardonic grin. My old teacher Royce had something of this perverse idealism.—L-88

Catholicism

Catholicism is the most human of religions, if taken
humanly: it is paganism spiritually transformed and made
meta-physical.—L-91

Orthodoxy and madness

Orthodoxy must be taken with a grain of salt, to keep it
beneficent and prevent it from turning into madness.—L-92

Body, character and mind

Body, character and mind are formed together by that single
hereditary organizing power which the ancients called psyche
or soul; so that however much the mind or the body may
be distorted by accident influences, at bottom they must always
correspond; and the innocent eye often catches this profound
identity. We are arrested by a beautiful body because the
sight of it quickens in ourselves the same vital principle that
fashioned that body.—L-93

Environment of Santayana

Granted that I was to awake in Spain in the nineteenth
century, I could have found myself in no place less degraded
than Avila; and granted that I was to be educated in America
and to earn my bread there, I could have fallen on no place
friendlier than Harvard. In each of these places there was
a maximum of air, of space, of suggestion; in each there
was a minimum of deceptiveness and of the power to enslave.—L-97

Birthplace of free spirit

For the freest spirit must have some birthplace, some *locus
standi* from which to view the world and some innate passion
by which to judge it.—L-97

Avila

At this altitude primitive bald nature has coexisted for ages with the tightest and most fortified civilization, ecclesiastical and military.—L-98

Superstition

Superstition may variously deceive the fancy; it never changes the allegiance of the heart, which I suppose is all that matters from a spiritual point of view.—L-107

Mother of Santayana

One evening, before putting me to bed, my mother carried me to the window, sitting on her arm, and pulled back the *visillo* or lace curtain that hung close to the glass. Above the tower of the Oñate house opposite, one bright steady star was shining. My mother pointed it out to me, and said: "Detrás de ese lucero está Pepín." Pepín, her lamented first-born, was behind that star. At the time, this announcement neither surprised nor impressed me; but something about my mother's tone and manner must have fixed her words mechanically in my memory. She seldom spoke unnecessarily, and was never emotional; but here was some profound association with her past that, for a moment, had spread its aura about me. Age 3.—L-117

American economy

Ours was the house to the left, not the one to the right. The pair were a product of that "producer's economy," then beginning to prevail in America, which first creates articles and then attempts to create a demand for them; an economy that has flooded the country with breakfast foods, shaving soaps, poets, and professors of philosophy.—L-141-142

Laissez-faire

The age was still enamored of *laissez-faire;* and its advantages were indeed undeniable. For the Government it meant a minimum of work, and for the public it meant a minimum of government.—L-142-143

History

The sectarian politics and moralizing of most historians

made history an impossible study for me for many years.—
L-145

Events in life of Santayana

More than once in my life I have crossed a desert in all that
regards myself, my thoughts, or my happiness; so that when
I look back over those years, I see objects, I see public events,
I see *persons and places,* but I don't see myself. My inner
life, as I recall it, seems to be concentrated in a few cases,
in a few halting-places, *Green Inns,* or Sanctuaries, where the
busy traveller stopped to rest, to think, and to be himself.
I say the *busy* traveller, because those long stretches of spiritual
emptiness were filled with daily actions and feelings, later
in my case often with giving lectures and writing books:
yet all was done under some mechanical stimulus, the college
bell, the desk, the pen, or the chapter planned: old thoughts
and old words flowing out duly from the reservoir, until
the college bell rang again, and the water was turned off. Of
myself in those years I have no recollection; it is as if I
hadn't existed, or only as a mechanical sensorium and active
apparatus, doing its work under my name. Somnambulistic
periods, let me call them; and such a period now seems to
begin and to last for two-thirds of my Latin School days.—
L-151

School time waste

In the best schools, almost all school time is wasted. Now
and then something is learned that sticks fast; for the rest
the boys are merely given time to grow and are kept from
too much mischief.—L-154

The demagogue and the people

I have mentioned declamation: that was another stimulus
to vanity. Inwardly it was one more dramatic indulgence, one
more occasion for fantastically playing a part. . . . Very useful, no doubt, for future lawyers, politicians, or clergymen—
training for that reversible sophistry and propaganda that
intoxicates the demagogue and misleads the people.—L-158

[164]

Hell and Heaven

In spite, then, of my religious and other daydreams, I was at bottom a young realist; I knew I was dreaming, and so was awake. A sure proof of this was that I was never *anxious* about what those dreams would have involved if they had been true. I never had the least touch of superstition. To follow the logic of dogma and keep the feasts, if not the fasts, of the Church, was a part of the game; and the whole allegorical pseudo-historical pageant passed through my mind unchallenged, because I felt intimately the dramatic logic that had inspired it. But no logic can upset the facts. . . . You are confusing poetry with fact. Never had I the least fear of a material hell or desire for a material heaven. The images were so violent, so childish, as to be comic.—L-173

Faith of Santayana
Comparison of business and the church

My faith was indeed so like despair that it wasn't faith at all; it was fondness, liking, what in Spanish is called afición; I indulged in it, but only north-northwest, and keeping my freedom. I heartily agreed with the Church about the world, yet I was ready to agree with the world about the Church; and I breathed more easily in the atmosphere of religion than in that of business, precisely because religion, like poetry, was more ideal, more freely imaginary, and in a material sense falser.—L-174

Soliloquies and ghosts

I now saw that there was only one possible play, the actual history of nature and of mankind, although there might well be ghosts among the characters and soliloquies among the speeches. Religions, *all* religions, and idealistic philosophies, *all* idealistic philosophies, were the soliloquies and the ghosts. —L-175

Rational belief

Rational belief must have other guides than sheer imagination, exploring infinite possibilities. Those guides can be, logically, nothing but accidents; but they have a compulsory presence and evoke an inescapable adhesion, confidence, and trust; which trust is fortified by experiment and found trustworthy.—L-177

Manual work

A little manual work or physical exercise changes the stops agreeably, lengthens the focus and range of vision, reverts to the realm of matter which is the true matrix of mind, and generally brings judgment and feeling back into harmony with nature.—L-188

Shamming. Professors and women

Besides, though I became a professor myself, I never had a real friend who was a professor. Is it jealousy, as among women, and a secret unwillingness to be wholly pleased? Or is it the consciousness that a professor or a woman has to be partly a sham; whence a mixture of contempt and pity for such a poor victim of necessity? In Fletcher, and in the nobler professors, the shamming is not an effect of the profession, but rather, as in inspired clergymen, the profession is an effect of an innate passion for shamming.—L-189

Closets

But an "improvement" had spoiled the dignity of these chambers. The rage for "closets" invaded America, why I am not antiquary enough to know.—L-192

"Lampoon". American joking

I never wrote for the *Lampoon;* even the text for my sketches was usually supplied for me by the others, who knew the idioms required. My English was too literary, too lady-like, too correct for such a purpose; and I never acquired, or liked, the American art of perpetual joking.—L-197

"Athletic Ode". "Six Wise Fools"

It was at the O. K. dinners in the 1890's, that I read my *Athletic Ode* and *Six Wise Fools*. Helped by the champagne, these trifles caught fire. The play of ordinary wit and sentiment, with a light touch and a masculine note, appeals to a side of the heart not reached in the standard poets; it moves from convention to sincerity, where the standard poets move from sincerity to convention.—L-200

American poetry. Swinburne

In verse he was scornful and revolutionary, with a good deal of verbal facility and technical ingenuity, after the manner of Swinburne. His versification was not slovenly, even when it was empty or trite. This was remarkable in America, and indicated a certain documentary precision and authority in his mind, that doubtless contributed to his subsequent official distinction.—L-201

Alone

They say dying animals go into hiding; and I could understand that instinct. There are phases of distress when help is neither possible nor desired. It is simpler, easier, more honest to be seasick alone, and to die alone. The trouble then seems something fated, not to be questioned, like life itself; and nature is built to face it and to see it out.—L-204

Prosperity

Liberalism, Protestantism, Judaism, positivism all have the same ultimate aim and standard. It is prosperity, or as Lutheran theologians put it, union with God at our level, not at God's level. The thing all these schools detest is the ideal of union with God at God's level, proper to asceticism, mysticism, and pure intelligence, which insist on seeing things under the form of truth and of eternity. You must be content, they say, to see things under the form of time, of appearance, and of feeling.—L-209

Lucretius. Santayana's father

It was not at long range only, like Lucretius, that my father could observe the evils occasioned by religion. . . . Here was a perpetual thorn in my father's side; and yet the prick was a stimulant. It enlivened him and kept his exasperation always pleasantly fresh and green . . . and he reverted to his fundamental tolerance and even deference towards all mankind.—L-210-215

Spanish people

The Spanish people is a poetic people and Spanish greatness a chivalrous greatness.—L-211

The sceptic and orthodoxy

Your genuine and profound sceptic sees no reason to quarrel with any ruling orthodoxy. It is as plausible as any other capable of prevailing in the world. If you do not think so, it is simply because that orthodoxy is not familiar to you, or not congenial. In a different age, or with a different endowment, you would have rested peacefully in it like the rest of mankind.—L-219

Our beliefs

It was not our fault that we were born. Is it our fault that we believe what we believe?—L-219

Women

The worst symptoms of infidelity that I saw in that family were in the women. Not unintelligibly. It was they who had suffered most from poverty, since there had always been enough to eat, but not enough to appear in the world as women like to appear. And it was they who had suffered most from the latent disgrace of their position, and the dread of gossip and insults. They owed society a grudge for making their life difficult. They had not sinned against nature, but the world had sinned against them by its cruel tyranny and injustice. They were therefore rebels, impotent rebels, against all the powers that be, celestial and earthly.—L-220

Rascals

Since we are all rascals, let us all be rascals at one level, with equal chances to worm our way to a false eminence. —L-221

Priests and women

For being a priest he has a keen scent for everything that concerns women.—L-223

The Jew—his view

To the Jew the earth seems a promised land, suggesting the millennium, the triumph of God in the human world. Swine, epicureans, and monks, on the contrary, not being legally edible, seem not only useless for that purpose, but positively unclean. This comes consistently enough of regarding God only as a power, the power that conditions our happiness.—L-231

Process of living. Prize of life

I was as convinced as I am now of the steady march of cosmic forces that we may, in a measure, enlist in our service, and thereby win the prize of life in the process of living, without laying any claims to dominate the universe, either physically or morally. But this is a comparatively mature, though very ancient, conclusion; and it is as well to become aware in the first place of the uncertainty and blindness of human opinion.—L-233

Tolerance toward social systems

I love Tory England and honor conservative Spain, but not with any dogmatic or prescriptive passion. If any community can become and desires to become communistic or democratic or anarchical I wish it joy from the bottom of my heart. I have only two qualms in this case: whether such ideals are realizable, and whether those who pursue them fancy them to be exclusively and universally right: an illusion pregnant with injustice, oppression, and war.—L-237

Lucretius. Nature

Even the physical and biological theories (of Lucretius) seemed instructive, not as scientific finalities, if science could be final, but as serving to dispel the notion that anything is non-natural or miraculous. If the theory suggested were false, another no less naturalistic would be true: and this presumption recommended itself to me and has become one of my first principles: not that a particular philosophy called naturalism must be true *a priori*, but that nature sets the standard of naturalness.—L-239

ℳ

Germany, impressions of

I used at that time to sum up my first impressions of Germany by saying that there were three good things there: the uniforms, the music, and the beer.—M-4

Beauty and Courage

For what is greater than beauty, and what is more beautiful than courage to live and to die freely, in one's chosen way?—M-6

Determinism. Bergson

He had thought and thought on that subject, yet he hadn't thought himself out of his half impulsive, half traditional horror of determinism, not because he couldn't think the argument out, but because, like Bergson, he didn't trust argument where he had intuition.—M-7

Happiness

A string of excited, fugitive, miscellaneous pleasures is not happiness; happiness resides in imaginative reflection and judgment, when the *picture* of one's life, or of human life, as it truly has been or is, satisfies the will, and is gladly accepted.—M-8

Epicurus. Solon. Peace, equanimity, intelligence
Beautiful moment, Beautiful death

Epicurus renounced most of the things called pleasures, for the sake of peace, equanimity, and intelligence, and Solon's heroes renounced life itself for the sake of a beautiful moment or a beautiful death.—M-8

Christ

He (Westenholz) always maintained an "Evangelical" conception of Christ very different from mine, which is Gnostic and free from all claims to be historical.—M-11

German characteristics

This joy in simplicity, this nostalgia for childishness, in highly educated, rich and terribly virtuous people surely is thoroughly German.—M-15

Protestantism

I think it must have been Protestantism that so completely extinguished Elizabethan genius.—M-23

Freedom vs. power. The Englishman

Even in the great respect that he (the Englishman) shows for wealth and station he honours freedom rather than power.—M-25

Prosperity in England

It is only the rich Englishman that can truly prosper in England.—M-26

Comparison of life in England, America, and The Continent

I was perfectly happy in the English climate and the English way of living. They were a great relief from America in softness and dignity, and from the Continent in comfort and privacy.—M-35

Matter compared with women. Defiance

Matter can be wooed, coaxed, and mastered like a woman, and this without being in the least understood sympathetically. On the contrary, the keen edge of the pleasure comes from defiance.—M-47

Catholicism. Whiskey

Perhaps, too, being Irish was closer to his inner man, and certainly more congruous with Catholicism and with whiskey.—M-55

Histrionic religion
And his religion too was genuine religion, if we admit that religion must be essentially histrionic.—M-56

Public opinion
A young man with a brilliant career open to him in the world is a fool to flout public opinion, even if he secretly despises it. Peace with the polite world is all important for one's comfort and euphoria so long as one lives in the polite world.—M-75

British society
British society is sustained by "created interests"; that is to say, by vain commitments into which people have been led unawares, but which it would be too disturbing now to abandon. The farce must be kept up, and it becomes a point of honor to drop dead at last upon the stage, in all one's paint and feathers.—M-75

Detached and sceptical philosophy
She possessed a rather detached and sceptical philosophy, one that teaches us that all conditions are bearable, all dignities trumpery, and wisdom simply the gift of making the best of whatever is thrust upon us.—M-78

Reason, definition of
I call it reason because reason in my philosophy is only a harmony among irrational impulses.—M-85

Wise religious zeal
Her religious zeal had become wiser, she let God look after His own interests, and didn't worry any longer about other people's salvation.—M-89

Incubus of life
Think what an incubus life would be, if death were not destined to cancel it, as far as any fact can be cancelled.—M-105

Laughter
Now laughter, as I have come to see in my old age, is the

innocent youthful side of repentance, of disillusion, of under-standing.—M-109

Eternal friendship with the beautiful

In each person I catch the fleeting suggestion of something beautiful and swear eternal friendship with that.—M-111

Women's opinions

When women's opinions waver, it means that their hearts are not at rest. Let them once settle their affections and see their interests, and theoretical doubt becomes impossible for them.—M-118

Ideal—love-affairs

His love-affairs, which were, as poetry should be, simple, sensuous, and short.—M-145

Materialist. Spirit

I think he distrusted me also for being a materialist, not so much in theory, for we never discussed that, but in my constant sense of the animal basis of spirit, and my disrespect for any claim on the part of spirit to govern the world.—M-149

Newman

It is tragic in such cases to look back to the lovely familiar world that one has abandoned for being false or wicked, and to seek in vain for compensations and equivalents in the strange system that one has decided to call good and true. So Newman must have suffered when he became a Catholic.—M-151

Lectures and sermons

I think, however, that lectures, like sermons, are usually unprofitable.—M-155

Materialist. Nature

Those liberal minds were thirsting for a tyrant. I, being a materialist, cynic, and Tory in philosophy, never dreamt of rebelling against the despotism of nature; and I accepted having feet, ugly and insufficient as they might be, because it would be much worse not to have them.—M-155

Beliefs of Santayana

So I believe, compulsorily and satirically, in the existence of this absurd world; but as to the existence of a better world, or of hidden reasons in this one, I am incredulous, or rather, I am critically sceptical; because it is not difficult to see the familiar motives that lead men to invent such myths.—M-155-156

Humanities

So are all systems of philosophy, so are all logical languages, so are all allegories and images of sense. The study of them is a part of the humanities, initiating us into the history of human life and mind; it is not the pursuit of science or salvation.—M-156

The virtues of Santayana. Eliot, President

My relations with President Eliot and with other influential persons had always been strained. I had disregarded or defied public opinion by not becoming a specialist, but writing pessimistic, old-fashioned verses, continuing to range superficially over literature and philosophy, being indiscernibly a Catholic or an atheist, attacking Robert Browning, prophet of the half-educated and half-believing, avoiding administrative duties, neglecting the intelligentsia, frequenting the society of undergraduates and fashionable ladies, spending my holidays abroad, and even appearing as a witness in the disreputable Russell trial.—M-159

Vague mind. Majority

There is solace to the vague mind in letting an anonymous and irresponsible majority be responsible for everything.—M-161

Slaves. Creatures of circumstance

Whereas individuals, especially in governments, are creatures of circumstance and slaves to vested interests.—M-169

[175]

Declaration of Independence

But the Declaration of Independence was a piece of literature, a salad of illusions.—M-169

"Cocktail words"

Phelps was irresistible. His every word was a cocktail, or at least a temperance drink. He made you love everything.—M-176

American luxury

It is an error into which too much domestic luxury has led American taste that all bread should be buttered.—M-176

Santayana vs. Emerson. Christianity

As Emerson said, "If God is anywhere, he is here," so this modern Christian should say, If heaven isn't here it's nowhere. A conclusion that in some sense I should be willing to accept, only that I shouldn't call it Christianity: rather Epicurean contentment in being an accident in an accident.—M-177

N

John Locke

He knew how many strange nations and false religions lodged in this round earth, itself but a speck in the universe. —N-2

Modern psychology

Locke was the father of modern psychology, and the birth of this airy monster, this half-natural changeling, was not altogether easy or fortunate.—N-2-3

Presuppositions and beliefs

Presuppositions are imposed on all of us by life itself: for instance the presupposition that life is to continue, and that it is worth living. Belief is born on the wing and awakes to many tacit commitments. Afterwards, in reflection, we may wonder at finding these presuppositions on our hands, and, being ignorant of the natural causes which have imposed them on the animal mind, we may be offended at them.—N-4-5

Poetical mind

Mind is incorrigibly poetical.—N-22

Frailty of philosophies

All philosophies are frail, in that they are products of the human mind, in which everything is essentially reactive, spontaneous, and volatile.—N-23

Locke's mind

Doubtless Locke might have dug his foundations deeper and integrated his faith better. His system was no metaphysical castle, no theological acropolis: rather a homely ancestral manor house built in several styles of architecture: a Tudor chapel, a Palladian front toward the new geometrical garden, a Jacobean parlour for political consultation and learned disputes, and even—since we are almost in the eighteenth century—a Chinese cabinet full of curios. It was a habitable philosophy, and not too inharmonious. There was no greater incongruity in its parts than in the gentle variations of English weather or in the qualified moods and insights of a civilised mind. Impoverished as we are, morally and humanly, we can no longer live in such a rambling mansion. It has become a national monument. On the days when it is open we revisit it with admiration; and those chambers and garden walks re-echo to us the clear dogmas and savoury diction of the sage—omnivorous, artless, loquacious—whose dwelling it was.—N-25-26

Philosophy and science

All modern philosophy, in so far as it is a description of experience and not of nature, therefore seems to belong to the sphere of literature, and to be without scientific value.—N-47

Moral consciousness

Moral consciousness in particular would never have arisen and would be gratuitous, save for the ferocious bias of a natural living creature, defending itself against its thousand enemies.—N-64

German idealism

German idealism is a mighty pose, an attitude always possible to a self-conscious and reflective being: but it is hardly a system, since it contradicts beliefs which in action are inevitable; it may therefore be readily swallowed, but it can never be digested.—N-67

English behavior

The modest English in these matters take shelter under the wing of science speculatively extended, or traditional religion prudently rationalised.—N-70

Twentieth century science

Since the beginning of the twentieth century, science has

gained notably in expertness, and lost notably in authority.
—N-71

Theoretical and applied science

Nevertheless, skill and understanding are at their best when they go together and adorn the same mind.—N-71-72

Technique of science and industry

The technique of science, like that of industry, has become a thing in itself; the one veils its object, which is happiness. —N-74

Space, time

The upright walls of space, the steady tread of time, begin to fail us; they bend now so obligingly to our perspectives that we no longer seem to travel through them, but to carry them with us, shooting them out or weaving them about us according to some fatality, which is left unexplained.—N-75

Science

Science, when it is more than the gossip of adventure or of experiment, yields practical assurances couched in symbolic terms, but no ultimate insight: so that the intellectual vacancy of the expert, which I was deriding, is a sort of warrant of his solidity. It is rather when the expert prophesies, when he propounds a new philosophy founded on his latest experiments, that we may justly smile at his system, and wait for the next.—N-79-80

Aspirations of science

If all the arts aspire to the condition of music, all the sciences aspire to the condition of mathematics. Their logic is their spontaneous and intelligible side: and while they differ from mathematics and from one another in being directed in the first instance upon various unintelligible existing objects, yet as they advance, they unite: because they are everywhere striving to discover in those miscellaneous objects some intelligible order and method. And as the emotion of the pure artist, whatever may be his materials, lies in finding in them some formal harmony or imposing it upon them, so the interest of the scientific mind, in so far as it is free and purely intellectual, lies in tracing their formal pattern. The mathematician can afford to leave to his clients, the engineers, or perhaps the popular philosophers, the emotion of belief: for himself he keeps the lyrical pleasure of metre and of evolving equations: and it is a pleasant surprise to him, and an added problem, if he finds that the arts can use his calculations, or that the senses can verify them; much as if a composer found that the sailors could heave better when singing his songs.—N-80-81

Popular habits of thinking

The soft-hearted, the muddle-headed, the superstitious are all raising their voices, no longer in desperate resistance to science, but hopefully, and in its name. Science, they tell us, is no longer hostile to religion, or to divination of any sort. Indeed, divination is a science too. Physics is no longer materialistic since space is now curved, and filled with an ether through which light travels at 300,000 kilometres per second —an immaterial rate. . . . All this I find announced in newspapers and even in books as the breakdown of scientific materialism: and yet, when was materialism more arrant and barbarous than in these announcements? Something no doubt has broken down: but I am afraid it is rather the ●habit of thinking clearly and the power to discern the difference between material and spiritual things.—N-82-83

The new science in democracy

The new science is unintelligible to almost all of us; it can be tested only by very delicate observations and very difficult reasoning. We accept it on the authority of a few professors who themselves have accepted it with a contagious alacrity, as if caught in a whirlwind. It has sprung up mysteriously and mightily, like mysticism in a cloister or theology in a council: a Soviet of learned men has proclaimed it. Moreover, it is not merely a system among systems, but a movement among movements. A system, even when it has serious rivals, may be maintained for centuries as religions are maintained, institutionally; but a movement comes to an end; it is followed presently by a period of assimilation which transforms it, or by a movement in some other direction. I ask myself accordingly whether the condition of the world in the coming years will be favourable to refined and paradoxical science. The extension of education will have enabled the uneducated to pronounce upon everything. Will the patronage of capital and enterprise subsist, to encourage discovery and reward invention? Will a jealous and dogmatic democracy respect the unintelligible insight of the few? Will a perhaps starving democracy support materially its Soviet of seers? But let us suppose that no utilitarian fanaticism supervenes, and no intellectual surfeit or discouragement. May not the very profundity of the new science and its metaphysical affinities lead it to bolder developments, inscrutable to the public and incompatible with one another, like the gnostic sects of declining antiquity? Then perhaps that luminous modern thing which until recently was called science, in contrast to all personal philosophies, may cease to exist altogether, being petrified into routine in the practitioners, and fading in the professors into abstruse speculations.—N-86

Nirvana

The relapse of created things into nothing is no violent fatality, but something naturally quite smooth and proper. —N-88

Myths

In what sense can myths and metaphors be true or false? In the sense that, in terms drawn from moral predicaments or from literary psychology, they may report the general movement and the pertinent issue of material facts, and may inspire us with a wise sentiment in their presence. In this sense I should say that Greek mythology was true and Calvinist theology was false.—N-92

Habits and obsessions

Every act initiates a new habit and may implant a new instinct. We see people even late in life carried away by political or religious contagions or developing strange vices; there would be no peace in old age, but rather a greater and greater obsession by all sorts of cares, were it not that time, in exposing us to many adventitious influences, weakens or discharges our primitive passions; we are less greedy, less lusty, less hopeful, less generous. But these weakened primitive impulses are naturally by far the strongest and most deeply rooted in the organism: so that although an old man may be converted or may take up some hobby, there is usually something thin in his elderly zeal.—N-95-96

Life

But the ineptitude of our aesthetic minds to unravel the nature of mechanism does not deprive these minds of their own clearness and euphony. Besides sounding their various musical notes, they have the cognitive function of indicating the hour and catching the echoes of distant events or of maturing inward dispositions. This information and emotion, added to incidental pleasures in satisfying our various passions, make up the life of an incarnate spirit.—N-97-98

Death

That the end of life should be death may sound sad: yet what other end can anything have? The end of an evening party is to go to bed; but its use is to gather congenial people together, that they may pass the time pleasantly. An invitation to the dance is not rendered ironical because the dance cannot last for ever; the youngest of us and the most vigorously wound up, after a few hours, has had enough of sinuous stepping and prancing. The transitoriness of things is essential to their physical being, and not at all sad in itself; it becomes sad by virtue of a sentimental illusion, which makes us imagine that they wish to endure, and that their end is always untimely; but in a healthy nature it is not so.—N-98

Spirit

It is only after the organs of spirit are formed mechanically that spirit can exist, and can distinguish the better from the worse in the fate of those organs, and therefore in its own fate. Spirit has nothing to do with infinite existence. Infinite existence is something physical and ambiguous; there is no scale in it and no centre. The depths of the human heart are finite, and they are dark only to ignorance. Deep and dark as a soul may be when you look down into it from outside, it is something perfectly natural; and the same understanding that can unearth our suppressed young passions, and dispel our stubborn bad habits, can show us where our true good lies. Nature has marked out the path for us beforehand; there are snares in it, but also primroses, and it leads to peace.—N-101

Fallaciousness of egotism

Seen in their infinite setting, which we may presume to be their ultimate environment, all things lose their central position and their dominant emphasis.—N-104

Immortality

Yet his whole gay world is secretly afraid of being found out, of being foiled in the systematic bluff by which it lives as if its life were immortal.—N-105

O

Reason. Prayer

I sought on earth a garden of delight,
Or island altar to the Sea and Air,
Where gentle music were accounted prayer,
And reason, veiled, performed the happy rite.—O-3

Wisdom

It is not wisdom to be only wise,
And on the inward vision close the eyes,
But it is wisdom to believe the heart.—O-5

Knowledge

Our knowledge is a torch of smoky pine
That lights the pathway but one step ahead
Across a void of mystery and dread.—O-5

Evil

Have patience; it is fit that in this wise
The spirit purge away its proper dross.
No endless fever doth thy watches toss,
For by excess of evil, evil dies.—O-11

Abjuration

Sweet are the days we wander with no hope
Along life's labyrinthine trodden way,
With no impatience at the steep's delay,
Nor sorrow at the swift-descended slope.
Why this inane curiosity to grope
In the dim dust for gems' unmeaning ray?
Why this proud piety, that dares to pray
For a world wider than the heaven's cope?

[184]

Farewell, my burden! No more will I bear
The foolish load of my fond faith's despair,
But trip the idle race with careless feet.
The crown of olive let another wear;
It is my crown to mock the runner's heat
With gentle wonder and with laughter sweet.—O-15

Beauties

Though I be mute, the birds will in the boughs
Sing as in every April they have sung,
And, though I die, the incense of heart-vows
Will float to heaven, as when I was young.
But, O ye beauties I must never see,
How great a lover have you lost in me!—O-25

Rebels. Slaves

My heart rebels against my generation,
That talks of freedom and is slave to riches,
And, toiling 'neath each day's ignoble burden,
    Boasts of the morrow.
No space for noonday rest or midnight watches,
No purest joy of breathing under heaven!
Wretched themselves, they heap, to make them happy,
    Many possessions.—O-73

Columbus and Magellan

Gathering the echoes of forgotten wisdom,
And mastered by a proud, adventurous purpose,
Columbus sought the golden shores of India
    Opposite Europe.
He gave the world another world, and ruin
Brought upon blameless, river-loving nations,
Cursed Spain with barren gold, and made the Andes
    Fiefs of Saint Peter;
While in the cheerless North the thrifty Saxon
Planted his corn, and, narrowing his bosom,
Made covenant with God, and by keen virtue
    Trebled his riches.

[185]

What venture hast thou left us, bold Columbus?
What honour left thy brothers, brave Magellan?
Daily the children of the rich for pastime
   Circle the planet
And what good comes to us of all your dangers?
A smaller earth and smaller hope of heaven.
Ye have but cheapened gold, and measuring ocean,
   Counted the islands.—O-75-76

Vain tongue

  How vain, how vain
The feeble croaking of a reasoning tongue
  That heals no pain
And prompts no bright deed worthy to be
  sung!—O-83

Life's rainbow

Lo! even in these days
  The world is young.
Life like a torrent flung
  For ever down
For ever wears a rainbow for crown.—O-86

Honor and success. Youth and age

Words soon are cold, and life is warm for ever.
One half honour is the strong endeavour,
Success the other, but when both conspire
Youth has her perfect crown, and age her
  old desire—O-87

Nature

The muffled syllables that Nature speaks
  Fill us with deeper longing for her word.—O-93

Faith

The four stone sentinels to heaven raise
  Their heads, in a more constant faith
  than man's.—O-105

They also will go forth, these gentle youths,
    Strong in the virtues of their manful isle,
Till one the pathway of the forest smooths,
    And one the Ganges rules, and one the Nile;

And to whatever wilderness they choose
    Their hearts will bear the sanctities of home,
The perfect ardours of the Grecian Muse,
    The mighty labour of the arms of Rome;

But, ah! how little of these storied walls
    Beneath whose shadow all their nurture was!
No, not one passing memory recalls
    The Blessed Mary and Saint Nicholas.—O-109

P

Absence of religion in Shakespeare

If, therefore, we were asked to select one monument of human civilisation that should survive to some future age, or be transported to another planet to bear witness to the inhabitants there of what we have been upon earth, we should probably choose the works of Shakespeare. In them we recognize the truest portrait and best memorial of man. Yet the archeologists of that future age, or the cosmographers of that part of the heavens, after conscientious study of our Shakesperian autobiography, would misconceive our life in one important respect. They would hardly understand that man had had a religion.

There are, indeed, numerous exclamations and invocations in Shakespeare, which we, who have other means of information, know to be evidences of current religious ideas. Shakespeare adopts these, as he adopts the rest of his vocabulary, from the society about him. But he seldom or never gives them their original value.—P-681

Oaths

Oaths are the fossils of piety.—P-682

Shakespeare's choice

In all this depth of experience, however, there is still wanting any religious image. The Sonnets are spiritual, but, with the doubtful exception of the one quoted above, they are not Christian. And, of course, a poet of Shakespeare's time could not have found any other mould than Christianity for his religion. In our day, with our wide and conscientious historical sympathies, it may be possible for us to find in other rites and doctrines than those of our ancestors an expression of some ultimate truth. But for Shakespeare, in the matter of religion, the choice lay between Christianity and nothing. He chose nothing; he chose to leave his heroes and himself in the presence of life and of death with no other philosophy than that which the profane world can suggest and understand.—P-684

Shakespeare's world
Shakespeare's world, on the contrary, is only the world of human society.—P-685

Paralysis of literature
When the Greek religion was eclipsed by the Christian . . . literature was paralyzed.—P-687

Drama. Secularism. Goethe. Wagner
Where Christianity was strong, the drama either disappeared or became secular; and it has never again dealt with cosmic themes successfully, except in such hands as those of Goethe and Wagner, men who either neglected Christianity altogether or used it only as an incidental ornament, having, as they say, transcended it in their philosophy.—P-688

Our civilization
The fact is that art and reflection have never been able to unite perfectly the two elements of a civilization like ours. —P-688

Antiquity
The more cultivated a period has been, the more wholly it has reverted to antiquity for its inspiration.—P-688

Secular Shakespeare. The Pious
We need not wonder that Shakespeare, a poet of the Renaissance, should have confined his representation of life to its secular aspects, and that his readers after him should rather have marveled at the variety of the things of which he showed an understanding than have taken note of the one thing he overlooked. To omit religion was after all to omit what was not felt to be congenial to a poet's mind.

[189]

The poet was to trace for us the passionate and romantic embroideries of life; he was to be artful and humane, and above all he was to be delightful. The beauty and charm of things had nothing any longer to do with those painful mysteries and contentions which made the temper of the pious so acrid and sad.—P-688

Good sense of Shakespeare. Shakespeare, Homer and Dante compared

We might say, for instance, that the absence of religion in Shakespeare was a sign of his good sense; that a healthy instinct kept his attention within the sublunary world; and that he was in that respect superior to Homer and to Dante. —P-689

Drama of Shakespeare

Shakespeare, however, is remarkable among the greater poets for being without a philosophy and without a religion. In his drama there is no fixed conception of any forces, natural or moral, dominating and transcending our mortal energies. Whether this characteristic be regarded as a merit or as a defect, its presence cannot be denied.—P-690

Q

Mental life of George Santayana

From childhood I have lived in the imaginative presence of interminable ocean spaces, coconut islands, blameless Malays, and immense continents swarming with Chinamen, polished and industrious, obscene and philosophical. It was habitual with me to think of scenes and customs pleasanter than those about me. My own travels have never carried me far from the frontiers of Christendom or of respectability, and chiefly back and forth across the North Atlantic—thirty-eight fussy voyages; but in mind I have always seen these things on an ironical background enormously empty, or breaking out in spots, like Polynesia, into nests of innocent particoloured humanity.—Q-4

Mental environment in youth of George Santayana
Catechism. Prayers. Religion

Thus, although I learned my prayers and catechism by rote, as was then inevitable in Spain, I knew that my parents regarded all religion as a work of human imagination: and I agreed, and still agree, with them there.—Q-7

Reality and science

Science expresses in human terms our dynamic relation to surrounding reality.—Q-8

Fairy tales. Conscience

Religions are the great fairy-tales of the conscience.—Q-8

Naturalism. Serious opinions

The necessity of naturalism as a foundation for all further serious opinions was clear to me from the beginning.—Q-9

Materialism
Democritus, Lucretius, Spinoza, Darwin

My naturalism or materialism is no academic opinion: it is not a survival of the alleged materialism of the nineteenth century, when all the professors of philosophy were idealists: it is an everyday conviction which came to me, as it came to my father, from experience and observation of the world at large, and especially of my own feelings and passions. It seems to me that those who are not materialists cannot be good observers of themselves: they may hear themselves thinking, but they cannot have watched themselves acting and feeling; for feeling and action are evidently accidents of matter. If a Democritus or Lucretius or Spinoza or Darwin works within the lines of nature, and clarifies some part of that familiar object, that fact is the ground of my attachment to them: they have the savour of truth; but what the savour of truth is, I know very well without their help. —Q-12-13

Wisdom

Wisdom lay rather in taking everything good-humouredly, with a grain of salt.—Q-14

Life and spirit

But life enlightened is spirit: the voice of life, and therefore aspiring to all the perfections to which life aspires, and loving all the beauties that life loves.—Q-23

Santayana's psychoanalysis of self
Reason and nature

I felt myself nearer than ever before to rural nature and to the perennial animal roots of human society. It was not my technical philosophy that was principally affected, but rather the meaning and status of philosophy for my inner man. The humanism characteristic of the *Sense of Beauty* and *Life of Reason* remained standing; but foundations were now supplied for that humanism by a more explicit and vigorous natural philosophy; a natural philosophy which, without being otherwise changed than as the growth of natural science might suggest, was itself destined to be enveloped later by the ontology contained in *Realms of Being*. These additions are buttresses and supports: the ontology justifies materialism, and the materialism justifies rational ethics and an aesthetic view of the mind.—Q-24

Lucretius compared with St. Augustine

My enthusiasm was largely dramatic; I recited my Lucretius with as much gusto as my Saint Augustine; and gradually Lucretius sank deeper and became more satisfying.—Q-24

Morality

The point of chief speculative interest is that morality, like health, is determined by the existing constitution of our animal nature, and the opportunities or denials that materially confront us; so that we are much deeper and more deeply bound to physical reality than our wayward thoughts and wishes might suggest.—Q-25

Essence

What I call essence is not something alleged to exist or subsist in some higher sphere: it is the last residuum of scepticism and analysis.—Q-28

Consciousness and nature

Consciousness was created by the muses; but meantime industrious nature, in our bodily organisation, takes good care to keep our actions moderately sane, in spite of our poetic genius.—Q-29

Deities and Dogmas

Platonic Ideas and the deities and dogmas of religion were ideal only: that is to say, they were fictions inspired by the moral imagination, and they expressed unsatisfied demands or implicit standards native to the human mind.—Q-497

Art

Art proper is that organic or external rearrangement of matter by which a *monument* or a *maxim* is established in

[193]

the world, and an element of traditional form is added to culture.—Q-501

Nature and reflection
Greece, England, America

If art *transports,* if it liberates the mind and heart, I prize it; but nature and reflection do so more often and with greater authority. If ever I have been captivated it has been by beautiful places, beautiful manners, and beautiful institutions: whence my admiration for Greece and for England and my pleasure in youthful, sporting, ingenuous America.—Q-501

Essences

For my essences are not washed out; they are *the whole* of what is actually visible, audible, imaginable or thinkable; and these manifestations in their pungency can come only to a warm soul from a world of matter.—Q-502

Analysis of knowledge. Moral emotions

My materialism indeed corroborates and justifies my analysis of knowledge, that it is faith mediated by symbols; since bodily life is, for the naturalist, the perfectly evident basis of moral emotions, pain, fear, attachment, and all kinds of desire.—Q-504

Matter and mind

For the realm of matter cannot admit mind into its progressive structure and movement.—Q-504

Spiritual life of Santayana

My whole description of the spiritual life is thus an extension of my materialism and a consequence of it.—Q-504

Materialism

I ask myself only what are the fundamental presuppositions that I cannot live without making. And I find that they are summed up in the word materialism.—Q-505

Existence

Existence is groundless, essentially groundless; for if I

[194]

thought I saw a ground for it, I should have to look for a ground for that ground, *ad infinitum.*—Q-505

Existence

The world I find myself in is irrational, but it is not mad. . . . In contrast with it, however, madness is possible in myself; as if, for instance, I insisted on finding a reason for existence, and started a perpetual and maddening vortex in my head.—Q-505

Intelligence, dawn of

Materialism marks the dawn of intelligence in the animal mind.—Q-506

Transcendental logic and materialism

Certainly I do not exclude transcendental logic; but I admit it only in what I think its place, consistently with materialism.—Q-506

Materialism

For this reason I have sometimes used the word naturalism instead of materialism to indicate my fundamental belief: but that word is open to even worse equivocations. . . . The term materialism seems to me safer, precisely because more disliked.—Q-508

Lodge. Spirit. Materialism

The spirit, Sir Oliver Lodge once said, was made of ether; and he thought he had refuted materialism. Ether might well be a name for the material agency that explodes in intuition and in action; but Lodge was a gross materialist in identifying *spirit* with ghost or with invisible magicians that might discover hidden treasure or make tables dance.—Q-509

Supernaturalism and materialism

Supernaturalism is indeed a phase of materialism, where imagination anticipates marvellous and morally interesting material discoveries; as we see in all the wonders of the Arabian nights, and in the orthodox notions of hell, of heaven, and of the resurrection of the body. There is nothing physically *inconceivable* in such miraculous extensions or complications in the cosmos: only they become *incredible* to an unprejudiced science.—Q-509

Matter

That matter is capable of eliciting feeling and thought follows necessarily from the principle that matter is the only *substance, power,* or *agency* in the universe: and this, not that matter is the only *reality,* is the first principle of materialism.—Q-509

Sceptic

The true sceptic merely analyses belief, discovering the risk and the logical uncertainty inherent in it. He finds that alleged knowledge is always faith.—Q-516

Scepticism. Faith. Common-sense

My scepticism remains merely the confession that faith is faith, without any rebellion against the physical necessity of believing. It enables me to believe in common-sense and in materialism and, like Landor, to warm both hands before the fire of life; and at the same time it gives me the key to the realms of dialectic and fancy, which I may enter without illusion.—Q-516-517

Scientific method. Beliefs, development of

There is no serious method except the scientific (and that wholly continuous with everyday thought)—no metaphysical method—of developing beliefs.—Q-519

Logical thoughts

Logical thoughts are not abstract but constructive, like poetry: they seem abstract only to persons incapable of attending to them, and interested only in something else.—Q-520

Empiricism. Sciences

Empiricism is current literary convention hypostasised, and only the sciences study reality.—Q-522

Mental events

I everywhere insist that mental events have physical grounds.
—Q-524

Essence

An essence is anything definite capable of appearing or being thought of; the existence of something possessing that essence is an ulterior question irrelevant to logic and to aesthetics.—Q-527

Superstitions

I am thus turned into a friend of outworn superstitions, when I am no friend even of the superstitions that prevail today.—Q-527

Ideolatry. Morals

Ideolatry is also common in morals, when certain precepts are felt to coerce the conscience by their intrinsic authority, without any vital or rational backing.—Q-528

Mind

For a materialist the mind will be simply sensibility in bodies.—Q-529

Nordic imagination

The truth is that the Nordic imagination has always interested and attracted me, because of a certain romantic mystery or aroma that hangs about it. It has the purity of a wintry atmosphere, rarefied but dark and comfortless, spiritual yet not bringing any sense of liberation or peace.—Q-552

Future and past

We must welcome the future, remembering that soon it will be the past; and we must respect the past remembering that once it was all that was humanly possible.—Q-560

Worth

The criterion of worth remains always the voice of nature, truly consulted, in the person that speaks.—Q-563

Spirit

Spirit, being a psychic faculty, cannot exist without an organ at a particular place and time, with a specific range. —Q-569

Lamprecht. Immortality

Lamprecht also wonders how at one time I avow a preference for being a rational animal rather than a pure spirit, and at another time profess to have no passionate love of existence and no desire for immortality.—Q-569

Spirit

If you conceive spirit to be, as I conceive it, the witness and not the actor in the soul.—Q-570

Spirit. Materialism

The reconciliation of spirit with nature does not rest, in my view, merely on moral grounds. It is inherent in my theory of the origin and place of spirit in nature. It follows from my materialism.—Q-572

Spirit. Dust of the earth. Beliefs and acts

We were not made of pure spirit but out of the dust of the earth. The motions of that dust, when organised, produce our sensations, with our *consequent* faith in them; we believe because we act, we do not act because we believe.—Q-581

Russell

In Russell's essay, as was to be expected, his well-known incisiveness and wit have been softened by kindness, and also enlightened by old acquaintance.—Q-582

Faith among Catholics. Faith among Protestants

For whereas faith among Catholics (except for the mystics) means intellectual assent to traditional dogmas, among Protestants it means an unspoken and sacrificial trust in the unfathomable power; not, in the deeper soul, confidence that we shall materially or personally prosper under it, or be publicly vindicated or saved, but rather willingness to have been born, to have drunk our cup to the dregs, and even to be eternally damned, because such was the will of God, intent on his own glory. *Worship* of this non-moral absolute Will seems to me canine and slavish, and excusable only as the sheer greatness of this universal power carries us with it dramatically, like a storm or an earthquake which we forget to fear because we identify ourselves with it and positively enjoy it.—Q-588

Religion and truth

I tolerantly observed religion always superposing itself upon truth.—Q-597

Naturalism. Democritus, Lucretius, Spinoza

My professed cosmological naturalism or materialism, which I consciously draw from Democritus, Lucretius and Spinoza. —Q-600

Mind

I believe profoundly in the animality of the mind.—Q-601

Truth

The truth is not impatient; it can stand representation and misrepresentation. The more we respect its authority, the more confidently and familiarly we may play round its base. —Q-604

R

Common sense vs. philosophy

I think that common sense, in a rough dogged way, is technically sounder than the special schools of philosophy, each of which squints and overlooks half the facts and half the difficulties in its eagerness to find in some detail the key to the whole.—R-v

Truth

I would lay siege to the truth only as animal exploration and fancy may do so, first from one quarter and then from another, expecting the reality to be not simpler than my experience of it, but far more extensive and complex.—R-vi

Materialist

Now in natural philosophy I am a decided materialist.—R-vii

Dogmatism

The more perfect the dogmatism, the more insecure. A great high topsail that can never be reefed nor furled is the first carried away by a gale.—R-7

Religious belief

Of this homely philosophy (of the common man) the tender cuticle is religious belief.—R-11

Religions

Without philosophical criticism, therefore, mere experience and good sense suggest that all positive religions are false, or at least (which is enough for my present purpose) that they are all fantastic and insecure.—R-12

Religion. History

The cruel mockery called religion, the sorry history and absurd passions of mankind.—R-21

Mystic. Illusion

The mystic must confess that he spends most of his life in the teeming valleys of illusion.—R-31

Richest philosophies

Often the richest philosophies are the most sceptical.—R-67

Expectations

Living beings dwell in their expectations rather than in their senses.—R-68

Scepticism

Scepticism is the chastity of the intellect.—R-69

Is

The little word *is* has its tragedies; it marries and identifies different things with the greatest innocence; and yet no two are ever identical, and if therein lies the charm of wedding them and calling them one, therein too lies the danger.—R-71

Honest mind. Illusion

It was the fear of illusion that originally disquieted the honest mind, congenitally dogmatic, and drove it in the direction of scepticism.—R-72

Mind and scepticism. Mind and dogma

Thus a mind enlightened by scepticism and cured of noisy dogma, a mind discounting all reports, and free from all tormenting anxiety about its own fortune or existence, finds in the wilderness of essence a very sweet and marvellous solitude. The ultimate reaches of doubt and renunciation open out for it, by an easy transition, into fields of endless variety and peace, as if through the gorges of death it had passed into a paradise where all things are crystallised into the image of themselves, and have lost their urgency and their venom. —R-76

Theatre. Life

The theatre, for all its artifices, depicts life in a sense more truly than history, because the medium has a kindred movement to that of real life, though an artificial setting and form.—R-102

Origins

All origins lie in the realm of matter, even when the being that is so generated is immaterial, because this creation or intrusion of the immaterial follows on material occasions and at the promptings of circumstance.—R-109

Spirit

The spirit that actually breathes in man is an animal spirit, transitive like the material endeavours which it expresses; it has a material station and accidental point of view, and a fevered preference for one alternative issue over another.—R-125

Experience

Belief in experience is the beginning of that bold instinctive art, more plastic than the instinct of most animals, by which man has raised himself to his earthly eminence: it opens the gates of nature to him, both within and without, and enables him to transmute his apprehension, at first merely aesthetic, into mathematical science. This is so great a step that most minds cannot take it. They stumble, and remain entangled in poetry and in gnomic wisdom. Science and reasonable virtue, which plunge their roots in the soil of nature, are to this day only partially welcome or understood. Although they bring freedom in the end, the approach to them seems sacrificial, and many prefer to live in the glamour of intuition, not having the courage to believe in experience.—R-144

Existence. Nihilism

I myself have no passionate attachment to existence, and value this world for the intuitions it can suggest, rather than for the wilderness of facts that compose it. To turn away from it may be the deepest wisdom in the end. What better than to blow out the candle, and to bed! But at noon this pleasure is premature. I can always hold it in reserve, and perhaps nihilism is a system—the simplest of all—on which we shall all agree in the end.—R-171

Ignorance

It is inattention and prejudice in men, not inconsistency in nature, that keeps them so ignorant, and the art of government so chaotic.—R-238

Myth. Theology

Myth is now extinct (which is a pity) and theology discredited; but the same confusion subsists in the quarters where it is not fashionable to doubt.—R-253

Universe. Ego

The universe is a novel of which the ego is the hero.—R-254

Immortality

I believe there is nothing immortal.—R-271

Matter. Spirit

I do not know what matter is in itself: but what metaphysical idealists call spirit, if it is understood to be responsible for what goes on in the world and in myself, and to be the "reality" of these appearances, is, in respect to my spiritual existence, precisely what I call matter; and I find the description of this matter which the natural sciences supply much more interesting than that given by the idealists, much more beautiful, and much more likely to be true.—R-287

Science and belief

It is for science and further investigation of the object to pronounce on the truth of any belief.—R-269

S

Suffering of Santayana

Other passages, I fear, betray how much I have suffered from a slack education, conflicting traditions, deadening social pressure, academic lumber, and partisan heat about false problems.—S-ix

Omissions of Santayana

I cannot help hoping that the ultimate recording angel may have the charity to erase as well as to preserve. Ah, if only he could recount, instead, my sins of omission, and bring to light the things I have not written but ought to have written!—S-x

Trivial routine

A straight philosophy might be a task reserved for some future age morally less distracted than ours, or possibly less comfortable outwardly, and freed from our suffocating compulsory trivial routine. If a single ripening tradition could bring some particular language and culture to perfection, the diversity of endowments at home and of foreign languages and cultures abroad, might raise understanding to a maximum without in the least confusing each man's moral allegiance.—S-x-xi

Resolution and intelligence

Hitherto resolution has gone too much with blindness, and intelligence with dissolution: a resolution therefore running its head against every stone wall, and an intelligence soon dying in vice, or wasted on trifles.—S-xi

Reason and the secular arm

Reason needs to be defended by the secular arm.—S-xi

Shakespeare. Characters and plots of Shakespeare

Perhaps no small part of Shakespeare's eminence is due to his having adopted plots and characters already current, already sanctioned by a certain proved vitality and power to charm.—S-41

Imagination

Imagination needs a soil in history, tradition, or human institutions, else its random growths are not significant enough and, like trivial melodies, go immediately out of fashion. A great poem needs to be built up and remodelled on some given foundation with materials already at hand.—S-41

Hamlet

The play (Hamlet) is an ordinary story with an extraordinary elaboration.—S-42

Middle Ages

The Middle Ages, when piety and obscenity, quaint simplicity and rant, could be jumbled together without offence. —S-43

Modern mind. Modern world. Byzantine culture

We must remember that the modern mind, like the modern world, is compacted out of ruins, and that the fresh northern spirit, inducted into that Byzantine labyrinth which we call civilization, feels a marked discord between its genius and its culture. The latter is alien and imperfectly grafted on the living stem from which it must draw its sap.—S-66

Man and government

Man is a social rather than a political animal; he can exist without a government.—S-88

The individual

The individual is the only seat and focus of social forces. If society and government are to be justified at all, they must be justified in his eyes and by his instincts.—S-88

Core of life

The core of his (man's) being has a closed, private, indomitable life.—S-88

Immortality

One of the assumptions of the pre-intelligent and pre-social soul is that it is immortal.—S-91

Social institutions

Social institutions must always remain questionable and oppressive in varying degrees, because they are not innate in the human race but are imposed upon us by circumstances.—S-91

Society—how formed

Society exists by a conspiracy of psychological, physiological forces; however rigid you may make its machinery, its breath of life must come from the willing connivance of a myriad fleeting, inconstant, half rational human souls.—S-93

Philosophies. Heresies

Viewed from a sufficient distance, all systems of philosophy are seen to be personal, temperamental, accidental, and premature. They treat partial knowledge as if it were total knowledge: they take peripheral facts for central and typical facts: they confuse the grammar of human expression, in language, logic, or moral estimation, with the substantial structure of things. In a word, they are heresies.—S-94

Folly of mankind

The more general the folly of mankind, the more likely is the critic himself to share it.—S-94

Orthodoxy

The great misfortune of human orthodoxy is the natural apathy to reason.—S-96

Truth, beauty of

The beauty of truth is not great enough to attract the eye for its own sake.—S-96

[206]

Knowledge

The sort of knowledge that successful practice involves and confirms need not be literal or exhaustive, but it must be knowledge of efficacious reality, knowledge of things as they are.—S-108

Unknowable

Those who a generation or two ago talked about the Unknowable were open to all sorts of attacks—for verbosity, for arrested scepticism, for lack of dialectical acumen, for a sham deference to religion.—S-116

Intuition

The playful and godlike mind of philosophers has always been fascinated by intuition: for philosophers—I mean the great ones—are the infant prodigies of reflection.—S-136

Knowledge of nature

Knowledge of nature is a great allegory, of which action is the interpreter.—S-140

Thoughts and reality

Our thoughts are not varied and plastic enough to cope with reality; yet our theories are always striving to make them more unitary and rigid. Poor indeed would human nature be, if philosophers had made it. Fortunately knowledge is of natural growth; it has roots underground, prehensile tendrils, and even flowers. It touches many miscellaneous things, some real and some imaginary, and it is a new and specific thing on its own account.—S-150

Art

Art is like a charming woman who once had her age of innocence in the nursery, when she was beautiful without knowing it, being wholly intent on what she was making or telling or imagining.—S-151

Pretence

It is really a sorry business, this perpetual pretence of being important and charming and charmed and beautiful.—S-151

Revivals

Fortunately, revivals now seem to be over.—S-155

Herbert Spencer

On the whole, with qualifications which will appear presently, I belong to Herbert Spencer's camp.—S-162

Spencer, Hegel, Bergson

When I rub my eyes and look at things candidly, it seems evident to me that this world is the sort of world described by Herbert Spencer, not the sort of world described by Hegel or Bergson.—S-163

Imagination vs. truth

Far be it from me to deride the imagination, poetic or dialectical; but after all it is a great advantage for a system of philosophy to be substantially true.—S-163

Metaphysicians and professors

Had he been expert in metaphysics and educated at a university, he might have missed the obvious.—S-166-167

Words

Words are weapons, and it is dangerous in speculation, as in politics, to borrow them from the arsenal of the enemy.—S-168

The unknowable

In this measure the emotion suggested by the term unknowable is a legitimate emotion. It expresses an integral part of the tragedy involved in being finite and moral—perhaps in being a mind or spirit at all. Poets and philosophers sometimes talk as if life were an entertainment, a feast of ordered sensations; but the poets, if not the philosophers, know too well in their hearts that life is no such thing: it is a predicament. We are caught in it; it is something compulsory, urgent, dangerous, and tempting.—S-169-170.

Feeling and the universe

What jurisdiction can any feeling have, or any logic, over what shall arise or not arise in the universe?—S-171

Substance

Calling substance unknowable, then, is like calling a drum inaudible, for the shrewd reason that what you hear is the sound and not the drum. It is a play on words, and little better than a pun.—S-173

Practical religion

Religion of the sober, practical, manly sort, Roman piety, is emphatically reverence for the nature of things, for the ways of substance. How far such manly piety may have been misled by superstition, or by hasty and sentimental science, so as to distort the laws of the world and found a *false* religion, is a question of fact for soberer science to examine. —S 177-178

Illusions

Illusions have their own specious reality and physiognomy, curious as folklore is curious; but it is substance as it exists that is momentous, since it determines events, including our illusions and the disappointments they entail.—S-185

Jewels and ladies

I have sometimes wondered at the value ladies set upon jewels: as centres of light, jewels seem rather trivial and monotonous. And yet there is an unmistakable spell about these pebbles; they can be taken up and turned over; they can be kept; they are faithful possessions; the sparkle of them, shifting from moment to moment, is constant from age to age. They are substances. The same aspects of light and colour, if they were homeless in space, or could be spied only once and irrecoverably, like fireworks, would have a less comfortable charm. In jewels there is the security, the mystery, the inexhaustible fixity proper to substance. After all, perhaps I can understand the fascination they exercise over the ladies; it is the same that the eternal feminine exercises over us. Our contact with them is unmistakable, our contemplation of them gladly renewed, and pleasantly prolonged; yet in one sense they are unknowable; we cannot fathom the secret of their constancy, of their hardness, of that perpetual but uncertain brilliancy by which they dazzle us and hide themselves. These qualities of the jewel and of the eternal feminine are also the qualities of substance and of the world. The existence of this world—unless we lapse for a moment into an untenable scepticism—is certain, or at least it is unquestioningly to be assumed. Experience may explore it adventurously, and science may describe it with precision; but after you have wandered up and down in it for many years, and have gathered all you could of its ways by report, this same world, because it exists substantially and is not invented, remains a foreign thing and a marvel to the spirit; unknowable as a drop of water is unknowable, or unknowable like a person loved.—S-187-188

Crime of society or nations

The internal morality of crime appears clearly when the criminal is not a single individual, but a band or a sect or a nation. Within that society, the most intrepid criminal is the most virtuous man. And he may really be an estimable person, sweet and mild in his domestic capacity, and heroic in the fray; the frontiers at which the crime begins may be so remote and the victim so foreign, that no self-reproach reverberates from them to the heart. Necessity and the blindness of war then turn ruthlessness into innocence.—S-266

The time to live

Why should a youth suppress his budding passions in favour of the sordid interests of his own withered old age? Why is that problematical old man who may bear his name fifty years hence nearer to him now than any other imaginary creature? The soul is not directed upon herself; more important than her temporal continuity is her reproduction, and more important than her material reproduction are her spiritual affinities, by which parity is established between the kindred exploits and the conspiring thoughts of the most remote persons. If it be frivolous to live in the present, is it not vain to live for the future? And how many are concentrated and contemplative enough to live in the eternal?— S-267-268

Money and religion

The domination of money is a sort of conventional miraculous domination, like the former domination of religion.— S-269

Life of reason

This life of reason is like the crystallizing principle that turns the common atoms of carbon into a diamond; it lends to our animal impulses a nobility which they never had in themselves and which they lose at once if they are liberated. —S-272

T

Greece and England

What I love in Greece and in England is contentment in finitude, fair outward ways, manly perfection and simplicity. —T-2

Bacon and Shakespeare

There may be some meaning in the stars, a sort of code-language such as Bacon put into Shakespeare's sonnets.—T-12

Change

A great principle of charity in morals is not to blame the fishes for their bad taste in liking to live under water. Yet many philosophers seem to have sinned against this reasonable law, since they have blamed life and nature for liking to change, which is as much as to say for liking to live.—T-20

Once

Is it not enough that matter should illustrate each ideal possibility only once and for a moment, and that Caesar or Shakespeare should figure once in this world?—T-21

Surprises of nature

The winds of February are not colder to a featherless chick than are the surprises which nature and truth bring to our dreaming egotism.—T-27

England

England is the paradise of individuality, eccentricity, heresy, anomalies, hobbies, and humours.—T-30

Women

The women—dear, dogmatic, fussy angels—are not here;

that is a relief; and yet you are counting the weeks before you can return to them at home.—T-34-35

The sea

There is a blessed simplicity about the sea, with its vast inhumanity islanding and freeing the humanity of man.—T-35

English mastery

The secret of English mastery is self-mastery.—T-35

Illusions

Illusions are mighty, and must be reckoned with in this world.—T-41

Religion of love

The dove of peace brings new wars, the religion of love instigates crusades and lights faggots.—T-42

Shams

The whole nation hugs its hallowed shams.—T-42

Orthodoxy of scholastics

There was always something slippery in the orthodoxy of scholastics, even in the Middle Ages.—T-43

Truth

For the truth is not itself luminous, as wit is; the truth travels silently in the night and requires to be caught by the searchlight of wit to become visible.—T-44

Mind and culture

The mind plays innocently with its own phosphorescence, which is what we call culture.—T-44

Snobbery. Evolution

Snobbery haunts those who are not reconciled with themselves; evolution is the hope of the immature. You cannot be everything. Why not be what you are?—T-47

Heredity vs. environment

Variations of fortune do not move a man from his inborn centre of gravity.—T-47

Moral world

The moral world is round like the heavens, and the directions which life can take are infinitely divergent and unreturning.—T-48

Friendship

Friendship is almost always the union of a part of one mind with a part of another; people are friends in spots. —T-55

Friends

One's friends are that part of the human race with which one can be human.—T-55

Loss of Christendom

If Christendom should lose everything that is now in the melting-pot, human life would still remain amiable and quite adequately human.—T-58

Christmas

In reviving Christmas, Dickens transformed it from the celebration of a metaphysical mystery into a feast of overflowing simple kindness and good cheer.—T-60

Compromise

Compromise is odious to passionate natures because it seems a surrender, and to intellectual natures because it seems a confusion; but to the inner man, to the profound Psyche within us, whose life is warm, nebulous and plastic, compromise seems the path of profit and justice.—T-83

Heretical Rome. Peter

It is obvious that Rome itself is heretical and schismatic on this theory, since it has laid an exaggerated weight on the text about Peter and the keys.—T-85

The church of England

It is national in its morals and manners, mincing in its scholarship, snobbish in its sympathies, sentimental in its emotions.—T-86

Origin of Christianity

Christianity was born of such a marriage between the Jewish soul and the Greek.—T-87

Protestant vs. Catholic faith

Protestant faith does not vanish into the sunlight as Catholic faith does, but leaves a shadowy ghost haunting the night of the soul.—T-88

Protestant compared with Catholic

And yet the Protestant can hardly go back, as the Catholic does easily on occasion, out of habit, or fatigue, or disappointment in life, or metaphysical delusion, or the emotional weakness of the death-bed. No, the Protestant is more in earnest, he carries his problem and his religion with him.—T-90

The cross

The cross is certainly a most violent image, putting suffering and death before us with a rude emphasis; and I can understand the preference of many for the serene Buddha, lifting the finger of meditation and profound counsel, and freeing the soul by the sheer force of knowledge and of sweet reason.—T-94

Christ and Buddha

Christ and Buddha are called saviours of the world; I think it must be in irony, for the world is just as much in need of salvation as ever. Death and insight and salvation are personal. The world springs up unregenerate every morning in spite of all the Tabors and Calvaries of yesterday. —T-96

Nature

The force that has launched me into this dream of life does not care what turns my dream takes nor how long it troubles me. Nature denies at every moment, not indeed that I am troubled and dreaming, but that there are any natural units like my visions, or anything anomalous in what I hate, or final in what I love.—T-96

The crucifix

I like to see the enamelled crucifix richly surrounded with scrolls, and encrusted with jewels; without a touch of this pagan instinct the religion of the cross would not be healthy nor just.—T-98

Birth and death

But since, as a matter of fact, birth and death actually occur, and our brief career is surrounded by vacancy, it is far better to live in the light of the tragic fact, rather than to forget or deny it, and build everything on a fundamental lie.—T-99

Death and life

The dark background which death supplies brings out the tender colours of life in all their purity.—T-99

Humanity slow to learn

Each generation breaks its egg-shell with the same haste and assurance as the last, pecks at the same indigestible pebbles, dreams the same dreams, or others just as absurd, and if it hears anything of what former men have learned by experience, it corrects their maxims by its first impressions, and rushes down any untrodden path which it finds alluring, to die in its own way, or become wise too late and to no purpose.—T-101

Reality

Ah, my delicate friends, if the soul of a philosopher may venture to address you, let me whisper this counsel in your ears: Reserve a part of your wrath; you have not seen the worst yet. You suppose that this war* has been a criminal blunder and an exceptional horror; you imagine that before long reason will prevail, and all these inferior people that

* First World War.

govern the world will be swept aside, and your own party will reform everything and remain always in office. You are mistaken. This war has given you your first glimpse of the ancient, fundamental, normal state of the world, your first taste of reality. It should teach you to dismiss all your philosophies of progress or of a governing reason as the babble of dreamers who walk through one world mentally beholding another. I don't mean that you or they are fools; heaven forbid. You have too much mind. It is easy to behave very much like other people and yet be possessed inwardly by a narcotic dream.—T-104

War

There is eternal war in nature, a war in which every cause is ultimately lost and every nation destroyed. War is but resisted change, and change must needs be resisted so long as the organism it would destroy retains any vitality. Peace itself means discipline at home and invulnerability abroad— two forms of permanent virtual war; peace requires so vigorous an internal regimen that every germ of dissolution or infection shall be repelled before it reaches the public soul. This war* has been a short one, and its ravages slight in comparison with what remains standing: a severe war is one in which the entire manhood of a nation is destroyed, its cities razed, and its women and children driven into slavery. In this instance the slaughter has been greater, perhaps, only because modern populations are so enormous; the disturbance has been acute only because the modern industrial system is so dangerously complex and unstable; and the expense seems prodigious because we were so extravagantly rich. Our society was a sleepy glutton who thought himself immortal and squealed inexpressibly, like a stuck pig, at the first prick of the sword. An ancient city would have thought this war, or one relatively as costly, only a normal incident; and certainly the Germans will not regard it otherwise.—T-104-105

* First World War.

Human nature. Shelley

He (Shelley) seems to have thought that human nature was not really made for puddings and port wine and hunting and elections, nor even for rollicking at universities and reading Greek, but only for innocent lyrical ecstasies and fiery convictions that nevertheless should somehow not render people covetous or jealous or cruelly disposed, nor constrain them to prevent any one from doing anything that any one might choose to do.—T-108

Intelligence

The only sublimity possible to man is intellectual; when he would be sublime in any other dimension he is merely fatuous and bombastic. By intelligence, so far as he possesses it, a man sees things as they are, transcends his senses and his passions, uproots himself from his casual stations in space and time, sees all things future as if they were past, and all things past as for ever present, at once condemns and forgives himself, renounces the world and loves it.—T-110

Vanity

The length of things is vanity, only their height is joy. —T-116

Dreams

We work dreaming. Consider what dreams must have dominated the builders of the Pyramids—dreams geometrical, dreams funereal, dreams of resurrection, dreams of outdoing some other Pharaoh! What dreams occupy that fat man in the street, toddling by under his shabby hat and bedraggled rain-coat? Perhaps he is in love; perhaps he is a Catholic, and imagines that early this morning he has partaken of the body and blood of Christ; perhaps he is a revolutionist, with the millennium in his heart and a bomb in his pocket. The spirit bloweth where it listeth: the wind of inspiration carries our dreams before it and constantly refashions them like clouds. Nothing could be madder, more irresponsible, more dangerous than this guidance of men by dreams. What saves us is the fact that our imaginations, groundless and chimerical as they may seem, are secretly suggested and controlled by shrewd old instincts of our animal nature, and by continual contact with things. The shock of sense, breaking in upon us with a fresh irresistible image, checks wayward imaginations and sends it rebounding in a new direction, perhaps more relevant to what is happening in the world outside.—T-122-123

Acts vs. professions

We profess to live up to the fine sentiments we have uttered, as we try to believe in the religion we profess.—T-133

Foolishness

The foolishness of the simple is delightful; only the foolishness of the wise is exasperating.—T-139

The Spanish

The Spanish nation boils the same peas for its dinner the whole year round; it has only one religion, if it has any; the pious part of it recites the same prayers fifty or one hundred and fifty times daily, almost in one breath; the gay and sentimental part never ceases to sing the same *jotas* and *malagueñas*. Such constancy is admirable. If a dish is cheap, nutritious, and savoury on Monday, it must be so on Tuesday, too.—T-153

Spanish religion

Spanish religion, again, is certainly most human and most super-human; but its mystic virtue to the devotee cannot alter the fact that, on a broad view, it appears to be a romantic *tour de force,* a desperate illusion, fostered by premature despair and by a total misunderstanding of nature and history. —T-154

Artists

Every artist is a moralist, though he need not preach.—T-158

Classic liberty

Classic liberty was a sort of forced and artificial liberty, a poor perfection reserved for an ascetic aristocracy in whom heroism and refinement were touched with perversity and slowly starved themselves to death.—T-168

Love. British liberalism. Victorian era

British liberalism has been particularly cruel to love; in the Victorian era all its amiable impulses were reputed indecent, until a marriage certificate suddenly rendered them godly, though still unmentionable.—T-184

Advertising

Advertising is the modern substitute for argument, its function is to make the worse appear the better article.—T-187

British philosophers and poets

Nevertheless the exotic tendency in so many British philosophers, as in so many disaffected British poets, is itself a mark of the British character. The crust of convention has solidified too soon, and the suppressed fires issue in little erratic streams that seem of an alien substance. In speculation as in other things, the Englishman trusts his inner man; his impulse is to soliloquize even in science.—T-190

Existence

There is a mystical happiness in accepting existence without understanding it.—T-201

Worldliness in England

In the real England there is a strong if not dominant admixture of worldliness.—T-204

Progress

This war (1914-1918) will kill the belief in progress, and it was high time.—T-207

Progress

What true progress is, and how it is usually qualified by all sorts of backsliding and by incompatible movements in contrary directions, is well illustrated by the history of philosophy.—T-208

Civilization and language

When a civilisation and a language take shape they have a wonderful vitality, and their first-fruits are some love-child, some incomparable creature in whom the whole genius of the young race bursts forth uncontaminated and untrammelled.—T-208-209

Indian philosophy

They (the Indians) saw that substance is infinite, out of scale with our sensuous images and (except in the little vortex that makes us up) out of sympathy with our endeavours; and that spirit in us nevertheless can hold its own, because salvation lies in finding joy in the truth, not in rendering fortune propitious, by some miracle, to our animal interests.—T-210

The Indian spirit

It does not deem it the part of piety to deny the fugitive, impotent, and fantastic nature of human life. It knows that the thoughts of man and his works, however great or delightful when measured by the human scale, are but the faintest shimmer on the surface of being. On the ruin of humanistic illusions (such as make up the religious philosophy of the West) it knows how to establish a tender morality and a sublime religion.—T-210

The spirit

But how could the spirit, if it had been free originally, ever have attached its fortunes to any lump of clay? Why should it be the sport of time and change and the vicissitudes of affairs?—T-211

Love of the ancient

I love the lore of the moral antiquary; I love rummaging in the psychological curiosity shop.—T-216

Paganism and Christianity

When breeding or conscience suppresses a man's genius, his genius often takes its revenge and reasserts itself, by some indirection, in the very system that crushed it. This happened to paganism when, being stamped out by Christianity, it turned Christianity into something half pagan.—T-231

Bad conscience

A bad conscience loves to be flattered and reassured; company consoles it for loss of honour.—T-242

Atheism of Spinoza

I can always say to myself that my atheism, like that of Spinoza, is true piety towards the universe and denies only gods fashioned by men in their own image, to be servants of their human interests; and that even in this denial I am no rude iconoclast, but full of secret sympathy with the impulses of idolaters.—T-246

Solipsism. Catholicism

But neither solipsism nor Catholicism were ever anything to me but theoretic poses or possibilities; vistas for the imagination, never convictions.—T-256

Moral sceptic

I am a pagan and a moral sceptic in my naturalism.—T-257

Critics of Santayana

My critics suppose, apparently, that I mean by the good some particular way of life or some type of character which is alone virtuous, and which ought to be propagated. Alas, their propagandas! How they have filled this world with hatred, darkness, and blood! How they are still the eternal obstacle, in every home and in every heart, to a simple happiness!—T-258

Happiness

I wish individuals, and races, and nations to be themselves, and to multiply the forms of perfection and happiness, as nature prompts them. The only thing which I think might be propagated without injustice to the types thereby suppressed is harmony; enough harmony to prevent the interference of one type with another, and to allow the perfect development of each type. The good, as I conceive it, is happiness, happiness for each man after his own heart, and for each hour according to its inspiration. I should dread to transplant my happiness into people; it might die in that soil.—T-259

Ideals

No man can set up an ideal for another, nor labour to realize it for him.—T-259

Theology

Homer tells us that Hermes was a thief; but the beauty of mythology is that every poet can recast it according to his own insight and sense of propriety; as, in fact, our solemn theologians do also, although they pretend that their theology is a science, and are not wide awake enough to notice the dreamful, dramatic impulse which leads them to construct it.—T-260

U

Evolution
The tide of evolution carries everything before it, thoughts no less than bodies, and persons no less than nations.—U-ix

Truth
The truth is cruel, but it can be loved, and it makes free those who have loved it.—U-x

Fiction
Often the art of fiction may tell us the truth about the fictions natural to the mind.—U-32

Superstition
Primitive imagination no doubt attributes power to wishes and prayers or to formal rhymes and coincidences in the aspects of things; but that is superstition; and we gradually discover the true order of nature by attentive observation of matter, and experiments with it, and calculation of its quantity and movement.—U-37

Conventions
Perhaps the speculative part of religion, pure myth or metaphysics or theology, will show the power of convention best, because here the inspiration is so potent that it overflows all barriers, overcomes the judgment and claims positive truth for its fictions.—U-56

Convention
The hold that convention has on mankind is not at all proportional to its rational justification.—U-58

Invisible world. Sceptic
Society does not present two separable worlds, one the world

of men's bodies and another less earthly one, that of men's minds. A world of mere minds, a heaven with its legions of invisible and bodiless angels, if conceived at all, exacts no belief from the sceptic. I am as far as possible a sceptic, and a world of that sort does not figure in my philosophy.—U-59

Moral ideas

Moral ideas are usually hybrid.—U-67

Moral judgment

The nerve of moral judgment is preference: and preference is a feeling or an impulse to action which cannot be either false or true.—U-67

Passion vs. truth

When passion usurps the name of truth, the very idea of truth is tarnished and defiled.—U-69

Moral dogmatism

Spiritually it is a sinister thing, a sin against spirit elsewhere.—U-76

Moral authority

Moral truth, therefore, even at its purest, by no means bestows moral authority over alien lives.—U-78

Mutation, personal

It is only when we ignore our own mutation that the truth seems to us to change.—U-86

Love of truth vs. hatred of truth

The love of truth is often mentioned, the hatred of truth hardly ever, yet the latter is the commoner.—U-102

Wild nature. Truth

Conviction always abounds in its own sense, as in theology: but what breaks at last through such a charmed circle is wild nature, within and without. A thousand contrary facts, a thousand rebel emotions, drive us from our nest. We find that *there can be no peace in delusion*: and perhaps in this negative and moral guise the idea of truth first insinuates itself into the mind.—U-107

Prostitution of truth

The more these self-indulgent minds fear and hate the truth, the more insistently they give the name of truth to the mask that hides it.—U-107

Truth, love of

We do not look about us because we love the truth, but we love the truth because we look about us.—U-112

Truth

The keen air of truth is not for all lungs.—U-131

Happiness

Happiness in the truth is like happiness in marriage, fruitful, lasting, and ironical.—U-134

Perfection of life. Truth and good

It would be inhuman and fanatical to set up the truth as the only good. The good is the perfection of life for each creature according to its kind; a perfection which man can never reach without knowledge of his immediate circumstances and his own nature.—U-140

V

Religious pretensions

It would naturally follow from this conception that religious doctrines would do well to withdraw their pretension to be dealing with matters of fact. That pretension is not only the source of the conflicts of religion with science and of the vain and bitter controversies of sects; it is also the cause of the impurity and incoherence of religion in the soul, when it seeks its sanctions in the sphere of reality, and forgets that its proper concern is to express the ideal. For the dignity of religion, like that of poetry and of every moral ideal, lies precisely in its ideal adequacy, in its fit rendering of the meanings and values of life, in its anticipation of perfection; so that the excellence of religion is due to an idealization of experience which, while making religion noble if treated as poetry, makes it necessarily false if treated as science. Its function is rather to draw from reality materials for an image of that ideal to which reality ought to conform, and to make us citizens, by anticipation, in the world we crave.—V-v-vi

Ideas and their misfortunes

The shortness of life, the distractions of passion, and the misrepresentation to which all transmitted knowledge is subject, have made the testing of ideas by practice extremely slow in the history of mankind.—V-5

Faith

When the prophecies of faith are verified, the function of faith is gone.—V-8

Mysticism vs. reason

The ideal of mysticism is accordingly exactly contrary to

the ideal of reason; instead of perfecting human nature it seeks to abolish it; instead of building a better world, it would undermine the foundations even of the world we have built already.—V-15

Human will

The wheels of the universe have a wonderful magnetism for the human will.—V-19

Mysticism

Mysticism is usually an incurable disease.—V-20

Mysticism's end

The only thing that can kill mysticism is its own uninterrupted progress, by which it gradually devours every function of the soul and at last, by destroying its own natural basis, immolates itself to its inexorable ideal.—V-20

The world

With a world so full of stuff before him, I can hardly conceive what morbid instinct can tempt a man to look elsewhere for wider vistas, unless it be unwillingness to endure the sadness and the discipline of the truth.—V-21

Mythology and religion

We of this generation look back upon a variety of religious conceptions and forms of worship, and a certain unsatisfied hunger in our own souls attaches our attention to the spectacle. We observe how literally fables and mysteries were once accepted which can have for us now only a thin and symbolical meaning. Judging other minds and other ages by our own, we are tempted to ask if there ever was any fundamental difference between religion and poetry. Both seem to consist in what the imagination adds to science, to history, and to morals. Men looked attentively on the face of Nature: their close struggle with her compelled them to do so: but before making statistics of her movements they made dramatizations of her life. The imagination enveloped the material world, as yet imperfectly studied, and produced the cosmos of mythology.—V-24

Phantoms, two

Our religion is the poetry in which we believe. Mere poetry is an ineffectual shadow of life; religion is, if you will, a phantom also, but a phantom guide.—V-26

God

A god is a conceived victory of mind over Nature. A visible god is the consciousness of such a victory momentarily attained. The vision soon vanishes, the sense of omnipotence is soon dispelled by recurring conflicts with hostile forces; but the momentary illusion of that realized good has left us with the perennial knowledge of good as an ideal. Therein lies the essence and the function of religion.—V-47

Customs

Many customs which a man may have occasion to conform to only once or twice in his life endure for ages and survive the ebb and flow of intellectual and political systems.—V-51

Mythology

Mythology thus ended with the conception of a single god whose body was the whole physical universe, whose fable was all history, and whose character was the principle of the universal natural order.—V-61

Gods, their disappearance
Anthropomorphism. Natural religion

Thus the reality which the naturalistic gods had borrowed from the elements proved to be a dangerous prerogative; being real and manifest, these gods had to be conceived according to our experience of their operation, so that with every advance in scientific observation theology had to be revised, and something had to be subtracted from the personality and benevolence of the gods. The moral character originally attributed to them necessarily receded before the clearer definition of natural forces and the accumulated experience of national disasters. Finally, little remained of the gods except their names. . . . All that the imagination had added to them by way of personal character, sanctity, and life must be rejected as anthropomorphism and fable.

Such is the necessary logic of natural religion.—V-62

Neo-Platonism

Yet Neo-Platonism, for all we can see, responded as well as Christianity to the needs of the time, and had besides great external advantages in its alliance with tradition, with civil power, and with philosophy.—V-76-77

Platonic influence in Christianity

The myths of the great dialogues, and above all, the fanciful machinery of the Timaeus, interpreted with an incredible literalness and naive earnestness, such as only Biblical exegesis can rival, formed the starting point of the new revelation. The method and insight thus obtained were then employed in filling the *lacunae* of the system and spreading its wings wider and wider, until a prodigious hierarchy of supernatural existences had been invented, from which the natural world was made to depend as a last link and lowest emanation.

The baselessness and elaboration of this theology were, of course, far from being obstacles to its success in such an age. On the contrary, the less evidence could be found in common experience for what a man appeared to know, the more deeply, people inferred, must he be versed in supernatural lore, and the greater, accordingly, was his authority.—V-78-79

Catholic church, its origin

The whole body of Catholic doctrine may have been contained in the oral teaching of Christ; or, on the other hand, a historical Jesus may not have existed at all, or may have been one among many obscure Jewish revolutionists, the one who, by accident, came afterward to be regarded as the initiator of a movement to which all sorts of forces contributed, and with which he had really had nothing to do. In either case the fact remains which alone interests us here;

that after three or four centuries of confused struggles, an institution emerged which called itself the Catholic Church. —V-81-82

Christ crucified

What overcame the world, because it was what the world desired, was not a moral reform—for that was preached by every sect; not an ascetic regimen—for that was practised by heathen gymnosophists and Pagan philosophers; not brotherly love within the Church—for the Jews had and have that at least in equal measure; but what overcame the world was what Saint Paul said he would always preach: Christ and him crucified. Therein was a new poetry, a new ideal, a new God. Therein was the transcript of the real experience of humanity, as men found it in their inmost souls and as they were dimly aware of it in universal history. The moving power was fable—for who stopped to question whether its elements were historical, if only its meaning were profound and its inspiration contagious? This fable had points of attachments to real life in a visible brotherhood and in an extant worship, as well as in the religious past of a whole people. —V-85-86

Christianity, morbid, visionary

Morbid as this species of faith (Christianity) may seem, visionary as it certainly was, it is not to be confused with an arbitrary madness or with personal illusions.—V-87

Wild fiction

For this reason the believer in any adequate and mature super-natural religion clings to it with such strange tenacity and regards it as his highest heritage, while the outsider, whose imagination speaks another language or is dumb altogether, wonders how so wild a fiction can take root in a reasonable mind.—V-88

Christian system—a great poem

The other circumstance that ennobled the Christian system was that all its parts had some significance and poetic truth, although they contained, or needed to contain, nothing empirically real. The system was a great poem which, besides being well constructed in itself, was allegorical of actual experience. —V-88-89

World made for man? Fallacy of Christianity

Was Christianity right in saying that the world was made for man? Was the account it adopted of the method and causes of Creation conceivably correct? Was the garden of Eden a historical reality, and were the Hebrew prophecies announcements of the advent of Jesus Christ? Did the deluge come because of man's wickedness, and will the last day coincide with the dramatic dénouement of the Church's history? In other words, is the spiritual experience of man the explanation of the universe? Certainly not, if we are thinking of a scientific, not of a poetical explanation. As a matter of fact, man is a product of laws which must also destroy him, and which, as Spinoza would say, infinitely exceed him in their scope and power.—V-91

Christian drama

The Christian drama was a magnificent poetic rendering of this side of the matter, a side which Socrates had envisaged by his admirable method, but which now flooded the consciousness of mankind with torrential emotions.—V-92

Christ—a product of the imagination

Let not the reader fancy that in Christianity everything was settled by records and traditions. The idea of Christ himself had to be constructed by the imagination in response to moral demands, tradition giving only the barest external points of attachment.—V-92

Efficacy of Christian doctrine

The whole of Christian doctrine is thus religious and efficacious only when it becomes poetry, because only then is it the felt counterpart of personal experience and a genuine expansion of human life.—V-94

Rewards and punishment

Take, as another example, the doctrine of eternal rewards and punishments. Many perplexed Christians of our day try to reconcile this spirited fable with their modern horror of physical suffering and their detestation of cruelty; and it must be admitted that the image of men suffering unending tortures in retribution for a few ignorant and sufficiently wretched sins is, even as poetry, somewhat repellent. The idea of torments and vengeance is happily becoming alien to our society and is therefore not a natural vehicle for our religion. Some accordingly reject altogether the Christian doctrine on this point, which is too strong for their nerves. Their objection, of course, is not simply that there is not evidence of its truth. If they asked for evidence, would they believe anything? Proofs are the last thing looked for by a truly religious mind which feels the imaginative fitness of its faith and knows instinctively that, in such a matter, imaginative fitness is all that can be required. The reason men reject the doctrine of eternal punishment is that they find it distasteful or unmeaning. They show, by the nature of their objections, that they acknowledge poetic propriety or moral truth to be the sole criterion of religious credibility.—V-94

Balance-sheet of life

Transitory life ends for the Christian when the balance-sheet of his individual merits and demerits is made up, and the eternity that ensues is the eternal reality of those values. —V-96

Christian fictions

Christian fictions were at least significant; they beguiled the intellect, no doubt, and were mistaken for accounts of external fact; but they enlightened the imagination; they made man understand, as never before or since, the pathos and nobility of his life, the necessity of discipline, the possibility of sanctity, the transcendence and the humanity of the divine. —V-98

The judgment

As for the Christian doctrine of the judgment, it is something wholly out of relation to empirical facts, it assumes the existence of a supernatural sphere, and is beyond the reach of scientific evidence of any kind. But if we look on religion as on a kind of poetry, as we have decided here to do,—as on a kind of poetry that expresses moral values and reacts beneficently upon life,—we shall see that the Christian doctrine is alone justified.—V-105

Mysticism

Mysticism is not a religion but a religious disease.—V-105

Imagination

Men became superstitious not because they had too much imagination, but because they were not aware that they had any.—V-108

Moral significance

In Darwinian language, moral significance has been a spontaneous variation of superstition, and this variation has insured its survival as a religion. For religion differs from superstition not psychologically but morally, not in its origin but in its worth.—V-108

Reason

Reason is powerless to found religions, although it is alone competent to judge them.—V-109

Graeco-Roman world

The Church's successes, however, were not all legitimate; they were not everywhere due to a real correspondence between her forms and the ideal life of men. It was only the inhabitants of the Graeco-Roman world that were quite prepared to understand her.—V-110

Fourth century compared with the sixteenth century

What the Fathers did for the Church in the fourth century, the Reformers did for themselves in the sixteenth, and have

continued to do on the occasion of their various appearances.
—V-112

Edifices of reason, their end

When the fruits of philosophic reflection, condensed into some phrase, pass into the common language of men, there does not and there cannot accompany them any just appreciation of their meaning or of the long experience and travail of soul from which they have arisen. . . .

It is not only the works of plastic art that moulder and disintegrate to furnish materials for the barbarous masons of a later age: the great edifices of reason also crumble, their plan is lost, and their fragments, picked where they happen to lie, become the materials of a feebler thought.—V-118-119

Words

Words are at least the tombs of ideas.—V-119

Chivalry

Chivalry is nothing but a fine emblazoning of the original manly impulse to fight every man and love every woman.—V-123

Triumphs of reason. Works of art

The triumphs of reason have been few and partial at any time, and perfect works of art are almost unknown.—V-173

Democracy

There is clearly some analogy between a mass of images without structure and the notion of an absolute democracy.—V-181

Whitman. Rousseau. Evolution

When Whitman made the initial and amorphous phase of society his ideal, he became the prophet of a lost cause. That cause was lost, not merely when wealth and intelligence began to take shape in the American Commonwealth, but it was lost at the very foundation of the world, when those laws of evolution were established which Whitman, like Rousseau, failed to understand.—V-183

Exalted life

Nothing is farther from the common people than the corrupt desire to be primitive. They instinctively look toward a more exalted life, which they imagine to be full of distinction and pleasure, and the idea of that brighter existence fills them with hope or with envy or with humble admiration.—V-185

Mysticism. Intelligence. Divinity

Mysticism makes us proud and happy to renounce the work of intelligence both in thought and in life, and persuades us that we become divine by remaining imperfectly human.—V-187

Experience

A more direct or impassioned grasp of experience than is given to mildly blatant, convention-ridden minds.—V-188

Passive religion

When a man's personal religion is passive, as Shakespeare's seems to have been, and is adopted without question or particular interest from the society around him, we may not observe any analogy between it and the free creations of that man's mind.—V-207

Nineteenth century

In every imaginative sphere the nineteenth century has been an era of chaos, as it has been an era of order and growing organization in the spheres of science and of industry.—V-215

Common sense vs. imagination

It is possible to think otherwise than as common sense thinks; there are other categories beside those of science. When we employ them we enlarge our lives. We add to the world of fact any number of worlds of the imagination in which human nature and the eternal relations of ideas may be nobly expressed. So far our imaginative fertility is only a benefit: it surrounds us with the congenial and necessary radiation of art and religion.—V-224

Religion

Religion is an imaginative echo of things natural and moral: and if this echo is to be well attuned, our ear must first be attentive to the natural sounds of which, in religion, we are to develop the harmony.—V-235

The Greeks

The Greeks, for all their clear consciousness of fate, hopeful without illusions and independent without rebellion.—V-243

Practical optimism and speculative pessimism

The practical optimism natural to an active being and the speculative pessimism inevitable to an intelligent one.—V-246

Abandoning illusions

That rare advance in wisdom which consists in abandoning our illusions the better to attain our ideals.—V-250

Science and common sense

Science and common sense are themselves in their way poets of no mean order, since they take the material of experience and make out of it a clear, symmetrical, and beautiful world.—V-270

Hysterical religion

The hysterical forms of music and religion are the refuge of an idealism that has lost its way; the waste and failure of life flow largely in those channels.—V-279

Poetry and religion

Poetry raised to its highest power is then identical with religion grasped in its inmost truth; at their point of union both reach their utmost purity and beneficence, for then poetry loses its frivolity and ceases to demoralize, while religion surrenders its illusions and ceases to deceive.—V-290

W

Character of the Gospels

Many a "Life of Jesus" has been composed in the effort to recast the narratives of the four Gospels into one consecutive and credible history. For a believer, if he were greatly inspired, such an understanding might be legitimate; yet it would be hardly required, since the narratives, though independent, fall together of themselves, in the pious mind, into a total and impressive picture. The history of Christian faith and of Christian art sufficiently proves it. But this presupposes an innocent state of mind that accepts every detail, no matter how miraculous, with unhesitating joy, and is ready sympathetically to piece out the blanks in the story, and to imagine ever more vividly how everything must have happened. So every orthodox preacher does in his glowing sermons, and every devout soul in its meditations.

If, however, the would-be biographer of Jesus is a cool critic, with no religious assumptions, his labours will be entirely wasted, because he has mistaken the character of his texts. The Gospels are not historical works, but products of inspiration. They are summonses and prophecies, announcing the end of this world, or at least of the present era, and prescribing the means by which individual souls may escape destruction, and enter into a Kingdom of Heaven which is at hand. Essentially, then, the Gospels are prophetic; they bring "glad tidings"; yet they are not written by the prophets themselves, but gathered together a generation or two later from oral tradition or from the inspirations of the Apostles and of anonymous believers through whom the spirit had not ceased to speak: nor is it excluded that the Evangelists themselves should have had original inspirations. In the Gospels, the unction, the freshness, the life-like details in many places are so many proofs of their poetic source. The writer is telling of something now standing before his eyes, of which his heart is full. He is not collecting reports, he is not remembering events that he himself has ever witnessed. If he overhears those discourses, it is by telepathy; if he sees those scenes, it is in a vision; if he knows those truths, it is by faith.—W-3-4

Are the Gospels inspired?
Gospels, Homer, Upanishads and Koran compared

For a sympathetic humanist and unprejudiced man of letters, there is no more reason for swearing by the letter of the Gospels than by that of Homer or the Upanishads or the Koran. We may prefer the spirit of one or another, but the moral beauty in them all is equally natural, equally human; and nothing but custom or a mystical conversion can lead us to regard the inspiration in one case only as miraculous, and a revealed mirror of the exact truth.—W-5

Inspiration

What is inspiration? We see in the Gospels that madmen were conceived to be possessed by devils; and antiquity in general regarded originality or genius in mankind as something infused by a magic spell, by the Muses, or by the spirit of some God; . . . Nevertheless, everybody knows . . . that the wilder inspiration produced by opiates and toxic gases, as well as that of spiritualist mediums, shows a strange mixture of dreamlike incoherence with bits of supernatural perception and prophecy.—W-7

Inspiration

It would appear from all this that the graphic and persuasive force of inspiration . . . springs from an innate poetic fertility and suppressed dreamfulness in the psyche.—W-7

Results of inspiration

In a word, inspiration remakes the image of the world, or

unmakes it, according to the mood of the soul. If the psyche is diseased, inspiration becomes madness; if the psyche is healthy and irrepressible, it becomes genius.—W-7

Faith and the miraculous

In religion, however, it is possible to entertain faith in the literal truth of certain inspirations, not by denying their psychological status and origin, but by positing a miraculous pre-established harmony between the inspired utterance and the absolute truth.—W-9

Christ. Saint Paul. Gospels, their origin

In the everyday light of profane history and literary criticism it appears that the life and the human person of Christ, far from being a present reality of which the Evangelists, notebook in hand, have set forth a few particulars, were little known or dwelt upon by the first generation of Christians. Saint Paul, the earliest of Christian writers, had seen Christ only in a vision; he had not read the Gospels, for they were not yet written.—W-11

Gospels and the church

The Gospels that we possess were . . . composed in the Church, by the Church, and for the Church.—W-14

Church vs. the Gospels

It was the Church that gave authority to the Gospels, not the Gospels that determined the faith of the Church.—W-14

Prayer and historical truths

Fasting and prayer and solitary meditation are certainly not likely to inform us about distant facts or historical truths.—W-16

Psyche

The influences and practices that tend to awaken inspiration are those that liberate and stimulate the inner man: therefore images and words that then come forward will rise from a relatively deeper and purer level and will reveal the native affinities of the psyche.—W-16

Illusions, their origin

If our inspirations are self-inspired, if our very senses are dependent on our organs, are they not rather fountains of illusion than revelation of the truth?—W-16-17

Matthew, Mark, Luke

A great part of the anecdotes and precepts that follow (in Luke) form a mere anthology, as in *Matthew* and *Mark*.—W-20

Hebrew and Oriental influence on Gospels

In all the Gospels the admirable quality of the scenes and the sayings is due less to the several Evangelists than to the tradition of Hebrew and of all oriental eloquence; and also perhaps to the fact that all these parables, maxims and episodes had been recounted orally numberless times before, here and there, they were set down on paper.—W-21

Evolution of the Christ idea

Preachers, prophets and evangelists would conspire to put into the mouth of Christ whatever words their inspiration thought to be worthy of him: the more memorable and impressive of these words would be retained and repeated; and the idea of Christ would grow and solidify in the minds of the faithful under the control of the very faith that evoked it. —W-21

Christ and Christianity

The idea of Christ is much older than Christianity.—W-42

Christ in Gospels explained

In suggesting this spiritual interpretation for the kingdom of God, and for the means of entering into it, I am far from wishing to insinuate into the idea of Christ in the Gospels any abandonment of the ordinary eschatology. Jesus is presented to us as having actually come down from heaven, and being about to ascend into heaven again, in order to come down once more with glory to judge all nations. The urgent note in his teaching presupposes such a material background, and would not be justified without it. But the reader knows that I am not attempting to reconstruct a Life of Jesus. I am only studying the idea of Christ in the Gospels. And in that idea, beneath the legendary figure of Jesus on earth, there is undoubtedly a theological and mystical figure of Christ the son of God, the eternal Word of the Father, and the *inner fountain* of salvation within the soul of the mystic.—W-104

Criticism

A critic must indeed have a criterion of criticism, and his own inspiration might serve that purpose in his private mind or in that of his sect. But if he is addressing the uninspired and unprejudiced public he should rely only on common sense and on secular history and science, as modest and unspeculative as possible.—W-173

Good

Vitally and intrinsically, good is whatsoever life aspires to in any direction; not, as in charity or kindness, the confluence of aspiration in one life with aspiration in another.—W-207

Spirituality and courage. Supernatural and truth

That spiritual minds should appeal to the supernatural is not to be wondered at. Few are courageous enough to accept nature as it is, and to build their spiritual house on the hard rock of the truth.—W-237

Origin of myths and gods

Expectation, memory, and dialogue transcend themselves in still another manner. The actual datum is a fictitious object like a person in a novel; but it is taken for evidence of a fact: and the credulous intellect is launched upon a sea of conversations with its past, its future, and an entire imagined society of gods and men.—W-241

Inspiration

Mankind is only too prone to trust inspiration, naively in prosperity and desperately in disaster.—W-244

World—saved by Christ crucified?

The idea of Christ crucified has had many worshippers, and has inspired many saints. But it has not converted the world or saved it. The world does not wish to be saved. If we say that the world thereby wills its own damnation, we are merely venting our private displeasure, without frightening the world. —W-254

X

Mutation, vanity

To perceive universal mutation, to feel the vanity of life, has always been the beginning of seriousness. It is the condition for any beautiful, measured, or tender philosophy.—X-23-24

Democritus

If Democritus could look down upon the present state of science, he would laugh, as he was in the habit of doing, partly at the confirmation we can furnish to portions of his philosophy, and partly at our stupidity that cannot guess the rest.—X-28

Nature

Nature is her own standard; and if she seems to us unnatural, there is no hope for our minds.—X-28

Materialism

Materialism, like any system of natural philosophy, carries with it no commandments and no advice. It merely describes the world, including the aspirations and consciences of mortals, and refers all to a material ground.—X-32

Lucretius—nature

Poetic dominion over things as they are is seen best in Shakespeare for the ways of men, and in Lucretius for the ways of nature. Unapproachably vivid, relentless, direct in detail, he is unflinchingly grand and serious in his grouping of the facts. It is the truth that absorbs him and carries him along. He wishes us to be convinced and sobered by the fact, by the overwhelming evidence of thing after thing, raining down upon us, all bearing witness with one voice to the nature of the world.—X-36

Love of life

The love of life is not something rational, or founded on experience of life. It is something antecedent and spontaneous.
—X-52

Greek religion

In Greek religion, as in all other religions, there was a background of vulgar superstition. Survivals and revivals of totem-worship, taboo, magic, ritual barter, and objectified rhetoric are to be found in it to the very end; yet if we consider in Greek religion its characteristic tendency, and what rendered it distinctly Greek, we see that it was its unprecedented ideality, disinterestedness, and aestheticism. To the Greek, in so far as he was a Greek, religion was an inspiration to grow like the gods by invoking their companionship, rehearsing their story, feeling vicariously the glow of their splendid prerogatives, and placing them, in the form of beautiful and very human statues, constantly before his eyes. This sympathetic interest in the immortals took the place, in the typical Greek mind, of any vivid hope of human immortality; perhaps it made such a hope seem superfluous and inappropriate. Mortality belonged to man, as immortality to the gods; and the one was the complement of the other.—X-63

Lucretius and superstition

Lucretius studies superstition, but only as an enemy; and the naturalistic poet should be the enemy of nothing.—X-67

Naturalism

A naturalism extended impartially over moral facts brings home a lesson of tolerance, scepticism, and independence.
—X-68

Dante

The political theory of Dante is a sublime and largely original one. It suffers only from its extreme ideality, which makes it inapplicable, and has caused it to be studied less than it deserves.—X-85

Middle Ages

The middle age saw the good in a vision. It is for the new age to translate those delightful symbols into the purposes of manhood.—X-104

Theory and sense

The life of theory is not less human or less emotional than the life of sense; it is more typically human and more keenly emotional. Philosophy is a more intense sort of experience than common life is, just as pure and subtle music, heard in retirement, is something keener and more intense than the howling of storms or the rumble of cities.—X-124

Poetry

Poetry is an attenuation, a rehandling, an echo of crude experience; it is itself a theoretic vision of things at arm's length.—X-124

Dante's poetry

Thus Dante, gifted with the tenderest sense of colour, and the firmest art of design, has put his whole world into his canvas. Seen there, that word becomes complete, clear, beautiful, and tragic. It is vivid and truthful in its detail, sublime in its march and in its harmony.—X-132

Lucretius and Dante

Lucretius was undoubtedly a philosophical poet; his whole poem is devoted to expounding and defending a system of philosophy. In Dante the case is almost as plain. The *Divine Comedy* is a moral and personal fable.—X-139

Goethe, a follower of Spinoza

Goethe was the wisest of mankind; too wise . . . to try to harness this wild world in a brain-spun terminology. It is true that he was all his life a follower of Spinoza, and . . . a naturalist in philosophy and a pantheist.—X-139

Goethe

Goethe was not a systematic philosopher. His feeling for the march of things and for the significance of great personages and great ideas was indeed philosophical, although more romantic than scientific. His thoughts upon life were fresh and miscellaneous. They voiced the genius and learning of his age.—X-140

Unheard philosophies

Heard philosophies are sweet, but those unheard may be sweeter. They may be more unmixed and more profound for being adopted unconsciously, for being lived rather than taught.—X-142

Goethe

Goethe is a romantic poet; he is a novelist in verse. He is a philosopher of experience as it comes to the individual; the philosopher of life, as action, memory, or soliloquy may put life before each of us in turn.—X-143

Greece

For Goethe, however, as for Byron, Greece was less a past civilization, to be studied scientifically, than a living idea, a summons to new forms of art and of sentiment.—X-176

Romantic poetry

In fact, the great merit of the romantic attitude in poetry, and of the transcendental method in philosophy, is that they put us back at the beginning of our experience. They disintegrate convention, which is often cumbrous and confused, and restore us to ourselves, to immediate perception and primordial will.—X-196

Romantic life

To be miscellaneous, to be indefinite, to be unfinished, is essential to the romantic life. . . . Herein we may see the radical and inalienable excellence of romanticism; its sincerity, freedom, richness, and infinity. Herein, too, we may see its limitations, in that it cannot fix or trust any of its ideals, and blindly believes the universe to be as wayward as itself, so that nature and art are always slipping through its fingers. It is obstinately empirical, and will never learn anything from experience.—X-198-199

Goethe-Lucretius-Dante

Goethe is the poet of life; Lucretius the poet of nature; Dante the poet of salvation.—X-204

Lucretius compared with Dante

So, too, if we rise from Lucretius to Dante, there is much left behind which we cannot afford to lose. Dante may seem at first sight to have a view of nature not less complete and clear than that of Lucretius; a view even more efficacious than materialism for fixing the limits of human destiny and marking the path to happiness. But there is an illusion here. Dante's idea of nature is not genuine; it is not sincerely put together out of reasoned observation. It is a view of nature intercepted by myths and worked out by dialectic. Consequently, he has no true idea either of the path to happiness or of its real conditions. His notion of nature is an inverted image of the moral world, cast like a gigantic shadow upon the sky. It is a mirage—X-208

Higher philosophy

Now, while to know evil, and especially good, in all their forms and inward implications is a far greater thing than to know the natural conditions of good and evil, or their real distribution in space and time, yet the higher philosophy is not safe if the lower philosophy is wanting or is false. Of course it is not safe practically; but it is not safe even poetically. There is an attenuated texture and imagery in the *Divine Comedy*. The voice that sings it, from beginning to end, is a thin boy-treble, all wonder and naiveté. This art does not smack of life, but of somnambulism; . . . man is not in the bosom of nature. He is, in a moral sense, still at the centre of the universe; his ideal is the cause of everything. He is the appointed lord of the earth, the darling of heaven, and history is a brief and prearranged drama, with Judea and Rome for its chief theatre.—X-208-209

Art

To the art of working well a civilized race would add the art of playing well. To play with nature and make it decorative, to play with the overtones of life and make them delightful, is a sort of art.—X-214

Y

Intellectual anarchy

Intellectual anarchy is full of lights; its blindness is made up of dazzling survivals, revivals, and fresh beginnings.—Y-1

Essence of spirituality

Nor is it easy to discern what the essence of spirituality may be, entangled as its manifestations have always been with all sorts of accidental traditions and prejudices.—Y-1

Platonic system

Plato's writings in particular show clearly that the eventual Platonic system was but a moral and poetic fable.—Y-20

Logic

But great is the power of logic, when the mind is single and the heart open. In a trice it will bring the humblest judgments into the clarifying presence of the highest good.—Y-21

Universe

To this descendant of Solon (Plato) the universe could never be anything but a crystal case to hold the jewel of a Greek City.—Y-27

Theology of Socrates and Plato

If the theology of Socrates and Plato was in this way domestic, the remnant of traditional religion in them was doubly so. Their attachment to ancient piety was childlike and superstitious when it remained personal, but more often it was expressly political and politic: they saw in religion a ready means of silencing dangerous questions and rebuking wickedness. It was a matter of moral education and police, and in no sense spiritual.—Y-28

Unchanging world

The great merit of an unchanging world is that all its inhabitants can be adapted to it.—Y-33

Existence

Existence, while it is the home of particular certitudes, is also a cage in which an inevitable and infinite ignorance sings and dies imprisoned.—Y-35

Spirit—defined*

Spirit, which is ultimately addressed to pure Being, is not itself this pure Being. It is the gift of intuition, feeling, or apprehension: an overtone of animal life, a realization, on a hypostatic plane, of certain moving unities in matter. So, at least, I understand the word; but its original meaning was a breath or wind, and hence, often, an influence. In this last sense it is used in Christian theology; the Holy Ghost is not the Father nor the Son, but proceeds from them and animates the world, or at least the souls of the elect. It is the fountain of grace. We also read in the gospel that God is a spirit, to be worshipped in spirit and in truth. Here the word evidently bears more than one sense; the spirit in which God is worshipped is a disposition of the mind, whereas God himself, we may presume, is a spirit in the mighty sense in which Jehovah swept the void, a breath or a word, bringing order out of chaos; the same voice that spoke to Job out of the whirlwind, with the sheer authority of power. Spirit thus seems to be sometimes a creative energy, sometimes a sanctifying influence. So in the Latin hymn:

Veni creator Spiritus
corda tuorum visitans
imple supernâ gratiâ
quae tu creasti pectora.

* Professor Santayana uses the word "spirit" so freely and frequently throughout his writings, and with apparently a variety of meanings, that this rather lengthy definition or brief disquisition of the word and its usage is quoted.

This double function of spirit, if we investigate its origin, would bring back the double source of Christian doctrines, here Hebraic and there Platonic: a profound dualism which custom scarcely avails to disguise or theology to heal. Creative power and redeeming grace point in opposite directions; but a complete religion needs to look both ways, feeding piously at the breast of nature, yet weaning itself spiritually from that necessary comfort to the contemplation of superhuman and eternal things. The object of piety is necessity, power, the laws of life and prosperity, and to call these things spirit is pure mythology; they are indeed a great wind, sometimes balmy, sometimes terrible; and it is the part of wisdom to take shelter from it, or spread wings or sails in it, according as it lists to blow. But to what end? To live, to have spirit, to understand all these things.

There is also a conventional modern sense in which we speak of the spirit of an age, a place, or a book, meaning some vague tendency or inspiration either actually dominating that thing or suggested by it to the mind of a third person. This is a verbal survival of myth, poetry become cant: spirit here means those characters of a thing which a myth-making mind would have attributed to a spirit.

In contrast to all these uses I am employing the word spirit to mean something actual; indeed, the very fact of actuality. The gleam of intuition or feeling. But this gleam ordinarily serves only to light up material life and the perspectives in which it moves in time and in space: an incessant sketchy sense of the affairs of the body and of its world. The digestion, and preparation of action (as the behaviourists have shown) is a physical matter. In that business the spirit is entirely superfluous. The behaviourists even affect to deny its existence on the ground that it is invisible and would be a useless luxury in nature: excellent economy, as if a man, the better to provide for his future, should starve himself to death. The spirit in us is that which, morally, we actually are: if anything is to be expunged from the complex face of reality it might rather be our material and social setting and all the strange and incoherent stories told us in history and science. Certainly all these apparent or reported facts would be perfectly vain, if they did not create the spirit, and teach it to observe and enjoy them. So we are brought back to the immediate revelation of things, which is also their ultimate value: we are brought back to the spirit. Its life is composed of feelings and intuitions, in many stages and degrees; and when spirit is free and collected it has no life but this spiritual life, in which the ultimate is immediate. All the experiences of the spirit, until they are so exorcized and appropriated—so enshrined in pure Being—are sheer distraction.—Y-47-50.

Material life
It is a lesson learned by experience, in view of the conditions of material life.—Y-52

Human mind
The human heart is full of political, religious, metaphysical ambition; it hugs all sorts of pleasant projects in art and in fortune.—Y-55

Spirit
Spirit is awareness, intelligence, recollection. It requires no dogmas, as does animal faith or the art of living.—Y-56

Spirit
Spirit itself is not human; it may spring up in any life; it may detach itself from any provincialism; as it exists in all nations and religions, so it may exist in all animals.—Y-56

Animal in man
But the animal in man is wretched unless he can imagine that his language, nation, arts, and sentiments are destined to be supreme in the world for ever; he is hardly content to suppose that he may not rise again to take part in celebrating some final, yet unending, victory; and he demands eternity not for the lovely essences which he may have beheld, which

have eternity in themselves already, but for the manifestation of those essences which cannot have it.—Y-59

Wistful thinking

The interests which these dogmas (of religion) expressed and sanctioned were respectable interests, political, moral, and emotional. The civilized mind is still very much more at home in such a cosy world than in the universal flux of nature, which not only opens material immeasurable abysses on every side of our human nest, but threatens us with an indefinite flux in our own being, in our habits, institutions, affections, and in the very grammar and categories of our thought.
—Y-62-63

Spirit and the Supreme Being

Even in rare moments of attainment, when the human spirit has seemed to be united or even identified with the supreme Being, the reports which reach us of that ecstasy indicate that the chasm has never really been bridged.—Y-76

Human morals

Human morals draw their vigour from earthly economy, and find their sanction there.—Y-91

Z

Matter

Matter seems an evil to the sour moralist because it is often untoward, and an occasion of imperfection or conflict in things. But if he took a wider view matter would seem a good to him, because it is the principle of existence: it is all things in their potentiality and therefore the condition of all their excellence or possible perfection.—Z-v

Realm of matter

From the point of view of origins, therefore, the realm of matter is the matrix and the source of everything: it is nature, the sphere of genesis, the universal mother. The truth cannot dictate to us the esteem in which we shall hold it: that is not a question of fact but of preference.—Z-xi

Provincialism

Nothing is dearer to a man or a nation than congenial modes of expression; I would rather be silent than use some people's language: I would rather die than think as some people think.—Z-5

Matter's creations

Why are human love and religion so tormented, if they are masters of the world? If they command miraculously and matter obeys, is it not because matter had first created them and dictated the commands which they were to issue?—Z-122

Nature vs. eloquence

The germination, definition, and prevalence of any good must be grounded in nature herself, not in human eloquence. —Z-131

Moral values and nature

Moral values cannot preside over nature.—Z-134

The soul

Avoiding, then, this poetical word, the soul, laden with so many equivocations, I will beg the reader to distinguish sharply two levels of life in the human body, one of which I call *the spirit* and the other *the psyche*. By spirit I understand the actual light of consciousness falling upon anything—the ultimate invisible emotional fruition of life in feeling and thought. On the other hand by the psyche I understand a system of tropes, inherited or acquired, displayed by living bodies in their growth and behaviour. This psyche is the specific form of physical life, present and potential, asserting itself in any plant or animal.—Z-139

Reason and the passions

Reason is not a force contrary to the passions, but a harmony possible among them. Except in their interests it could have no ardour, except in their world, it could have no point of application, nothing to beautify, nothing to dominate.—Z-147

Physical basis of psychology

I find, then, that in the psychological sphere, apart from pure feeling or intuition, everything is physical. There is no such thing as mental substance, mental force, mental machinery, or mental causation. If actual feelings or intuitions have any ground at all this ground is physical; if they have a date, place, or occasion they have it only in the physical world. —Z-188-189

Psychology and matter

Thus psychology reports certain complications in the realm of matter: and the interpretations which may be added in terms of spirit depend entirely for their truth on the existence and spiritual fertility of that material background.—Z-189

Dominance of the material

When the heart is bent on the truth, when prudence and

the love of prosperity dominate the will, science must insensibly supplant divination, and reverence must be transferred from traditional sanctities to the naked power at work in nature, sanctioning worldly wisdom and hygienic virtue rather than the maxims of zealots or the dreams of saints. God then becomes a poetic symbol for the material tenderness and the paternal strictness of this wonderful world. —Z-204-205

MISCELLANEOUS

Temptation of writers.
Traditional religions and moralities

Now in my mental life there have been two great impediments, two congenital vices, two initial temptations: the temptation of the primitive poet to believe his fables, and the temptation of the spontaneous agent to lose himself in his world. The primitive poet falls into that first temptation inevitably; his inspiration is passive and not an art; he lends credence to his obsessions as to a higher kind of knowledge, and proclaims each new intuition to be a revelation of the truth. The Jews, says Spinoza, whenever they think something, say God told them. Prophets indeed do this explicitly and with full conviction, opposing their sudden intuitions to the current views of mankind. They are even more credulous and absorbed in life than are ordinary people, only in some extraordinary direction. Yet, unlike madmen, good prophets proclaim new ideas the world can be led to take seriously and to weave into its conventions, at least for a time and in some sect; whence all traditional religions and moralities. —Atlantic, Dec., 1948. Mis. 1

Christian Weltanschauung

All her life my sister Susana was a little troubled because, as she said, she feared that I was "moving away from God." Yet at heart I was not *moving* at all. I was only *seeing* what

[257]

a catastrophe the Christian *Weltanschauung* was pregnant with, if you took it for history and cosmology, and not for a symbolic myth.—Atlantic, Dec., 1948. Mis. 2

The Christian myths

I had been childishly absorbed in religious ideas, and it was a true though bloodless sacrifice for me to wash them clean of all pretensions to historical or material truth; yet I was able to do so when quite young, readily and even gladly, because when I learned to conceive those myths as poetry, their meaning and beauty, far from being lost, seemed to me clearer and more profound than ever.—Atlantic, Dec., 1948. Mis. 3

Utopias and religions

Religion and social utopias proposed nothing that I respected.—Atlantic, Dec., 1948. Mis. 4

Imagination

Cultivate imagination, love it, give it endless forms, but do not let it deceive you.—Atlantic, Dec., 1948. Mis. 5

Lucretius

The great master of sympathy with nature, in my education, was Lucretius.—Atlantic, Jan., 1949. Mis. 6

Matter. Nature. Lucretius. Bacon

Matter has been kind to me, and I am a lover of matter. Not only esthetically but dynamically, as felt by Lucretius, nature to me is a welcome presence; and modern progress in mechanical invention and industrial luxury has excited joyously my materialistic imagination, as it did prophetically that of Bacon.—Atlantic, Jan., 1949. Mis. 7

Unreason. Twentieth century wars

The contemporary world has turned its back on the attempt and even on the desire to live reasonably. The two great wars of the twentieth century were adventures in enthusiastic unreason.—Atlantic, Jan., 1949. Mis. 8

Unfit. Proletariat

There have always been beggars and paupers in the world, because there is bound to be a margin of the unfit—too bad or too good—to keep in step with any well-organized society; but that the great body of mankind should sink into a proletariat has been an unhappy effect of the monstrous growth of cities, made possible by the concentration of trade and the multiplication of industries, mechanized and swelling into monopolies.—Atlantic, Jan., 1949. Mis. 9

(Is it possible there could be too many people?—Ed.)

Education

A child educated only at school is an uneducated child.—in "Why I Am Not a Marxist", Modern Monthly 9:77. Mis. 10

Sentimentalism and Romanticism

Sentimentalism in the observer and Romanticism in the artist are examples of aesthetic incapacity. Whenever beauty is really seen and loved, it has a definite embodiment, the eye has precision, the work has style, and the object has perfection.—from "The Sense of Beauty." Mis. 11

Restless man

Man in particular is not a grazing animal, and he would never stay long in a paradise where everybody has four meals a day and nothing else ever happens.—(Mercury 37:377) reviewing Russell's "Religion and Science." Mis. 12

Enlightenment

Every wave of enlightenment extinguishes some lights.—(Mercury 37:377) reviewing Russell's "Religion and Science." Mis. 13

Philosophers

Philosophers like fish, move often in schools, and each sect is bitterly exclusive.—(Mercury 37:377) reviewing Russell's "Religion and Science." Mis. 14

Sanity, nature's care of

Doubtless nobody is quite sane; but nature, against our reasonings and expectations, continually redresses the balance, killing off the worst fools; and the non-theoretical strain in us keeps us alive, with only our more harmless illusions.— (Mercury 37:377) reviewing Russell's "Religion and Science." Mis. 15

Anti-clerical propaganda

Why should a mind of the highest distinction, in the van of science and social reform, stop to repeat the commonplaces of anti-clerical propaganda, and inform us again that witches and heretics were burned and that Galileo was imprisoned?—(Mercury 37:377), reviewing Russell's "Religion and Science." Mis. 16

Politics and Religion

All ancient religions are political. Either in spots, like paganism, or thoroughly and minutely, as in the Jewish law and the Koran, they set out private conscience. Their regimen is held out to be the sole means of making men sane in this world and happy in the next. If, therefore, the Catholic church ever became dominant in America, it would without doubt, by virtue of its concrete mission, transform American life and institutions. In the measure of its power and prudence it would abolish religious liberty, the freedom of the press, divorce and lay education.—New Republic, Jan. 15, 1916. Mis. 17

Intolerance

Mystics themselves being inwardly illuminated, are fiercely intolerant.—New Republic, Jan. 15, 1916. Mis. 18

Persecution

It is not worldly ecclesiastics that kindle the fires of persecution, but mystics who think they hear the voice of God. —New Republic, Jan. 15, 1916. Mis. 19

Intelligence

Those who have lost the instinct for expression cannot imagine that those who retain it have anything to express.— New Republic, Jan. 15, 1916. Mis. 20

Mystical passion and devout fancy

Mystical passion and devout fancy intervene spontaneously and powerfully in mundane affairs, and in so doing they at once quicken and confuse science, morals, and politics.—New Republic, Jan. 15, 1916. Mis. 21

Evolution

Spencerian cosmology, where various principles of evolution are traced through all departments of nature, and represented as a sort of framework of eternal necessity on which the frail web of phenomena is stretched, and must be stretched in all future time.—"The Unknowable," p. 221, of Fadiman's "Reading I've Liked." Mis. 22

Literature. Experience

"Only literature can describe experience, for the excellent reason that the terms of experience are moral and literary from the beginning." Thus, continues Santayana, life, concerned with practical matters, is transformed by the mind into "pleasures and pains, and into many-colored ideas."—Philosophy in Literature, by Julian L. Ross. Mis. 23

MH

God

The Jews, says Spinoza, whenever they think something, say God told them.—MH-3

Christian Weltanschauung

I am only *seeing* what a catastrophe the Christian *Weltanschauung* was pregnant with, if you took it for history and cosmology, and not for a symbolic myth.—MH-3

Peace with Destiny

Each religion, by the help of more or less myth which it takes more or less seriously, proposes some method of fortifying the human soul and enabling it to make its peace with its destiny.—MH-4

Vanity and Truth

Being a philosopher, I couldn't accept a solution not based on the truth. If all is vanity—and I heartily agreed to that—the solution must be built on remembering that fact, not on forgetting it; and if drinking and comradeship have a good side—and I heartily agreed to that too—the solution must recognize the good side of drink, and also of wealth, women, travel, fame, and war.—MH-6

Catholicism or Judaism

Was Catholicism, in principle, much better than Judaism? Wasn't it still worldliness, transferred to a future world, and thereby doubly falsified?—MH-10

Salvation

The question is whether the paraphernalia of salvation are not in all cases accidental, sometimes pleasing and poetical, sometimes dangerously superstitious; and whether they do not encumber the spirit with other-worldliness.—MH-11

Perfect Lover

The perfect lover must renounce pursuit and the hope of possession.—MH-14

Reformers

Reformers don't like one another.—MH-25

Faith versus Intelligence

It is a vendetta of faith against intelligence that perpetuates hostilities.—MH-26

Facts

Facts are all accidents. They all might have been different. They all may become different. They all may collapse altogether.
—MH-26

Ideals

Ideals are relative to the will.—MH-33

Greatest Wrong

I could forgive the world everything except the ignorance and arrogance of thinking its condition alone possible or alone right.—MH-33

Realist

In spite of my longing for unexampled things, I have always been a realist about the facts and suspicious of all desiderata and utopias.—MH-33

Imagination

Imagination is potentially infinite.—MH-33

European Life

European life surely has a hereditary skeleton, an indisputable structure, that must be reproduced, of course with variations, so long as moral continuity and progress remain possible in our world.—MH-38

Religious Fables

But the poor little girl's imagination had been excited and deranged by religious fables. When would such follies die out?
—MH-40

Handicap of Tradition

Both Lucretius and Empedocles are said to have killed themselves, or voluntarily become gods: in any case they saw the world as the gods would: that is to say, as we all should, if we could surmount our accidental humanity and let the pure spirit in us speak through our mouths. I wonder if a mushroom civilization, by its very thinness and sudden brilliancy, like fire in straw, may not be easier for the spirit to profit by and to transcend than a more deeply rooted tradition.—MH-42

Palestine Visited by Santayana

It was not as a pious pilgrim that I went to Palestine; nothing that I could expect to find there would affect my personal religion or philosophy. I went as a skeptic, to visit the birthplace of religion in others and if possible to understand that religion better. These parched Semitic deserts have been the fountain of inspiration to the whole modern West and to a great part of the East: only pagan antiquity, India, and China have reflected rationally upon the subject, and leaving inspiration to take the forms it likes, have naturalized it in a calm philosophy.—MH-47-48

Intolerance

Turkish soldiers kept guard at the supposed birthplace of Christ, lest Christian sects should come to blows over it: and everywhere ecclesiastical quarrels and modern desecration vulgarised sacred and poetic things.—MH-50

How to Live

The full-grown human soul should respect all traditions and understand all passions; at the same time it should possess and embody a particular culture, without any unmanly relaxation or mystical neutrality. Justice is one thing, indecision is another, and weak. If you allow all men to live according to their genuine natures, you must assert your own genuine nature and live up to it.—MH-53

Dissolution of Christendom

For this reason I too preferred to live in Paris and to read French books: not that, like Mortimer, I detested the old France or the old England, but because the new France afforded a more lucid medium through which to observe the dissolution of Christendom. This dissolution might be regretted; yet it was imperative to understand the forces and know the facts that were bringing it about. Harvard, also, if you were morally an outsider, afforded such a medium; but there, as in England, the intellectual grab-bag was offered by a missionary hand and with a single purpose, though perhaps an unconscious one: namely to equip everybody as well as possible in the service of national wealth and industrial dominance. The intellectual result, if you forgot that political purpose, was utter confusion; yet this chaos itself was welcome to the dilettante, the parasite, and the *viveur*. It enabled him to pick sweets out of the grab-bag at will, and to indulge all his impulses for the moment, yet sadly in the end: an intellectual brothel.—MH-92-93

Strachey

Strachey, who was then youngish, looked like a caricature of Christ: a limp cadaverous creature, moving feebly, with lank long brown hair and the beginnings of a beard much paler in colour, and spasmodic treble murmurs of a voice utterly weary and contemptuous. *Obscene* was the character written all over him;

and his expertness in secret history and in satire expressed that character intellectually.—MH-94

Santayana's Foibles

It was the antithesis and the scornful enemy of the Oxford I could love. Unfortunately this lovable Oxford was imaginary or extinct or evanescent. It could be recaptured only in odd persons and stray glimpses. My bad scholarship, my Romanism, my connection with America and my friendship with the Russells made me unpalatable to the very people that I might have liked best.—MH-95

England's Danger to Santayana

In the year 1919, when the peace of Versailles was being debated, Robert Bridges made a determined effort to induce me to settle for good in England. He said I had things to say that the English needed to hear. Save for the deference I always showed him, who was the only real friend I ever had much older than myself, I might have replied that it would be more becoming and more efficacious for *him* to say these things, if he thought them worth saying. He was poet laureate, official prophet to royalty, psalmist and vicar of King David. He knew the chords to strike and had the ear of the public; and if the public didn't pay much attention to him, what attention would they ever pay to me, a foreigner and a skeptic? Moreover, it was not my vocation to address the British public or any public, but to record as best I could the inwardness of things for a free spirit.

I loved England only too much. Living there I was in danger of losing my philosophical cruelty and independence.—MH-96

What Germans and Americans Needed to Hear

They didn't understand, though they may have felt instinctively, that the egotism I attacked was far from being exclusively German, but was present in them and in the Americans whenever they turned their national ideal into something cosmic and eschatological, and felt themselves to be the chosen people.

That if they did so they were themselves neither good philosophers nor good Christians was one of the things they needed to hear: but they wouldn't listen.—MH-96-97

Ever the Learner

Oh, no: I had never wished to teach. I had nothing to *teach*. I wished only to learn, to be always the student, never the professor. And with being eternally a student went the idea of being free to move, to pass from one town and one country to another, at least while enough youth and energy remained for me to love exploration and to profit by it.—MH-98

England

He said that my abandonment of England was "deplorable." Yet nothing was further from my thoughts than to "abandon" England. I hoped to return often, and I had never lived there except as a stranger and a guest. I was simply avoiding a misunderstanding, a false position. I could never abandon *my* England, because that was a part of myself, just as *my* America and *my* Spain are parts of myself: but these are not to be confused with the real, public, ever-changing England, Spain or America of geography and politics. My England was only the illusion with which the real England had inspired me. This illusion contained some truth; but it sprang from a few contacts, many of them indirect, and supplied by other poetic fictions. Shakespeare and Dickens were important sources, and especially Shakespeare's comedies and comic scenes in the histories and tragedies; for the histories officially depict mediaeval passions that are not English now, nor elements in my England. They are noisy. But in the songs, and in Shakespeare's wit and wistfulness everywhere, I find the spirit of my England purer than in any later poet. He was not puritan, he smacked of the country air and of young blood. I am well aware that the real England has many a virtue appreciable from points of view other than mine, virtues that are their own reward; but that is not my affair. It would have been treason to myself and a false profession of faith to have *wedded* the real England or the real America. They are variable material complexes: I could draw from them the pleasures and lessons of travel, but they are not ideal objects to which I would pledge my troth.—MH-99-100

Democracy in England and America

I felt (in 1920) in my bones, and divined everywhere, the tyrant flood of democracy in England and of commercial imperialism in America, visibly undermining my England in England, and swallowing up my America in America.—MH-100

Reason in Comedy

The happy presence of reason in human life is perhaps better exemplified in comedy than in tragedy. In comedy we see no terrible sub-human or super-human fatality to render reason vain. Reason therefore can make its little runs and show its comic contradictions and clever solutions without disturbing the sound vegetative substance and free flowerings of human society. In comedy we laugh at our foolish errors, correct them with a word, and know no reason why we shouldn't be happy ever after.—MH-101-102

Passing of the Aged

People do not grow better when they grow older; they remain the same, but later circumstances cause them to exhibit their character sometimes in a minor key with the soft pedal, so that they seem to us grown sweeter, and sometimes more harshly and disagreeably, when we think them soured or depraved. No: we are no longer charmed by their virtues or interested in their vices.—MH-103

Unselfishness of Santayana

I am profoundly selfish in the sense that I resist human contagion, except provisionally, on the surface, and in matters indifferent to me. For pleasure, and convivially, I like to share the life about me, and have often done it; but never so as, at heart, to surrender my independence. On the other hand, I am not selfish in a competitive way. I don't want to snatch money or position or pleasures from other people, nor do I attempt to dominate them, as an unselfish man would say, for their own good. I sincerely wish them joy in their native ways of living, as if they were wild animals; but I decidedly refuse to hunt with them unless the probable result recommends itself to me independently.

To heartlessness of this kind I am ready to plead guilty, and see clearly that it is unhuman. Sympathy with nature, however, is the source of it, and not any aggressive selfishness.

—MH-103-104

Peace

I on the contrary have been enjoying peace for thirty years, in the midst of prodigious wars.—MH-108

Friendship

It is characteristic of spontaneous friendship to take on trust, without enquiry and almost at first sight, the unseen doings and unspoken sentiments of our friends: the part known gives us evidence enough that the unknown parts cannot be much amiss. Nor does this imply that the unknown parts must be intelligible to us or after our own taste; on the contrary, it is almost better that they should extend into the inimitable. Friendship may then be touched at the edges with admiration and love.—MH-109

French Mind

The French mind is an exquisite medium for conveying such things as can be communicated in words.—MH-120

Intelligence Unpopular

That I was a philosopher, that I could identify myself willingly only with intelligence and with the truth, offended my friends in Avila, as it now seems to offend some of my friends in other places.—MH-122

Sometimes

When you transplant the species, it suffers constraint and becomes sickly or intrusive or both at once.—MH-123

Appeal of the Numen to Santayana

It was precisely this indifference to physical identities that made me episodical in friendship and Platonising in love . . . It was only the *numen* that I loved, who, as I passed by abstracted, whispered some immortal word in my ear.—MH-130

Inability of Youth to Appreciate the Old in Any Category

Old places and old persons in their turn, when spirit dwells in them, have an intrinsic vitality of which youth is incapable; precisely the balance and wisdom that comes from long perspectives and broad foundations.—MH-131-132

Value of the Modest and Judicial Mind

Thus recognition and honor flow out to all things, from the mind that conceives them justly and without egotism; and thus mind is reconciled to its own momentary existence and limited vision by the sense of the infinite supplements that embosom it on every side.—MH-132

World Not for Man

Mine was a blue sea family: our world was that of colonial officials and great merchants. From the beginning I learned to think of the earth as a globe with its surface chiefly salt water, a barren treacherous and intractable waste for mankind, yet tempting and beautiful and swarming with primitive animals not possible to tame or humanize but sometimes good to eat. In fine, I opened my eyes on the world with the conviction that it was human: not meant for man, but habitable by him, and possible to exploit, with prudence, in innumerable ways: a conviction that everything ever since has confirmed.—MH-133

Man's Place in Nature

The vastness and violence of nature, in challenging and often decimating mankind, by no means tend to dehumanise it.

—MH-134

Santayana Ever a Foreigner

For by chance I was a foreigner where I was educated; and although the new language and customs interested me and gave me no serious trouble, yet speculatively and emotionally, especially in regard to religion, the world around me was utterly undigestible. The times also were moving, rapidly and exultingly, towards what for me was chaos and universal triviality.—MH-135

Modern Science

Now modern sciences and inventions are not vicious in this sense; on the contrary, they bring notable additions to human *virtù*. And I think that the Renaissance, with the historical learning and humanism which it fostered, was also a great gain for human happiness and self-knowledge.—MH-137

Unreason of Twentieth-Century Wars

The contemporary world has turned its back on the attempt and even on the desire to live reasonably. The two great wars (so far) of the twentieth century were adventures in enthusiastic unreason. They were inspired by unnecessary and impracticable ambitions.—MH-139

Requirements for Rational Living

What is required for living rationally? I think the conditions may be reduced to two: First, knowledge of the world to perceive what alternatives are open to you and which of them are favorable to your true interests.—MH-139

Society Ever in a State of Hazardous Flux

Every generation is born as ignorant and wilful as the first man; and when tradition has lost its obvious fitness or numinous authority, eager minds will revert without knowing it to every false hope and blind alley that had tempted their predecessors long since buried under layer upon layer of ruins. And these eager minds may easily become leaders; for society is never perfect; grievances and misfortunes perpetually breed rebellion in the oppressed heart; and the eloquent imagination of youth and of indignation will find the right words to blow the discontent, always smouldering, into sudden flame. Often things as they are become intolerable; there must be insurrection at any cost, as when the established order is not only casually oppressive, but ideally perverse and due to some previous epidemic of militant madness become constitutional. Against that domination, established in wilful indifference to the true good of man and to his possibilities, any political nostrum, proposed with the same rashness, will be accepted with the same faith. Thus the blind in extirpating the mad may plant a new madness.—MH-142-143

Civilizations all Ephemeral

It would be preposterous to expect any one civilization to last forever.—MH-144

DP

Human Race

That mankind is a race of animals living in a material world is the first presupposition of this whole inquiry. I should be playing false to myself and to the reader if I did not assume it.—DP-6

Philosopher versus Prophet

I should not wish to be a philosopher, if that meant being a prophet with a message.—DP-7

Cause and Effect

Life and spirit are not the cause of order in the world but its result.—DP-9

Santayana's Status

The most brutal form of naturalism is materialism, and I have repeatedly confessed that I am a materialist.—DP-18

Verity of Nature

A materialist is therefore fundamentally a naturalist, and begins, not with any theory of the essence of matter, but with the natural assumption made by children and poets that he is living in an existing and persisting world in which there are rocks and trees, men and animals, feelings and dreams; yet the philosophic naturalist has stopped to observe how these things change and grow, often passing into one another, and eating one another up: so that they suggest to him the belief that something continuous runs through them, makes them up, or causes them to appear. But the appearances are not parts of the material object, since they change with the distance, position, and condition of the observer; often, too, when no such object exists, as in the case of illusions and dreams. If on examination and in the practice of the arts the naturalist thinks this theory verified, he has become a materialist.—DP-18-19

History—Its Abuse

History is a chaos, if we endeavor to impose our moral notions upon it. If we would find its true order, we must allow it to flow unguided, continually offering fresh suggestions of ideals which it never realizes or at last betrays.—DP-33

Chaos

Chaos is a name for any order that produces confusion in our minds.—DP-33

Illusions—Their Possible Source

Figures of speech often leave behind them metaphysical illusions.—DP-46

Dreams

We think we could live happy if eternally free in a world we might build around us and constantly rebuild, like a happy dream, to suit our secret disposition. This feeling is not too extravagant to be the guiding inspiration of some romantic philosophers, notably of Fichte; and in a less articulate form it underlies much modern sentiment in politics. Reformers when they utter the word "liberty," and peoples when they take up arms in response to that cry, seldom have a clear idea of what they will do with their liberty when they have won it.—DP-47

Egotism

Fundamentally, every vitally integrated tribe, nation, or government, unless in straits, looks on all others as nuisances or dangers, that it would be a relief to get rid of. Their territory ought to be annexed, the inhabitants assimilated, exterminated, or reduced to slavery. A treaty of peace or of commerce is a temporary compromise dictated by necessity or minor conveni-

ence. The political ideal remains always infinite, vacant freedom surrounding a chosen way of life. This ideal has been
loudly proclaimed by every militant religion, as today by the
apostles of both kinds of democracy. It was frankly expressed
by Virgil for the Romans and by Dante for the Holy Roman
Empire; and it is betrayed by the Soviets now in their continual demand for unanimity.—DP-48

The Reformer

There is always more in the reformer than his reforming
zeal, especially if he is an artist; and there is always more in
the world than the vacant freedom that the Will in its blindness had hoped to find.—DP-49

Freedom

Logical freedom must therefore be well understood to in-
clude freedom not to change: and the modern sense of mal-
adjustment, with sweeping hatred of the past and the present,
must not be regarded as native to liberty or to the love of
liberty.—DP-51

Conformity

The crowd compels us to adopt its language, manners, morals,
and religion; and it is a rare freedom in human life when even
a slight personal originality in any of these matters—or even
in dress—is not crushed at once by universal obloquy and
persecution. This is not because the public is wicked but because
it is the public—which is hardly its own fault. Society suffocates
liberty merely by existing, and it must exist, and all its members are equally its slaves.—DP-64-65

Tyranny of the Populace

But the point to remember is this: any ideal enthusiasm, any
loyalty to duty or commandment, is incidental in man. It cannot be relied upon. You must fortify it by personal appeals,
by wages in this world or the other, by some smiling prospect
opened to the social conscript. This was long ago discovered

by wise religions, which promised the saints heaven and gave the clergy the earth; but foolish governments and philosophies in our day sometimes try to get on without reconciling the individual. The result, sooner or later, is disaster; their constituency deserts them with a wonderfully sharp and sudden revulsion of feeling. Converts, infidels, and revolutionaries have bad memories and worse tempers. To justify their apostasy and heal the wounds it may have caused they require the balm of libelling their past and lording it over their new surroundings. They are the founders of the worst tyrannies.—DP-72-73

Victims of Legality

Not all the heroic victims of legality are martyrs to a nobler cause.—DP-82

Man's Stature Relative

You can't play the whale in a box of sardines.—DP-114

Religion, Its Character

For religion too is easily diffused and histrionically popular, but seldom transforms or even touches the radical motives guiding a man's life.—DP-126

Patriotism

Patriotism, like the government it radiates from, may become a vice.—DP-130

Language, One of Its Faults

Language is the great instrument of fanaticism.—DP-140

Religious Trends

Indeed the most characteristic function of religion would seem to lie in lifting the soul out of its earthly environment altogether and bringing it into an imagined commerce with supernatural things. But by the irony of fate this heroic means of escaping convention becomes at once conventional and compulsory. The human soul is anxious, agitated, and ignorant; she cannot wait for confirmation of any reports first coming to hand; she dare not neglect any casual suggestion, any mystic impulse, however irrational, that reaches her in her distress. The omens she reads everywhere, the fancies and dreams that visit her, pass for facts and forces not to be neglected: terrible divine dangers, or divine helps, more important than any calculable agency. Thus groping anxiety glides into random experiments, these into fixed rites, and these again into sacred laws, disobedience to which is death. Religion has then been reduced to an art, ostensibly necessary to social welfare; it has been swallowed up in authority, in mock science, and arbitrary law; it has become the most tyrannous element in that hostile, hopeless world from which it has come to deliver us. Religious impulse is therefore always rebelling against its own creations, the positive religions, even more violently than against the dogmas of science or the stupid moralities of the world.

—DP-161

Loyalty, Its Hazards

Loyalty to clan or monarch and religious or political faith, however intense or rapturous, have an insecure tenure in the moral nature of man. The doctrinaire who for this reason turns upon human nature and calls it sinful or corrupt may be right metaphysically, but his conviction that he is right should give him no confidence that he can force his particular system upon mankind. He may pile controversial proof or may organize a dogmatic education like the Catholic Church or the Russian State and proclaim inexorable laws, like the Pentateuch, the Koran, or the Medes and Persians. Indomitable aliens will still surround and resist him. His own children will whisper incessant heresies; his very soul will trouble him with doubts or with treacherous extensions of orthodoxy; and nothing he can do will prevent the ground from crumbling under his feet, and the world from moving on to some other unexpected convention.—DP-202

Society

Society exists by a conspiracy of physiological forces; however rigid you make its machinery, its breath of life must come from the willing connivance of a myriad fleeting, inconstant, half-conscious human souls.—DP-203

The Missionary Sermon

A missionary sermon is an unprovoked attack; it seems to entice, to dictate, to browbeat, to disturb, and to terrify; it ends, if it can, by grafting into your heart, and leaving to fructify there, an alien impulse, the grounds of which you do not understand, and the consequences of which you never have desired.
—DP-203

Similarity in Man and Simian

In walking through a Zoological Garden we may admire the dignity of the animals—except the monkeys and the peering spectators.—DP-213

Sins of Christians

A Christian, for instance, calls himself a sinner, but he seldom regrets his sins, and hardly ever corrects them.—DP-221

Consecrated Phrases

The world has caught us in a trap; but it did so when we were born, and we are used to the feeling. Consecrated phrases wrap our minds up in a cloud; we can no more stop using them than we can stop breathing. These are fatalities to which it is wise to yield gracefully; they are unavoidable and they are sometimes pleasant.—DP-222

Conscience

One of the inspirations of man is his conscience; but if you give this inspiration free rein, it may end by persuading you that it is murder to boil an egg.—DP-227

Despotisms

Most despotisms end by being tolerant in religious matters, that is by leaving every sect to oppress those born within its pale.—DP-227

Misplaced Credit for Human Achievement

The abusive rhetorician and the smashing victorious general get all the ovations, and the man who has proved his mastery over the fruitful world is never entrusted with the government. War and revolution are public and dramatic events in which everyone participates at least in imagination; but the private discoveries and inventions of the adventurous mind work the transformation of society often without being noticed at all.—DP-245

Advertisement

Instead of comparatively innocent cries of vendors or heralds announcing their wares or their news, we now have advertising and propaganda: arts explicitly bent on bending the public mind to party advantage. The process is like that of a lottery, catering to human weakness and popular delusions for the benefit of partial interests themselves probably hollow and deceptive.—DP-249

Selfishness

Experience since the world began seems powerless here against the presumptions of egotism and ignorance, and against that rooted belief with which all animals seem to be born, that the world exists for their benefit.—DP-268

Christianity

Christianity is a revealed and militant religion. It would die out at once if it were not expressly inculcated.—DP-288

Rational Thinking

Ordinary rational decisions make only short, clear runs amid the turbid rapids of existence.—DP-307

The mere existence of enlightenment softens the fury of contending sects.—DP-318

Liberty

Equality and, later, democracy have been nominal battlecries of liberalism; but liberals have never really desired such things. Real equality is incompatible with that private wealth and that moral liberty which were at bottom the aspiration of this school. Moral liberty invites diversity, and presupposes it.—DP-319

Communism

The moral inspiration of communism is brotherly, pacifist, ascetic, and saintly. Christianity was originally communistic, and all the religious Orders continue to be so in their internal economy and discipline.—DP-320

Reason—Its Problem

So that in the end what reason can best do is to disinfect existence as far as possible of illusion, pride, and wanton militancy.—DP-333

Evolution of Christianity

But let me turn back from the outburst of militant Will that devised this philosophy, and that deceived the nineteenth century and blasted the twentieth, to the purer phases of Will on which it fed. Fundamental and most influential was Biblical prophecy: Jehovah guiding history for the salvation, chastisement, and ultimate glory of his Chosen People. This glory, though miraculously bestowed, was to be thoroughly earthly, temporal, and public. The godly man would be rich and long-lived and the People and their Law universally dominant.

The chastisement included in this providential plan proved severe; but far from discouraging the faithful, it led them, in the Prophets, to revise the notion of what allegiance to Jehovah implied: not merely ritual and legal obedience but righteousness, loving kindness, and spiritual exaltation. When this

insight became dominant and dropped altogether the political and earthly reign of Jehovah, and on the contrary foretold a speedy destruction of this world and the beginning of a celestial, purely religious, life, Judaism became Christianity. Progress, according to this bi-mundane cosmology (for the goal was still to be a temporal and social existence of the elect with their risen bodies), meant conversion of mankind to militancy in the Church here and mystical ecstasy in the other world.
—DP-335

Political Utopia

Any moral or political utopia may be advocated in opposition to the special vices of one's own society; the difficulty lies in catching such a moral meteor and caging it in an earthly system of government—DP-346

New Democracy

Hence the contrast, notorious in the middle of the twentieth century, between a democracy formed by a concourse of adventurers migrating separately into a new and relatively empty world and a democracy of crowds, accustomed to troop in armies or in gangs of workingmen, like flocks of sheep scientifically guided by expert shepherds and their well-trained sheep-dogs.—DP-346

Democracy—Two Kinds

In spite of this diversity of origin, I think that the two kinds (Russian and American democracy) of democracy may generate similar regimens. Both aspire to be universal; and under either of them, if absolutely dominant, mankind might become safe, law-abiding, sporting, and uniform.—DP-347

Saints—Their Origin

While the pagan gods survived nominally it was in vain to multiply them; but when quite fallen and forgotten, they left an inner vacuum that the saints came to fill.—DP-380

Reason—Its Results

Reason never rules the world, but it sometimes beckons in the conscience and seems to shine in a specious harmony of chosen words or ideas.—DP-411

Our Neighbor

The belief that we know what is good for others better than they do may be foolish or wise; foolish when it rests on the presumption that life is everywhere radically addressed to what we address it; wise when we see the difficulties and the failures that external and persistent circumstances prepare for the unwary.—DP-430

Liberalism

The virtue of liberalism is a sort of intellectual kindness or courtesy to all possible wills.—DP-436

War—Its Madness

The dust, the thunder, the carnage, and the ruin of war seem to make visible some deeper disorder, some suicidal madness in the human race.—DP-439

Infinity of the Will

There is a sort of subterranean chaos, sometimes bursting through the crust of civilization; and something in the individual heart rejoices at that eruption, feels that at last the moment has come to break through its own crust, and build itself, as well as the world, on some different plan. Not a better plan, since there is no deeper organism to pronounce on the matter or to have any stake in it; but simply a relief from this plan, from this routine and this morality, from these surroundings, and these prospects. It is what Descartes called the infinity of the will, contrasted with the finitude of reason . . . A sort of self-hatred and self-contempt: a wild throw for something different, and a deep, dark impulse to challenge and to destroy everything that has the impertinence to exist.—DP-439-440

Paradox of Liberalism

Liberty habitually exercised presupposes peace; but the price of peace, as men are actually constituted, is the suppression of almost all their liberties. The history of liberalism, now virtually closed, illustrates this paradox.—DP-447

Where There Is Danger of War

Between two nothings there is eternal peace; but between two somethings, if they come within range of each other, there is always danger of war.—DP-449

Communism, Its Possibilities

Perhaps the Soviets might be better fitted than any other power to become the guardians of universal peace. In the first place, they are a real power, with an autonomous army, navy, and air force, grown out of the remnants of the old Russian armaments: this is the first prerequisite to accomplish anything. Secondly, the Soviets are theoretically international, and might become thoroughly so if extended further; they might become absolutely neutral in matters of race, nationality, education, and religion. Thirdly, they represent the Dictatorship of the Proletariat, that is, of the nondescript masses of human beings without country, religion, property, or skill. We are all born proletarians, and remain such all our lives long in our physical being and in respect to these radical animal wants which are alone coercive. The dictatorship is therefore not artificial here, but simply a recognition of the fundamental conditions of our existence. At that level, and in those respects, we live under the control of universal material forces; it would be childish not to recognize them and irrational not to confront them with foresight and method. Lastly, such foresight and method are foreshadowed in the Soviet doctrine of Historical Materialism. Supposing the Hegelian verbiage contained in this to be discarded, there would remain an explicit recognition of the physical basis of society. In regard to tenure of land, and to the management of industry and communications, if the management were competent, a universal communism, backed by irresistible armed force, would be a wonderful boon to mankind. Imaginations might still quarrel, but only with the arms of imagination; and the equal and safe possession of one's daily pittance would liberate the mind, where mind existed, for higher flights.—DP-455

Traditional Progress

A traditional great government, comparable to the Roman, might have arisen in the United States and might legally, and by general consent, have established its universal jurisdiction.

Would such an American hegemony have operated justly and deserved to endure?

There are several respects in which it would seem eminently capable of doing so. In the first place, the American people are good; their mentality is settled and pervasive; they are devoted and ingenious in improving the instruments and methods of material economy: and it is precisely in this sphere that they would have been called upon to act for the welfare of all mankind. They would have done so honestly, diligently, guided by experts in every department; and while a cumbrous official system, with much pedantry and delay and some false and premature theories, might have intervened, there need not have been, in their government, that open, perhaps unconscious, selfishness which many imperial governments have shown in the past. And this not because Americans are super-humanly unselfish, but because in questions of universal peace and universal trade their self-interest coincides with that of all other nations, or would at least do so if it were clearly understood and strictly confined to material economy.

But would an American management of international affairs be really confined to the economic sphere? It is no doubt the desire to keep American enterprise alive and progressive, by establishing everywhere rational commercial relations advantageous to both sides, that fundamentally inspires what the Russians call American imperialism; but quickness and sagacity in the economic arts are human virtues, and in the human psyche which is the agent in politics, they cannot stand alone. By the obvious well-being which they bring, they breed self-satisfaction and complacency; and the technically just belief that national trade is profitable even to the less enterprising party excites a pleasing passion for doing good. And there are so many other goods, like education and training, that help to secure prosperity and in turn are favored by it! The authority that controlled universal economy, if it were in American hands, would irresistibly tend to control education and training also.

—DP-458-459

English versus American

The British Empire, which was not founded or held exclusively for economic reasons, had a way of governing at once more reserved and more spectacular than the American system seems likely to be. There was military pomp and official grandeur about it; and the sportsmen of aristocratic breeding who chiefly carried it on meddled as little as possible with the natives. If the measures dictated to them from Whitehall were sometimes oppressive and designed to maintain British trade, even perhaps in opium, the thoughts of the military men and civil servants who actually governed were fixed rather on national prestige and on home and family affairs. It was as Englishmen that they fought and ruled, not as experts in an impartial and international economy. The very idea of a rational moral regimen for mankind was unknown to them, and they quite naturally associated prosperity rather with brave military enterprise than, as Americans naturally associate it, with a rising volume of irresistible trade. The fruits of monopolist adventure and incessant mechanical invention have dangled in America before the eyes of ambitious youth and of capitalist old age; it was a world in progress and ulterior repercussions and settlements were not considered.—DP-460

New Serfdom

It is only now that the multiplication of mechanisms has become a nightmare, omnipresent advertisements a plague, the overgrown proletariat a quicksand beneath the feet of wealth, and the hierarchy of occupations a reversion to a sort of serfdom. In Europe this tragedy of commercialism is perceived; in America it seems to rumble still invisible below the horizon. And it may be a serious question whether universal government in American hands would not attempt to revitalize the commercial optimism of the nineteenth century, by the aid of new inventions and better coordination of resources.—DP-460

LE

Human Nature

The works of nature first acquire a meaning in the commentaries they provoke.—LE-4

In imagination, not in perception, lies the substance of experience, while science and reason are but its chastened and ultimate form.—LE-8

Philosophers have sometimes said that all ideas come from experience; they never could have been poets and must have forgotten that they were ever children—LE-9

To separate things so closely bound together as are mind and body, reason and nature, is a violent and artificial divorce, and a man of judgment will instinctively discredit any philosophy in which it is decreed.—LE-15

If we must speak, therefore, of causal relations between mind and body, we should say that matter is the pervasive cause of the distribution of mind, and mind the pervasive cause of the discovery and value of matter. To ask for an efficient cause, to trace back a force or investigate origins, is to have already turned one's face in the direction of matter and mechanical laws: no success in that undertaking can fail to be a triumph for materialism.—LE-18

Ideal society is a drama enacted exclusively in the imagination. Its personages are all mythical, beginning with that brave protagonist who calls himself I and speaks all the soliloquies.
—LE-20

That life is worth living is the most necessary of assumptions and, were it not assumed, the most impossible of conclusions.

—LE-26

Only the cruel workings of compulsion and extermination keep what is spontaneous in any creature harmonious with the world it is called to live in.—LE-28

Science is nothing but developed perception, interpreted intent, common-sense rounded out and minutely articulated.

—LE-32

Mind, which calls itself the organ of truth, is a permanent possibility of error.—LE-32

Yet reason has the indomitable persistence of all natural tendencies; it returns to the attack as waves beat on the shore. To observe its defeat is already to give it a new embodiment.

—LE-33

Immense as are the uses and wide the applications of mathematics, its texture is too thin and inhuman to employ the whole mind or render it harmonious.—LE-34

Religion

All the doctrines that have flourished in the world about immortality have hardly affected men's natural sentiment in the face of death, a sentiment which those doctrines, if taken seriously, ought wholly to reverse.—LE-50

Prayer, among sane people, has never superseded practical efforts to secure the desired end; a proof that the sphere of expression was never really confused with that of reality.

—LE-50

Religious doctrines would do well to withdraw their pretension to be dealing with matters of fact.—LE-51

The mass of mankind is divided into two classes—the Sancho Panzas who have a sense for reality, but no ideals, and the Don Quixotes with a sense for ideals, but mad.—LE-51-52

The environing world can justify itself to the mind only by the free life which it fosters there.—LE-52

Men become superstitious, not because they have too much imagination, but because they are not aware that they have any.—LE-54

In spite of the theologians, we know by instinct that in speaking of gods we are dealing in myths and symbols.—LE-55

Nor should we wonder at this enduring illusion. Man is still in his childhood; for he cannot respect an ideal which is not imposed on him against his will, nor can he find satisfaction in a good created by his own action. He is afraid of a universe that leaves him alone.—LE-68

Can it reform its claims, or can it overwhelm all opposition and take the human heart once more by storm? The future alone can decide. The greatest calamity, however, would be that which seems, alas! not unlikely to befall our immediate posterity, namely, that while Christianity should be discredited, no other religion, more disillusioned and not less inspired, should come to take its place.—LE-79

Indeed we may say that the typical Protestant was himself his own church and made the selection and interpretation of tradition according to the demands of his personal spirit.—LE-82

A soul is but the last bubble of a long fermentation in the world.—LE-83

Mankind at large is, to some minds, an object of piety. But this religion of humanity is rather a desideratum than a fact.
—LE-84

The universe is the true Adam.—LE-86

Art and Poetry

Art, like life, should be free, since both are experimental.
—LE-117

Men are habitually insensible to beauty—LE-117

The value of art lies in making people happy.—LE-119

It will further be observed that the moralists are much more able to condemn than to appreciate the effects of the arts.
—LE-121

Nothing but the good of life enters into the texture of the beautiful.—LE-123

In the happiest and most prosperous moments of humanity, when the mind and the world were knit into a brief embrace, that natural beauty has been best perceived and art has won its triumphs.—LE-123

This incapacity of the imagination to reconstruct the conditions of life and build the frame of things nearer to the heart's desire is fatal to a steady loyalty to what is noble and fine.
—LE-124

Science, on the contrary, seeks to disclose the bleak anatomy of existence, stripping off as much as possible the veil of prejudice and words.—LE-138

Literature has its piety, its conscience; it cannot long forget, without forfeiting all dignity, that it serves a burdened and perplexed creature, a human animal struggling to persuade the universal Sphinx to propose a more intelligible riddle. Irresponsible and trivial in its abstract impulse, man's simian chatter becomes noble as it becomes symbolic; its representative function lends it a serious beauty, its unity endows it with moral worth.—LE-138-139

The great function of poetry is precisely this: to repair to the material of experience, seizing hold of the reality of sensation and fancy beneath the surface of conventional ideas, and then out of that living but indefinite material to build new structures, richer, finer, fitter to the primary tendencies of our nature, truer to the ultimate possibilities of the soul. Our descent into the elements of our being is then justified by our subsequent freer ascent toward its goal; we revert to sense only to find food for reason; we destroy conventions only to construct ideals.—LE-140

Lying is a privilege of poets because they have not yet reached the level on which truth and error are discernible. Veracity and significance are not ideals for a primitive mind.—LE-147

To have to distinguish fact from fancy is so great a violence to the inner man that not only poets, but theologians and philosophers, still protest against such a distinction.—LE-147

Popular poets are the parish priests of the Muse, retailing her ancient divinations to a long since converted public.—LE-152

Poets and Philosophers

When chaos has penetrated into the moral being of nations they can hardly be expected to produce great men.—LE-159

Inexperience, pedantry, and mysticism—three obstacles to wisdom—were not absent from those academic geniuses by whom transcendentalism was first brought forth. They became consequently entangled in their profundity, and never were masters of their purpose or of their tools.—LE-176

Homer, the first of the poets, was also the best and the most poetical.—LE-182

The purpose of education is to free us from these prejudices. For the barbarian is the man who regards his passions as their own excuse for being; who does not domesticate them by understanding their cause or by conceiving their ideal goal. He is the man who does not know his derivations nor perceive his tendencies, but who merely feels and acts, valuing in his life its force and its filling, but being careless of its purpose and its form. His delight is in abundance and vehemence; his art, like his life, shows an exclusive respect for quantity and splendor of materials. His scorn for what is poorer and weaker than himself is only surpassed by his ignorance of what is higher.
—LE-190-191

To be miscellaneous, to be indefinite, to be unfinished, is essential to the romantic life.—LE-196

It (romanticism) is obstinately empirical, and will never learn anything from experience.—LE-196

Intelligence is the power of seeing things as they are.
—LE-204

Both Christianity and romanticism accustomed people to disregard the intrinsic value of things. Things ought to be useful for salvation, or symbols of other greater but unknown things: it is not to be expected that they should be simply good in themselves. This life was to be justified, if justified at all, only as servile work or tedious business may be justified, not as health or artistic expression justify themselves. Unless some external and ulterior end could be achieved by living, it was thought that life would be vanity. Remove now the expectation of a millennium or of a paradise in the sky, and it may seem that all serious value has disappeared from our earthly existence. Yet this feeling is only a temporary after-image of a particular education.—LE-214

Materialism and Morals

Materialism has its distinct aesthetic and emotional colour, though this may be strangely affected and even reversed by contrast with systems of an incongruous hue, jostling it accidentally in a confused and amphibious mind. If you are in the habit of believing in special providences, or of expecting to continue your romantic adventures in a second life, materialism will dash your hopes most unpleasantly, and you may think for a year or two that you have nothing left to live for. But a thorough materialist, one born to the faith and not half plunged into it by an unexpected christening in cold water, will be like the superb Democritus, a laughing philosopher. His delight in a mechanism that can fall into so many marvelous and beautiful shapes, and can generate so many exciting passions, should be of the same intellectual quality as that which the visitor feels in a museum of natural history, where he views the myriad butterflies in their cases, the flamingoes and shell-fish, the mammoths and gorillas. Doubtless there were pangs in that incalculable life, but they were soon over; and how splendid meantime was the pageant, how infinitely interesting the universal interplay, and how foolish and inevitable those absolute little passions. Somewhat of that sort might be the sentiment that materialism would arouse in a vigorous mind, active, joyful, impersonal, and in respect to private illusions not without a touch of scorn.—LE-227

Contempt for mortal sorrows is reserved for those who drive with hosannas the Juggernaut car of absolute optimism. But against evils born of pure vanity and self-deception, against the verbiage by which man persuades himself that he is the goal and acme of the universe, laughter is the proper defence.

—LE-227-228

What matters then is quality. The reasonable and humane demand to make of the world is that such creatures as exist should not be unhappy, and that life, whatever its quantity, should have a quality that may justify it in its own eyes.

—LE-230

There is nothing cheaper than idealism. It can be had by merely not observing the ineptitude of our chance prejudices, and by declaring that the first rhymes that have struck our ear are the eternal and necessary harmonies of the world

—LE-233

Throw open to the young poet the infinity of nature; let him feel the precariousness of life, the variety of purposes, civilizations, and religions even upon this little planet; let him trace the triumphs and follies of art and philosophy, and their perpetual resurrections. If, under the stimulus of such a scene, he does not some day compose a natural comedy as much surpassing Dante's divine comedy in sublimity and richness as it will surpass it in truth, the fault will not lie with the subject, which is inviting and magnificent, but with the halting genius that cannot render that subject worthily.—LE-233-234

We shall then be making that rare advance in wisdom which consists in abandoning our illusions the better to attain our ideals.—LE-235

We owe to Democritus this ideal of practical intelligibility; and he is accordingly an eternal spokesman of reason.—LE-236

Mechanism is not one principle of explanation among others. In natural philosophy, where to explain means to discover origins, transmutations, and laws, mechanism is explanation itself. But it does not ask to be worshipped.—LE-236

Virtue is then seen to be admirable essentially, and not merely by conventional imputation.—LE-237

I cannot help thinking that a consciousness of the relativity of values, if it became prevalent, would tend to render people more truly social than would a belief that things have intrinsic and unchangeable values, no matter what the attitude of any one of them may be. If we said that goods, including the right distribution of goods, are relative to specific natures, moral warfare would continue, but not with poisoned arrows. Our private sense of justice itself would be acknowledged to have but a relative authority, and while we could not have a higher duty than to follow it, we should seek to meet those whose aims were incompatible with it as we meet things physically inconvenient, without insulting them as if they were morally vile or logically contemptible. Real unselfishness consists in sharing the interests of others. Beyond the pale of actual unanimity the only possible unselfishness is chivalry—a recognition of the inward right and justification of our enemies fighting against us. This chivalry has long been practised in the battlefield without abolishing the causes of war; and it might conceivably be extended to all the conflicts of men with one another, and of the warring elements within each breast. Policy, hypnotization, and even surgery may be practised without exorcisms or anathemas. When a man has decided on a course of action, it is a vain indulgence in expletives to declare that he is sure that course is absolutely right.—LE-240-241

It is unmeaning to say that what is beautiful to one man ought to be beautiful to another.—LE-241

Rational life is an art, not a slavery; and terrible as may be the errors and the apathy that impede its successful exercise, the standard and goal of it are given intrinsically.—LE-245

Those who are guided only by an irrational conscience can hardly understand what a good life would be. Their Utopias have to be supernatural in order that the irresponsible rules which they call morality may lead by miracle to happy results.
—LE-245

Reason as such represents or rather constitutes a single formal interest, the interest in harmony.—LE-246

Nature is innocent, and so are all her impulses and moods when taken in isolation; it is only on meeting that they blush.
—LE-247

There is nothing people will not maintain when they are slaves to superstition.—LE-252

Perhaps the art of politics, if it were practised scientifically, might obviate open war, religious enmities, industrial competition, and human slavery.—LE-257-258

It is war that wastes a nation's wealth, chokes its industries, kills its flower, narrows its sympathies, condemns it to be governed by adventurers, and leaves the puny, deformed, and unmanly to breed the next generation. Internecine war, foreign and civil, brought about the greatest set-back which the life of reason has ever suffered; it exterminated the Greek and Italian aristocracies. Instead of being descended from heroes, modern nations are descended from slaves; and it is not their bodies only that show it.—LE-261

To call war the soil of courage and virtue is like calling debauchery the soil of love.—LE-262

A man's feet must be planted in his country, but his eyes should survey the world.—LE-263

Knowledge of what is possible is the beginning of happiness.
—LE-267

The acceptable side of industrialism, which is supposed to be inspired exclusively by utility, is not utility at all but pure achievement.—LE-267

We may say, therefore, that a zeal sufficient to destroy selfishness is, as men are now constituted, worse than selfishness itself.—LE-268

To ambition, to the love of wealth and honour, to love of a liberty which meant opportunity for experiment and adventure, we owe whatever benefits we have derived from Greece and Rome, from Italy and England.—LE-268

Individualism is in one sense the only possible ideal; for whatever social order may be most valuable can be valuable only for its effect on conscious individuals.—LE-269

Faith in the supernatural is a desperate wager made by man at the lowest ebb of his fortunes.—LE-273

The philosophers addicted to each sect, and brought up under its influence, may exhaust criticism and sophistry to show that all faith and effort would be vain unless their particular nostrum was accepted; and so a curious party philosophy arises in which, after discrediting nature and reason in general, the sectary puts forward some mythical echo of reason and nature as the one saving and necessary truth. The positive substance of such a doctrine is accordingly pre-rational and perhaps crudely superstitious; but it is introduced and nominally supported by a formidable indictment of physical and moral science, so that the wretched idol ultimately offered to our worship acquires a spurious halo and an imputed majesty by being raised on a pedestal of infinite despair.—LE-276-277

So men have feverishly conceived a heaven only to find it insipid, and a hell to find it ridiculous.—LE-278

To be happy you must be wise.—LE-280

Knowledge, affection, religion, and beauty are not less constant influences in a man's life because his consciousness of them is intermittent. Even when absent, they fill the chambers of the mind with a kind of fragrance. They have a continual efficacy, as well as a perennial worth.—LE-285

Beauty is a pledge of the possible conformity between the soul and nature, and consequently a ground of faith in the prevalence of the good.—LE-286

Index

Index

[303]

[304]

Dreams—Luc-134, A-128, F-27, T-122, DP-47
Dreams, dangerous—T-122
Drunkard—B-69
Dual minds—F-3
Dunce—J-60
Dust of the earth—Q-581
Dying language—A-154

—E—

Early Christians—C-99
Earthly economy—Y-91
East—G-1
Eccentricity—T-30
Ecstasy—E-14
Edifices of reason, their end—V-118
Education—A-192, B-54, S-ix, Mis-10
Education, lay—Mis-17
Education's effect—A-141
Edwards, Jonathan—G-91, J-9
Efficacy of Christian doctrine—V-94
Ego—H-32, H-90, R-254
Egotism—C-125, H-7, H-162, DP-48, DP-268
Egotism, dreaming—T-27
Egotism, Hebraic—H-180
Egotism, its origin—H-178
Egotism of Germans and Americans—MH-96-7
Elan vital—G-107
Elementary beauties—D-197
Eliot, Pres.—M-159
Emancipated democracy—G-1
Ember days—C-102
Emerson—G-192, G-193, G-197
Emerson myths—G-197
Emotion—D-212
Emotions—A-141
Emotions, moral—Q-404
Emotions, transformations of—B-187
Emotions vs. necessities—D-210
Empedocles—MH-42
Empires—F-174
Empiricism—Q-522
End, of Christendom—J-vii
End of mythology—V-61
Enduring illusion—LE-68
Energetic—C-124
Engineer in art—D-126

Engines, formidable—C-81
England—B-48, Q-501, T-2, T-30, MH-99-100
England, her metamorphosis—K-287
England's danger to Santayana—MH-96
English behavior—N-70
English liberty, assumptions of—J-205
English mastery—T-35
English psychology—G-62
English vs. American—DP-460
Englishmen—M-25
Enlightenment—E-83, DP-318, Mis-13
Environment—E-22
Environment, mental, of George Santayana—Q-7
Environment of Santayana—L-97
Envy—V-185
Epicurean contentment—M-177
Epicurus—M-8
Epidemic prejudices—E-188
Equality—DP-319
Equanimity—M-8
Equivocal religious spirit in Germany—H-104
Equivocation—G-8
Equivocation with conscience—H-59
Equivocations—Z-139
Error—LE-32
Essence—Q-28, Q-527, R-76
Essence of knowledge—H-18
Essences—Q-502
Eternal feminine—S-187
Eternal friendship with the beautiful—M-111
Eternal truth—G-118
Eternity—C-270, F-32, F-174, V-96
Ethics—A-55, E-244
Ethics, of Greece—E-262
Ethics of pleasure and pain—A-236
Ethics, religious—D-5
European life—MH-38
Europeans—C-59
Evangeline—J-2
Events in life of Santayana—L-151
Events, mental—Q-524
Ever the learner—MH-98
Evidence—V-94
Evil—O-11
Evils of religion—L-210

[306]

[307]

Greeks—C-51, C-276, H-139, J-18, V-243
Greeks, their day—F-38
Grow—G-108

—H—

Habit—D-35
Habit of using old names for new delusions—H-24
Habits and obsessions—N-95
Habits of moralists—LE-121
Habits of Protestantism—G-137
Hamlet—I-12, S-42
Handicap to early science—E-4
Happiness—LE-280, A-223, C-225, C-279, E-253, H-103, I-66, M-8, N-74, T-259, U-134
Harlots—B-187
Harmony—LE-246, G-214, T-259, Z-147
Harmony in impulses—D-208
Harmony, want of it—D-208
Harvard—L-97
Harvard and dissolution of Christendom —MH-92, MH-93
Hatred, fanatical—K-244
Hatred of own condition—A-225
Hawthorne—G-192, G-193
Healthy life—A-xii
Heart of man—D-229
Heart of nature—D-229
Heathen—H-144
Heathenism—H-149
Heaven—LE-278, G-35, H-59, K-22
Heaven and Hell—D-190
Hebraic pretensions—C-98
Hebraism—C-106
Hebrew—C-69
Hebrew and Oriental influence on gospels —W-21
Hebrew prophets—B-191
Hebrew tradition—C-14
Hebrews—C-51, C-276
Hegel—A-x, E-195, H-22, H-25, S-163
Hell—LE-278, D-190
Hell and heaven—L-173
Hell and morality—C-247
Hell-fire—G-193
Hell's fires—E-93
Heredity vs. environment—T-47

Heresies—S-94
Heresy—C-152, T-30
Heretical Rome—T-85
Heroes and gods, how created—B-159
Hiawatha—J-2
Hierarchy—V-78
Historical criticism—E-5
Historian—A-197
Historian's work—A-197
Historical materialism—DP-455
Historicity of Christ—W-11
History—A-197, E-45, G-10, L-143, R-21, R-102
History, its abuse—DP-33
History, modern—I-18
History, rationalistic—G-43
History, secular—W-173
History—when it becomes chaos—DP-33
Histrionic religion—M-56
Hobbies—T-30
Holiness, strained—I-74
Home—B-45
Homer—LE-182, B-159, P-689, T-260, W-5
Honest humanity—F-38
Honest mind—R-72
Honesty—A-236
Honor—LE-268, B-46
Honor and success—O-87
Hope—C-118, C-274, J-viii, V-185
Hope of science—E-33
Hope of the church—G-56
Hope, vital—G-157
Hopes, irrational—D-124
Hostilities???—MH-26
Hostility to supernaturalism—G-38
How to live—MH-53
Human experiences—B-196
Human ideas—A-x
Human mind—facts and principles— J-163
Human nature—A-269, D-206, G-2, G-190, H-103, T-108
Human perception—E-193
Human prejudices—G-63
Human progress—A-4
Human Race—DP-6
Human weakness and prayer—C-274
Human will—V-19

Human world—K-114
Humanism—I-74
Humanists—J-2
Humanists of renaissance—I-4
Humanities—M-156
Humanity—A-5
Humanity of man—T-35
Humanity, religion of—C-189
Humanity slow to learn—T-101
Hume—G-70
Humorous view of the world—K-321
Humours—T-30
Husband—B-54
Huxley—G-70
Hypnotisations—C-59
Hysterical religion—V-279

—I—

Ideal—A-279, C-272, V-v, V-47
Ideal love affairs—M-145
Ideal of renaissance—G-38
Ideal principles—A-194
Ideal science—A-133
Ideal society—LE-20
Ideal world—A-131
Idealism—LE-233
Idealism, cheap—A-193
Idealists—C-46
Ideality—B-6, C-265
Ideality, unprecedented—X-63
Idealization—A-153, J-178
Ideals—A-3, H-137, T-259, MH-33
Ideals in forms—D-120
Ideals, nineteenth century—G-7
Ideals vs. demands of living—A-260
Ideals vs. experience—C-249
Ideals vs. illusions—LE-235
Ideals vs. personal effects—DP-72, DP-73
Ideas—A-141, D-129, D-199
Ideas and conceived things—A-169
Ideas and their misfortunes—V-5
Ideas in mind—G-62
Ideation—A-5
Idiots, sanctified—F-144
Idolatry—A-279, C-14, Q-258
Ignominy—H-129
Ignorance—C-9, C-118, L-2, H-238, DP-268, MH-33
Ignorance of self—D-206

Ignorant mind—A-187
Illusion—E-253, G-57, G-63, R-31, R-72, V-47
Illusion, desperate—T-154
Illusion vs. truth—J-87
Illusions—C-77, F-68, G-63, K-201, S-185, T-41, V-87
Illusions of religion—V-290
Illusions, their origin—W-16
Illusions, their source—DP-46
Imagination—LE-8, LE-124, G-20, S-41, V-108, MH-33, Mis-5
Imagination—civilized—D-207
Imagination, Nordic—Q-553
Imagination, Oriental—G-35
Imaginative achievements—C-12
Immaterial—R-109
Immortality—LE-50, N-105, Q-569, R-569, R-271, S-91
Immortals—C-272
Impediments of Santayana—Mis-1
Impossible history—L-145
Imposture—C-226
Impotence—C-33, G-43
Impotence vs. pride—J-17
Impotency of will—D-6
Inattention—R-238
Inconstancy in nature—R-238
Incubus of life—M-105
Independence—B-55, X-68
Indeterminism—A-124
India—B-46, C-59
Indian philosophy—T-210
Indian philosophy compared with Occidental—E-56
Indian spirit, the—T-210
Indifference, of nature—F-22
Individual—C-69
Individual, the—S-88
Individual, the, in English liberty, compared with the Oriental—J-199
Individualism—LE-269, B-53
Individualism vs. social order—B-53
Individualists—G-157
Individuality—T-30
Indoctrinated virtue—B-134
Industrial future—G-1
Industrialism—G-19
Inequality—L-13

[313]

[316]

[317]

Qualities required for intelligence—A-202

Quality of Shelley's mind—G-170

Quality vs. quantity—G-5

—R—

Rabble, oriental—B-74

Race (human), its present condition—B-110

Race, superior—H-175

Rascals—G-36, L-221

Rational—G-20

Rational animal—J-18

Rational belief—L-177

Rational ethics—E-244, E-248

Rational formation—C-265

Rational Life—LE-245, A-2, D-192

Rational living, requirements for—MH-139

Rational morality—E-239

Rational philosophy—C-51

Rational purpose—C-194

Rational thinking—DP-307

Rationalists—theologians—H-5

Rationality—C-272, D-126

Realist—MH-33

Reality—E-253, Q-522, S-108, S-150, T-104, V-v

Reality and science—Q-8

Reality, the only—G-12

Realm of matter—Z-xi

Reason—LE-8, LE-15, Luc-54, Luc-89, A-4, A-5, A-129, C-6, D-192, E-34, E-232, G-70, H-184, I-66, J-118, O-3, S-96, S-272, V-109

Reason and ideals—C-265

Reason and nature—Q-24

Reason and the passions—Z-147

Reason and the secular arm—S-xi

Reason, defeat of—A-176

Reason, definition of—M-85

Reason, fearless—K-513

Reason in comedy—MH-101-102

Reason, insult to—E-255

Reason, its character—LE-33

Reason, its foundation—D-191

Reason, its problems—DP-333

Reason, its results—DP-411

Reason, Life of—G-9

Reason, origin and evolution of—A-205

Reason, persistence of—A-176

Reason, speculative—A-176

Reason, sweet—T-94

Reason, triumphs of—V-173

Reason vs. religion—L-35

Reason vs. supernaturalism—I-64

Reason's danger—E-314

Reason's severity—F-23

Rebellions—G-36

Rebels—G-157, O-73

Rebels, women—L-220

Reconstruction of history—E-49

Reflection—A-xii, D-192, E-92, P-688, S-136

Reflective man—A-193

Reform—G-8

Reformation—I-8

Reformers—K-244, MH-25, DP-49

Relations material—E-54

Relativity of Values—LE-240-1

Religion—LE-285, A-vi, A-119, A-156, B-46, B-49, C-5, C-118, D-5, E-3, E-255, E-307, F-65, F-98, G-10, I-12, Q-7, R-21, S-269, V-235, Z-122, Mis-4, Mis-17

Religion, absence of in Shakespeare—P-681

Religion among nations—F-44

Religion and idealism in America—J-180

Religion and madness—I-11

Religion and philosophies adjudged—H-154

Religion and philosophy—L-85

Religion and truth—Q-597

Religion arises—C-33

Religion, drink, women—K-201

Religion, essence of—V-47

Religion, false—H-7, L-174

Religion, Greek—P-687

Religion, illusions of—C-77

Religion ineffective—DP-126

Religion, its character—DP-126

Religion of humanity is?—LE-84

Religion of love—T-42

Religion of melancholy—A-189

Religion, origin of—C-68

Religion, profound—G-200

Religion, sublime—T-210

Religion to be omitted—L-74

Scent, of a priest—L-223
Sceptic—Q-516, U-59
Sceptic, moral—T-257
Sceptic, the, and orthodoxy—L-219
Scepticism—C-118, E-70, Q-516, R-69, R-72, X-68
School time waste—L-154
Schopenhauer—H-25
Science—LE-8, A-176, B-45, C-10, C-51, C-130, C-277, D-190, E-302, E-307, G-10, G-70, N-79, Q-8, R-144, S-187, V-v, W-173, X-28, Mis-21
Science and belief—R-296
Science and common knowledge—E-18
Science and common sense—V-270
Science and existence—LE-138
Science and experience—E-38
Science and human life—E-302
Science and philosophy—E-304
Science and virtue—E-243
Science as a disciplinarian—E-25
Science defined—E-307
Science, foundation—C-265
Science in society—E-237
Science (its content)—LE-32
Science, its handicaps—E-4
Science, its merits and defects—E-22
Science, modern—MH-137
Science, theoretical and applied—N-71
Science, twentieth century—N-71
Science, uses of—A-xiii
Science vs. divination—Z-204
Sciences—G-10, Q-522
Scientific army—E-98
Scientific formulas—C-55
Scientific method—Q-519
Scientific methods—E-98
Scientific politics—LE-257-8
Sea, the—T-35
Second life—E-90, E-298
Secularism—P-688
Self-analysis—H-32
Self deceit—K-201
Self-indulgent minds—E-73
Self mastery—T-35
Selfishness—LE-268, B-134, DP-268
Seneca—L-15
Sense, good, of Shakespeare—P-689
Senses—R-68

Sensibility—I-8
Sentience—A-202
Sentiment—C-9
Sentimentalism—Mis-11
Serfdom, new—DP-460
Serious vs. tragic and comic—A-vi
Seriousness—X-23
Servants in Spain—L-27
Servitude—C-85
Shadow of life—V-26
Shakespeare—I-10, S-41, V-207, X-36
Shakespeare, absence of religion—P-681
Shakespeare, secular—P-688
Shakespeare's choice—P-684
Shames, irrational—D-124
Shamming—L-189
Shell of Christendom—G-1
Shelley—G-157, K-158, G-162, G-175, G-178, G-163, T-108
Shrines—C-231
Similarity in man and simian—DP-213
Simple life—reward—C-194
Simplicity—T-2
Simplicity and rant—S-43
Sin—E-292
Sin of Adam—G-178
Sins of Christians—DP-221
Sincerity—C-118
Singer—G-183
Sinister, spirituality—U-76
"Six Wise Fools"—L-200
Slavery—LE-252
Slavery in America—J-209
Slaves—M-169, O-73
Sleep—Luc-17
Smiles—K-382
Snobbery—T-47
Snobs—L-13
Social and intellectual trends—G-10
Social democracy—B-128
Social disease—C-206
Social imagination—E-126
Social inertia—E-87
Social institutions—S-91
Social life—C-125
Social order—B-53
Socialistic future—G-1
Society—B-53, B-185, D-199, DP-203

[323]

What Germans and Americans needed to hear—MH-96-97

What God thinks of world—B-188

What religion—C-5

Whiskey—M-85

White race—L-37

Whitman—Walt—G-202, V-183

Wife—B-54

Wild nature—U-107

Wilfulness in morals—H-7

Will—F-26

Will against reason—DP-439-440

Will of God—Q-588

Will, religion of—H-149

Will vs. experience—D-6

Winds of doctrine—G-v

Wisdom—Luc-147, D-35, E-253, F-26, G-23, G-157, J-90, O-5, Q-14, V-250

Wisdom, maniacal—A-197

Wise—LE-280

Wise governor—A-156

Wise religious zeal—M-89

Wisest mind—Luc-18

Wistful thinking—C-189, N-82

Wit—F-25

Women—L-220, T-30

Women, prejudices with reference to—B-46

Women vs. men—B-148

Women's affections—M-118

Women's opinions—M-118

Word, most false—H-168

Word, most odious—H-168

Words—S-168, V-119

Work—G-108

Work, motives for—B-124

Works of art—V-173

Works of nature—LE-4

World—B-176, G-2

World and early mind—A-128

World and its people—K-227

World, how ruled—E-76

World, intellectual—G-35

World is inhuman—MH-133

World, its qualities—S-187

World not for man—MH-133

World of human society—P-685

World made for man?—V-91

World of matter—Q-502

World of modern minds—A-128

World, profane—P-684

World, the—V-21

World—saved by Christ crucified?—W-254

World, Shakespeare's—P-685

World, spiritual—A-133

World, sublunary—P-689

World, unchanging—Y-33

Worldliness—C-226

Worldliness in England—T-204

World's conventions—B-194

Worth—Q-563

Worth, real—B-49

Worst to come—Luc-149

—Y—

Yellow men—G-5

Youth and age—O-87

—Z—

Zeal—LE-268, C-152

Zeal, native—I-44

Zealots—Z-204